Healthy Starts Here!

140 Recipes That Will Make You Feel Great

Peace, Love, + Fibre,
M Smith

MAIRLYN SMITH, PHEc

whitecap

EDITED BY Julia Aitken
COPY EDITED BY Viola Funk
INTERIOR DESIGN BY Working Format
PHOTOGRAPHY BY Mike McColl/General Chefery
FOOD STYLING BY Joan Ttooulias, Michale Brode, and Barb Holland
SET DESIGN AND PROP STYLING BY Erin Spencer

PRINTED IN China

Library and Archives Canada Cataloguing in Publication

Smith, Mairlyn
Healthy starts here! : 140 recipes that will make you feel great / Mairlyn Smith.

Includes bibliographical references and index.
ISBN 978-1-77050-039-6

1. Cooking. 2. Low-fat diet—Recipes. I. Title.

TX714.S593 2011 641.5'63 C2011-900459-3

The publisher acknowledges the financial support of the Government of Canada through the Canada Book Fund (CBF) and the Province of British Columbia through the Book Publishing Tax Credit.

13 14 15 5 4 3 2

Contents

To my dad and mom, Jack and Roberta, for being amazing gardeners and fabulous parents, and for encouraging me to enter the wonderful world of food when I was just a kid.

Knowledge is power.

The more we know about a subject, the better able we are to make excellent choices. This theory explains in part why I've been married so many times; I didn't know a lot about men back in the day and I made a couple of choices that seemed like a good idea at the time, but which didn't pan out.

Every day we make choices, and some of them are more important than others: Do I sleep in or get up when the alarm goes off? Do I marry that guy or not? Do I eat a plate of poutine or have an apple?

Not all our choices are a matter of life or death. Sleeping in won't affect your life in the long run; marrying the wrong person may, while, in the big picture, eating that plate of poutine instead of the apple probably will.

Heart disease, type 2 diabetes, osteoporosis, and fatty liver disease aren't something you catch from someone on public transit. In general, these diseases happen as a result of years of eating the wrong foods, not exercising, not coping with stress, and neglecting your general health.

We can choose to eat healthy, fabulous-tasting foods, or not. We can become more active, or not. We can choose to always look on the bright side of life, or not. It's our decision.

Everyone knows someone who eats junk food, smokes like a chimney, and wears the couch as the latest look in lounging outfits, and they're doing just fine. There will always be exceptions, but if you're banking on your future turning out like that person's life, you need to re-evaluate your attitude. There is an old saying that goes, if I had known I was going to live this long I would have taken better care of myself. You don't want to be *that* person.

I want to live a fabulous life and I want to feel great every day. Choosing healthy foods and an active lifestyle gives me a leg up. It's an investment in my health GIC with a much better rate of return than my local bank is giving.

I have cancer on both sides of my family and heart disease on one, so my genes aren't helping me out any. But although genetics play a role in our long-term health, they are only responsible for approximately 30 percent of our future. So I have 70 percent input into what my longevity will be. I know that if I follow my own advice, I have a really great shot at living to see my son married with children. I'm so optimistic that I am planning on living to be 100 and still remembering my name.

Bags of chips, fast food, sleeves of cookies, bowls of ice cream, cans of pop, mindless eating, no exercise, no stress management, and hours of sitting at the computer or watching TV eventually take their toll.

If you've been riding your couch instead of a bike, getting in your car to get to the corner store, or standing around drinking a double-double while your dog runs around the park like a lunatic, it's time to get your act together. You don't have to join a gym, but you do have to get moving every single day.

The future is right now. There has never been a better time to take your health into your own hands and make a change.

Writing a cookbook has a serious job hazard: the inevitable weight gain from trying out all your creations, over and over and over again. But I had an ace up my sleeve this time. I didn't quit my workout routine. I didn't hole up in my kitchen and office for months on end. I continued walking my dog, going to the gym, aquafit, and hot yin yoga, and attending a drum circle every week just for my soul. And I only gained a couple of pounds. Unfortunately for my wardrobe, they all ended up on my derrière, plus some jiggly stuff on my triceps, and where on earth did the back fat come from? Oh, don't get me started. Anyway, I *feel* great. I am fiftysomething, and I feel fabulous.

Health is not the absence of illness. Health is a combination of mind, body, and spirit working together. It's choosing healthy foods and a healthy, active lifestyle. Throw in some stress management strategies like yoga, tai chi, meditation, helping others, or volunteering and you have the formula for a fabulous life.

There is no magic bullet. It's the sum of all these parts that equals health. It's never too late to start living a healthy lifestyle; you just have to make a commitment to yourself, because you are totally worth it. My hope is that this book will kick-start your own personal journey to healthy living.

Peace, love, and fibre,

About This Book

There is a common misconception that healthy doesn't taste good. I believe that healthy does taste good; in fact, better than good—it tastes fabulous.

I've been eating seasonal and locally grown foods since I was a kid growing up in Vancouver. My parents had a vegetable garden the size of a badminton court and a composter the size of a Mini Cooper. My dad used compost and organic fertilizer even before it was hip and cool to grow vegetables organically. Every summer we would have amazingly colourful vegetable-garden dinners where everything on our plates was homegrown and delicious.

I eat as much Canadian-grown food as possible because fresher does taste better. Plus, it lowers my impact on the environment by reducing the distance food needs to be transported, and it supports Canadian farmers. I am never going to buy a raspberry in January, unless it's frozen and grown in Canada.

But, and there's always a but, I am never giving up bananas, mangoes, or chocolate just because these foods don't grow north of the 49th parallel.

When I was working on this book, front and centre in my mind was creating recipes with amazing flavours, using local and seasonal fare, making sure every recipe was nutrient dense, and incorporating foods that could reduce the chances of developing heart disease, type 2 diabetes, cancer, and Alzheimer's.

A study published recently in the *Archives of Neurology* looked at 2,148 healthy seniors over the age of 65 who didn't have dementia, and recorded their eating habits every 18 months for 3.9 years.

The seniors who more frequently ate nuts, fish, poultry, fruits (including tomatoes), dark green leafy and cruciferous vegetables, and salad dressings made with healthy fats, and who less frequently ate high-fat dairy products, red meat, organ meat, and butter were found to be less at risk of developing Alzheimer's.

This cookbook is packed with recipes using all the good stuff those seniors ate, plus some beta-carotene-rich veggies, whole grains, mushrooms, alliums, yogurt, and a little bit of chocolate for your heart *and* your soul.

A Constellation on Your Plate

There isn't a single food or an element in a single food that can protect you from cancer all by itself. But according to the American Institute for Cancer Research (AICR), scientists believe that combinations of foods, mostly from plants, can have a strong impact on reducing your chances of developing cancer.

When is this math calculation ever correct: 1 + 1 = 3? It wasn't when I was going to school, but this formula, in which the sum of the parts is greater than the individual elements, is called synergy. This is one of the ways scientists explain how eating combinations of certain foods boosts their individual anti-cancer effects. The research keeps piling up that diets high in fruits and vegetables may help you live a healthy life. Antioxidants, such as phenolics, flavonoids, and carotenoids from fruits and vegetables, may play a key role in reducing chronic disease risk.

Antioxidants are the good guys in the fight against the evil free radicals. Conjure up Amazon warriors armed and dangerous in the long-term war on disease and you'll have a pretty accurate picture of these courageous fighters. For healthier lives we need these antioxidants in our diets. To get the biggest impact, choose intensely colourful fruits and vegetables.

But to get those powerful fruits and vegetables onto your plate, you need to make room for them. The AICR recommends you fill your plate in the following proportions:

Two-thirds or more should be fruits, vegetables, whole grains, and beans. One-third (or less) should be all other protein sources.

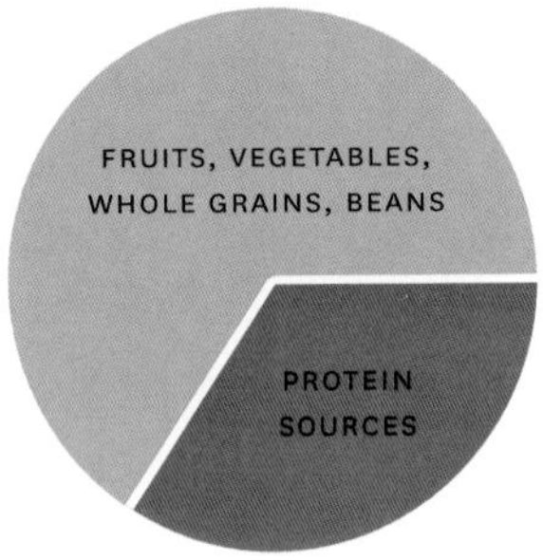

The Canadian Diabetes Association (CDA) takes a slightly different approach but still puts the emphasis on fruits, vegetables, and whole grains. The CDA recommends you fill your plate with one-half fruits and vegetables and one-quarter whole grains. The remaining one-quarter should be a protein source.

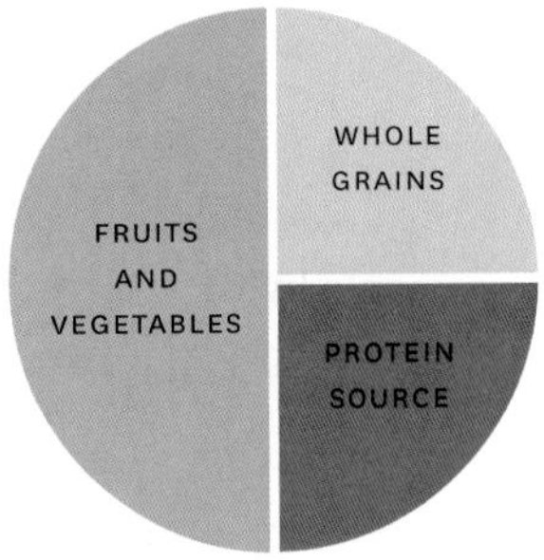

Whichever plate plan you pick, they'll both steer you in the right direction for healthy eating.

How Much Is Enough?

All my recipes include the total amount that the recipe makes, followed by how much one serving is. If you've never measured a serving, hold onto your seat; these correct serving sizes may throw you for a loop.

- One serving of cooked whole grains or pasta is ½ cup (125 mL)
- One serving of protein is only 2½ oz (75 g). If you're accustomed to eating, say, an 8 oz (250 g) steak, then 2½ oz looks pitiful, but that's the amount recommended by Canada's Food Guide
- One serving of prepared fresh, frozen, or canned fruits and veggies is ½ cup (125 mL)
- One serving of leafy greens is 1 cup (250 mL) raw or ½ cup (125 mL) cooked
- One serving of fruit is one medium piece of fruit, ½ cup (125 mL) 100% fruit juice, or ¼ cup (60 mL) dried fruit
- One serving of dairy is 1 cup (250 mL) milk, ¾ cup (185 mL) yogurt, or 1½ oz (50 g) cheese

Go out and buy yourself a set of dry measuring cups for grains, pasta, cut-up veggies, and fruit; a glass measuring cup for liquids; and a food scale for meat, fish, poultry, and cheese, and you will be totally on the plan. Members of Weight Watchers, people living with diabetes, and those who have gotten into the habit of measuring out portions are already on board.

And if your plate doesn't look full enough, just add some of those disease-lowering, antioxidant-rich fruits and vegetables.

A Note about Nutrient Breakdowns

For recipe analysis, I used the nutrient breakdowns that manufacturers provided on the labels of their products sold in Canada, and had a database created using that information. Mine is the only Canadian cookbook I know that calculates nutrient information this way.

Where there is a choice of ingredients in a recipe, the nutrient breakdown is calculated based on the first choice given. Also, nutrient breakdowns don't include any optional ingredients.

If you've been cooking from recipes that don't include nutrient breakdowns, you may be shocked when you see how many calories, grams of fat, or milligrams of sodium a recipe has. As an educator, I wanted to provide these numbers to help you make healthier decisions.

DIABETES FOOD CHOICE VALUES

I wanted people living with diabetes to be able to use all my recipes, so I asked Yvonne MacRae, RD, CDE, a clinical dietitian who has been a diabetes educator for more than 14 years, to do the calculations.

Diabetes values were calculated manually based on the Canadian Diabetes Association Food Values in the table below. Carbohydrate choices are based on the *available carbohydrate* (total amount of carbohydrate less dietary fibre).

	NUTRIENTS PER CHOICE		
FOOD GROUP	CARBOHYDRATE	PROTEIN	FAT
GRAINS, BEANS, AND STARCHES	15 g	3 g	0 g
FRUITS	15 g	1 g	0 g
MILK (1%) AND ALTERNATIVES	15 g	8 g	2.5 g
OTHER CHOICES	15 g	VARIABLE*	VARIABLE*
VEGETABLES	<5 g	2 g	0 g
MEAT AND ALTERNATIVES	0 g	7 g	3 TO 5 g*
FATS	0 g	0 g	5 g
EXTRAS	<5 g	0 g	0 g

* WHERE THERE IS A RANGE, THE LOWER NUMBER IS USED

Retraining Your Sodium Taste Buds

We are swimming in a pool of salt, and getting way over our heads. A diet high in sodium is linked with an increased risk of high blood pressure (a major risk factor for strokes), heart disease, and kidney disease.

In Canada, the daily amount of sodium considered adequate to promote good health is 1,500 mg for adults, but most Canadians average around 3,100 mg per day. Health Canada recommends that adults not exceed 2,300 mg sodium per day. One teaspoonful (5 mL) of salt contains about 2,400 mg of sodium.

So, you can see that lowering our sodium intake will require some proactive steps.

I don't mean to pick on chicken broth, but it really is a great example of how high in sodium our packaged and canned foods are. Depending on the brand, regular commercial chicken broth contains anywhere from 760 to 1,350 mg sodium per cup (250 mL).

Broth that claims to be 25% lower in sodium can contain 480 to 560 mg sodium per cup (250 mL), while some lower-sodium brands can contain 85 mg sodium per cup (250 mL).

To calculate the nutrient breakdowns of the recipes in this book, we used lower-sodium packaged products available at local grocery stores in the Greater Toronto Area. If, for example, you use higher-sodium regular chicken broth in, say, the Jamaican-Spiced Pumpkin Soup on page 119, the sodium content in your version will be higher.

We need to retrain our sodium taste buds. And at the risk of putting you off, this can take up to 12 weeks, because at first your food may taste really bland.

As with all dietary changes, going cold turkey is hard, so when switching to lower-sodium chicken or vegetable broth, start by blending half of the broth you regularly buy with the lowest-sodium version you can find.

There is no standardization of measurements for any packaged item. For example, the label on one brand of chicken broth may say it contains 650 mg sodium per serving, while another brand's label may state 450 mg sodium per serving. But before you grab the one containing 450 mg, check the serving size.

The serving size of the first brand may be 1 cup (250 mL) and that of the second, ½ cup (125 mL). This would make the second choice, the one that looks at first glance to be lower in sodium, the worse pick. Doing some quick math reveals the second brand would contain 900 mg sodium per cup (250 mL). It really is buyer beware, so read those labels and brush up on your math skills.

Now, let's get cooking.

Must-Have Kitchen Toys and Why You Need Them

Ask any cook what kitchen tools they can't do without, and you'll get a unique list based on how they cook. Here is my list, in order of importance.

A GREAT KNIFE

One really good-quality chef's knife is essential. It needs to fit comfortably in your hand, so make sure that you hold it and, if possible, try using it before you buy. I have two spectacular knives. My Henckels chef's knife has lasted longer than three of my cars and has a tiny bend in the tip; my latest toy is a Japanese-style santoku knife that is a cross between a chef's knife and a cleaver, and has a semi-melted handle from a kitchen accident. Even with these flaws, they are both amazing.

FOOD PROCESSOR

My number-two-ranked kitchen toy, my KitchenAid food processor, and I go way back. Sure, I have to haul it out of the cupboard many times a week, but I like to think of it as weight training. It holds 9 cups (2.25 L), and my only regret is that I should have bought the 12-cup (3 L) one.

It shreds, chops, purées, grinds, and mixes. It makes pizza dough, coleslaw, hummus, puréed marinades, and baby food. Without a food processor you won't be able to make my Fantastic Frozen Yogurt on page 89. And this alone is reason to put it on your wish list.

VITA-MIX BLENDER (OR OTHER REALLY HIGH-POWERED BLENDER)

My Vita-Mix is my hippy-dippy-weirdo-blender-drink countertop toy, and I use it several times a week. I'm not a fan of juicers because they remove the fibre, and with it, a lot of the great stuff in fruits and veggies. My Vita-Mix liquefies the whole shebang. Want fresh apple juice with antioxidants from the peel? Just wash, core, and throw in an apple, and voilà, real apple juice.

I can whirl up apples, parsley, watercress, spinach, ginger, cucumber, ice cubes, and a lime to make a delicious but truly icky-looking green drink faster than you can say, "Wow, that's one icky-looking drink!" It's more powerful than any other blender I have owned, or burned the motor out on. It's a keeper.

HAND-HELD IMMERSION BLENDER

I really like puréed soups. Yes, I could transfer the soup into the Vita-Mix but that would mean I would have to wash the Vita-Mix afterwards. When I want a *quick* puréed soup, I stick my hand-held immersion blender in the pot and blend. If I want it silky smooth, I use the Vita-Mix.

Better for smaller jobs, hand-held immersion blenders are great for making salad dressings and smoothies for one. Mine is in my cupboard right above the stove for easy access, thanks to Joanne Sigal who, after working in my kitchen testing the recipes for this book, reorganized all my cupboards. A true friend.

MICROPLANE GRATER

This tool was called a woodworking rasp until foodies discovered it, and now it's called a Microplane grater. Different name, but it still does the same thing: shaves the antioxidant-rich, flavour-enhancing zest—one of my favourite ingredients—off citrus fruit.

MEAT THERMOMETER

Gone are the days when you just eyeballed a piece of meat to see if it was cooked. We're much more aware of food safety issues now. You really need to take the internal temperature of cooked meat and poultry to make sure it is safe to eat.

a great knife (or two)

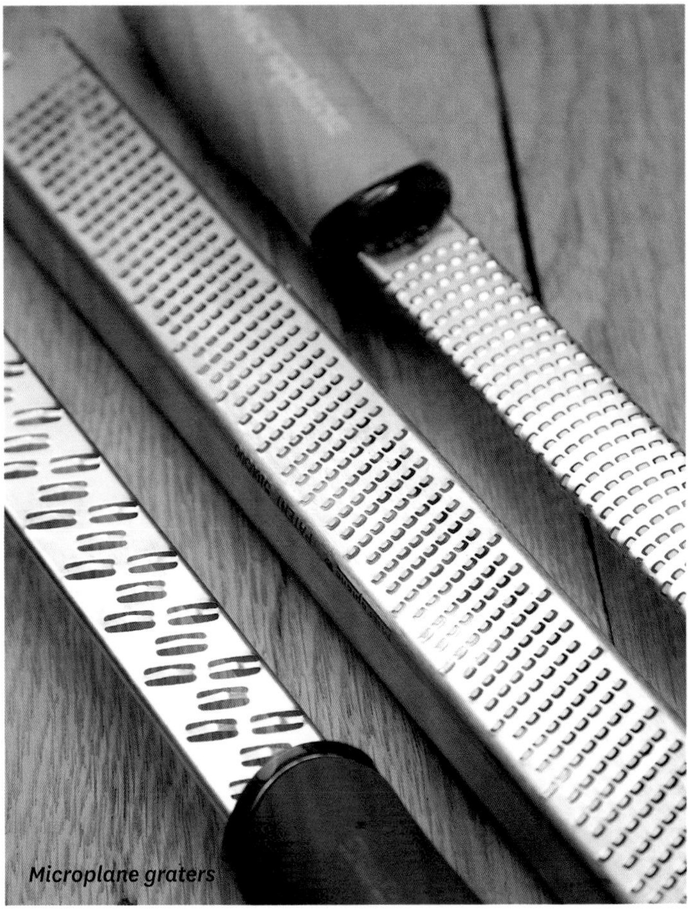

Microplane graters

meat thermometers

rice paddles

scoops

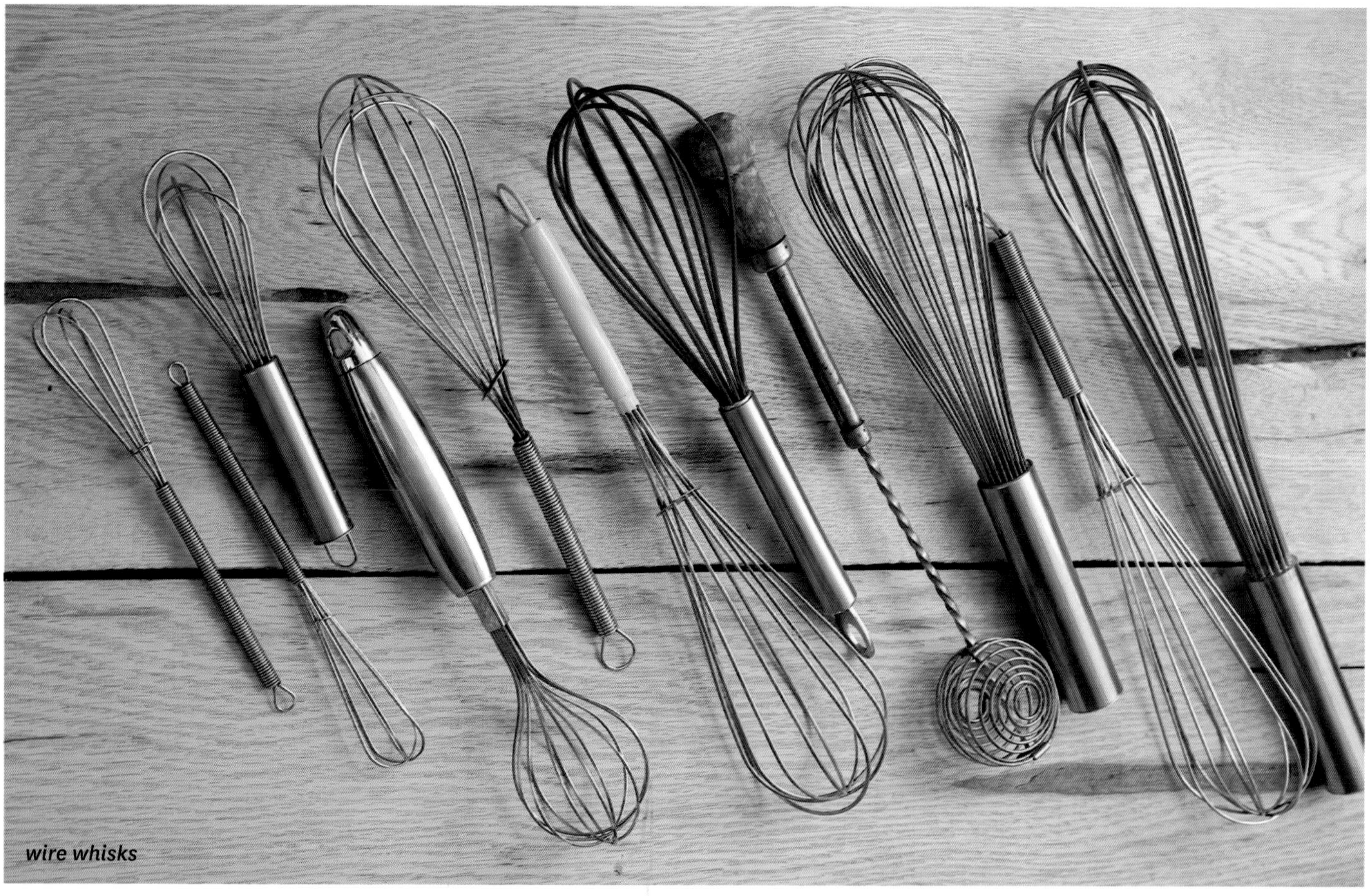
wire whisks

HIGH-END SAUCEPANS

I have three Le Creuset pots that have lasted longer than my original hair colour. They're made of enamelled cast iron, which distributes heat slowly and evenly. My other absolute favourite saucepans are the stainless steel ones made by Calphalon.

NON-STICK SKILLET

Buy a really good one that is heavy (I like Calphalon's), and make sure to follow the care instructions. Most of them require you to cook only on medium heat to protect the coating. When using any non-stick cookware, make sure to stir with either wooden utensils or utensils made for non-stick ware. If you scratch non-stick cookware, you have to throw it out.

PARCHMENT PAPER

If I had to choose between a spa pedicure and parchment paper, the paper would come out on top. It's the perfect cake-pan and baking-sheet liner, never lets anything stick to it, and makes cleaning up a breeze.

Parchment paper is also perfect for lining baking dishes when you're making a casserole or anything with moisture in it. Tear off enough to line the dish with about an inch (2.5 cm) to spare. Crinkle the paper up under cold running water, wring out the excess water, then use it to line the dish. Easy cleanup, here we come!

RICE PADDLE

To get the best possible, most evenly cooked rice, you need a *shamoji*, a.k.a. a rice paddle. This great little toy brings the wetter rice at the bottom of the pot up to the top. Rice paddles are inexpensive and a must-have if you cook a lot of rice.

RICE COOKER

If you cook rice often, you'll love the convenience of a rice cooker. All you do is add the correct amounts of rice and water, turn it on, and walk away, and it does all the cooking and even keeps the rice warm until you're ready to serve it.

Look for a size that works for you; there's no point in getting a huge one for two people. I like the type with a removable pot for easy cleanup, like the ones made by Rival.

SALAD SPINNER

I know it's fun to put salad greens in a clean tea towel and whip it around your head, but it spells "flying greens." Get a salad spinner for really dry greens—and a tidier kitchen.

SCOOPS

Scoops come in many sizes. A tiny ice cream scoop with a release button is perfect for making cookies. I use the 2 tsp (10 mL) size most often. Without one, you will never, ever get the amount of cookies I say a recipe will make. A scoop makes each cookie exactly the right size, and is the secret of food stylists everywhere. For perfect muffins I use a ¼-cup (60 mL) scoop.

MANDOLINE

Yes, we all need a couple of tunes in the kitchen, and what's better than having an old-fashioned wooden lute on hand to help you strum them out? Except that's *mandolin*, no *e*. A kitchen mandoline is a hand-operated slicing and julienning tool that's fabulous when you want to make sweet potato fries or apple chips, or have only a little bit of shredding to do. You don't need to buy an expensive one; my plastic mandoline is wonderful.

WIRE WHISKS

The more wire loops a whisk has, the better. I have several in different sizes, including a tiny cocoa whisk, which is perfect for whisking a mug of Chai-Infused Cocoa (page 291) or Old-Fashioned Hot Cocoa (page 290). (Two cocoa whisks are pictured on the far left.)

Ordinary and Not-Quite-So-Ordinary Ingredients

There are some ingredients I just can't live without. Neither should you.

APPLE CIDER VINEGAR

I prefer organic apple cider vinegar; it may cost more, but the flavour is well worth the expense. I use it mostly in salad dressing and marinades. Grocery Store Search: It's either with the regular vinegars or in the health food section.

APPLE JUICE

I buy natural apple juice, which is made using the entire apple, peel and all. The antioxidants are in the peel so this type of apple juice will be higher in nutrients than regular clear apple juice. Natural apple juice is cloudy, but don't worry; it's just all that antioxidant-rich peel. Grocery Store Search: Depending on the brand, you'll find natural apple juice in the juice aisle or with the refrigerated juices.

AVOCADOS

Avocados are full of heart-healthy monounsaturated fat. They contain fibre, vitamins C and K, folate, and potassium.

Pick firm unripe avocados that are a deep green and let them ripen on your counter. A perfectly ripe avocado slices well and keeps its shape, isn't mushy, and has a buttery flavour. Store any leftover avocado in the fridge, covered and with the peel on and the pit intact (this will help keep it from turning black); use within two days.

CAPERS

Capers are the unripened flower buds of a plant native to the Mediterranean and some parts of Asia. These tiny buds are picked, then cured. They have a lemony, salty flavour. I always rinse them lightly under cold water, then drain them before using. Grocery Store Search: You can usually find capers with the olives and pickles.

CHICKEN BROTH

It can be hard to find, but the lowest-sodium chicken broth I have seen in grocery stores is President's Choice Blue Menu chicken broth. With only 85 mg sodium per 1 cup (250 mL), it's right on target for helping Canadians lower their sodium consumption. For more information on sodium, see Retraining Your Sodium Taste Buds (page 7).

CHILI SAUCE

I like to use Thai-style chili sauce, which has a sweet, spicy, tangy flavour. My favourite brand is Kikkoman because it tastes great and doesn't contain any MSG. Grocery Store Search: Check out the Asian section of large grocery stores.

COCOA NIBS

Cocoa nibs are what chocolate is made from, minus the sugar and milk products. They aren't sweet. I repeat, they aren't sweet. They aren't even *close* to sweet but they do contain a ton of flavanols, more than any other version of chocolate or even natural cocoa powder. Cocoa nibs aren't for a chocolatey snack; I use them as an ingredient in my Triple-Chocolate Brownie Cookies (page 284).

I have tried many a cocoa nib and in all honesty some are so bitter they are absolutely awful to eat. After hours of grocery shopping and sampling, I can report Organic Traditions cocoa nibs are the best. I buy mine at a health food store; if your store doesn't carry them, it's worth the time and effort to ask the owner to order this brand.

COCOA POWDER

To maximize flavour, cocoa manufacturers traditionally ferment the beans, use high heat to roast them, and add an alkali in a process known as Dutching, to improve the colour, texture, and flavour. The big problem is that all these steps reduce the amount of antioxidants present. The impact of alkalizing alone reduces the total flavanol content by two-thirds. For heart health, buy natural cocoa powder that hasn't been alkalized. Brands sold in Canada include Hershey's Natural Unsweetened Cocoa and Ghirardelli Natural Unsweetened Cocoa. Grocery Store Search: You can find Hershey's at Wal-Mart in Ontario, and in Save-On-Foods grocery stores in the West; Ghirardelli is sold in higher-end grocery stores.

CRYSTALLIZED GINGER

This is fresh ginger that has been sliced or chopped into pieces and cooked in a sugar syrup, then coated with sugar. It will keep for up to one year in your cupboard. Grocery Store Search: Look for crystallized ginger in the baking section of your grocery store, or in bulk food stores.

DATES

Dates come in two different forms: pitted and not. Pitted baking dates have had the pits removed and are pressed into a cake or bar. They tend to be firmer and drier and better for baking. Grocery Store Search: Look for them in the baking aisle.

Dried dates with pits are great for eating as a snack, and if reasonably fresh, tend to be fairly soft. Medjool dates are my favourite variety. Grocery Store Search: These dates are usually found in the produce department.

Chopping dates is a pain. A better method is to use kitchen scissors to cut them up. If the scissors get too sticky, rinse them in hot water, wipe, and continue. I have tried to chop pitted baking dates in the food processor, but nearly burned the motor out. My advice? Go with the kitchen scissors for any type of date.

EGGS

We don't get enough omega-3 fatty acids in our diets and I believe that every bit counts so, many years ago, I switched to buying omega-3 eggs. The hens are fed flaxseed, and convert the plant-based omega-3 into a more accessible type of omega-3 called DHA, which is the same kind as found in fish.

EVAPORATED FAT-FREE MILK

This comes in a can, and when added to cream-based soups instead of cream, has a million times less fat. Okay, I am exaggerating, but in pursuit of reducing the amount of saturated fat grams in our diets, we need to find alternatives, and this is mine. Pour any leftovers into a clean, airtight container, store in the fridge, and use within five days.

FLAXSEED

Flaxseed is a rich source of plant lignans that may reduce your chances of developing cancer. It is also a rich source of fibre — 1 tbsp (15 mL) contains a whopping 2.25 g fibre, which is the same amount found in 1 cup (250 mL) broccoli. That's a lot of fibrous clout for a really small amount of food.

Flaxseed provides both soluble and insoluble fibre. The first lowers your cholesterol, and the second keeps your digestive system moving. Add 1 to 2 tbsp (15 to 30 mL) per day to your diet.

Flaxseed comes whole or ground. I buy mine whole and grind it myself in my coffee grinder. (Whole flaxseed will keep for up to one year stored in a cool dark place.) I have tried every other grinding machine in my house — the blender, the food processor, the immersion blender, a hammer — just to see what would happen. They were all abysmal. Stick with the coffee grinder.

I grind enough flaxseed to last me about two weeks and store it in an airtight container in the fridge (although it can be refrigerated for one month). No coffee grinder? You can buy flaxseed already ground, usually packed in vacuum-sealed bags. Store the package in the fridge after you open it.

You can sprinkle ground flaxseed onto your cereal or over yogurt, or try one of my muffin recipes, like Really, Really High-Fibre Banana Chocolate Chip Muffins (page 186), Apple-Date Muffins (page 32), or Double-Chocolate Banana Muffins (page 281).

FROZEN ORANGE JUICE CONCENTRATE

This is one of my secret ingredients. Loaded with tons of flavour, it gives new life to salad dressing and marinades. I even use it as an ingredient in my Crustless Orange-Ricotta Cheesecake with Chocolate Glaze (page 313).

I like McCain Old South because of its flavour and amazing, *almost* resealable lid. Don't tear off the lid. Leave it attached, scoop out what you need of the frozen concentrate, then put the can back in the freezer. Grocery Store Search: It's with the frozen juices. Wow, that was easy!

FROZEN PEAS

I always keep a bag of peas in my freezer. They are great as an addition to soups, stir-fries, or salads, or just served as is. If using frozen peas for a salad, place them in a colander and rinse under cold water to thaw, then drain well.

GARLIC

If the amount of garlic I use in recipes is anything to go by, I could never be accused of being a vampire. But as always, size matters. Check out what a small, a medium, and a large clove of garlic look like. In this book, unless otherwise stated in the recipe, I use medium garlic cloves. Two small garlic cloves or half of a large one equals one medium clove.

And why do my recipes say "mince garlic and set aside"? For its antioxidants to become more bioavailable, garlic needs to oxidize before it is added to a recipe. By letting it sit there "breathing," the oxidation can take place.

GOAT'S MILK FETA CHEESE

In the original Mediterranean diet, goat's milk was the norm. Personally, I don't like the way goat's milk tastes, but I do prefer goat's milk feta to cow's milk feta. Feel free to use your favourite feta in any of the recipes that call for this ingredient. Grocery Store Search: It's usually in the deli section.

HONEY

I prefer to use liquid honey as a sweetener in salad dressings, sauces, and drinks. I like the way it tastes and the subtle sweetness it gives. But if you are a person living with diabetes and prefer to use granular Splenda, go for it. (For more on substituting with granular Splenda, see page 17.)

LEEKS

Ever wander down the produce aisle and spot an enormous green onion? If you answered yes, you've probably experienced a leek sighting. Leeks are usually sold with the roots intact and have a really big green top. See Handy How-Tos (page 23) for my favourite way to clean leeks.

MAPLE SYRUP

The sweet, boiled-down sap from the maple tree is about as Canadian as you can get. Yes, you can buy the fake stuff that's less caloric and less expensive, but it tastes like pure sugar with a hint of maple. I say, no. Buy real pure maple syrup, use a little, and always store the opened bottle in the fridge.

MISO PASTE

Miso paste is a fermented soybean paste that is used to make soups and sauces. I prefer the red (*aka*) miso paste, which has a more pronounced flavour than *shiro* miso (*shiro* means "white"). Miso paste is very salty, so I only use a little bit, but that little bit really adds an authentic Asian flavour. Grocery Store Search: Most large grocery stores carry it in the Asian section of the store.

OAT BRAN

Oat bran is the outer husk of the whole oat grain and contains most of the fibre and some of the fat. Keep it in a cool dry place. I store mine in the fridge or freezer. Look for plain oat bran, such as Rogers or Quaker brand. Can't find these brands? Read the label to be sure that the list of ingredients says only oat bran.

ONIONS

When a recipe calls for an onion, I mean one medium onion. Store onions in a cool, dark place. See How to Dice and Mince an Onion on page 22.

PEANUT BUTTER

Regular peanut butter contains sugar, and depending on the brand, a lot. I was raised on natural peanut butter, which means no sugar, just tons of peanuts. Yes, the oil is on top, and yes, you do have to mix it in, but as far as I am concerned, natural peanut butter is the best choice.

I think it comes down to what you were raised on. My partner, Scott, loves Skippy, my friend Michale swears by Kraft, and my dad loves whatever's on sale. Go

small
medium
large
garlic

large
medium
small
shallots

ROSEMARY

ahead and buy your favourite, but for me and my health, it's natural all the way. A couple of my favourite brands are Kraft All-Natural Peanut Butter, and Adams 100% Natural Peanut Butter.

For an easy way to mix natural peanut butter, store the unopened jar upside down for a couple of days, then open it and place it in the sink. Using a long, dull knife, spoon, or skinny rubber spatula, churn or stir the peanut butter well to redistribute the oil. Once mixed, store it in the fridge, right side up!

If you decide to use regular peanut butter in my recipes, you may find them to be on the sweet side. Unfortunately you can't reduce the sugar in the baked recipes or they won't work, but you can eliminate the sugar in the Chocolate Monkey Smoothie (page 289).

PSYLLIUM

Psyllium (pronounced SILL-*ee-um*; the *p* is silent) is powerful stuff. Aside from keeping you regular, this soluble fibre can lower your cholesterol, helping to reduce your chances of developing heart disease. And if you have diabetes, it can help manage blood glucose levels.

You can find psyllium husks in the health section of larger grocery stores or at your local health food store. Don't use powdered psyllium unless you are planning on making lawn ornaments. Powdered psyllium is the type that you dissolve in water to drink; it will turn the muffins on page 186 into cement blocks.

PUMPKIN

When buying canned pumpkin, always look for 100% pure pumpkin. Never, ever buy pumpkin pie filling, which is full of sugar and spices. One-hundred-percent pure pumpkin is just that.

If you buy a large can and have leftovers, freeze in ¼ cup (60 mL) portions. Make sure to label the little containers so you know what the heck is in your freezer. I use canned pumpkin in Pumpkin-Date Spice Cookies (page 190), Pumpkin-Cornmeal Griddle Cakes (page 179), Double-Chocolate Pumpkin Muffins (page 120), and Jamaican-Spiced Pumpkin Soup (page 119).

RIBENA

This blackcurrant concentrate is made in the UK, and I use it to add intense flavour and a fabulous colour to salad dressings, marinades, and sauces. High in sugar, a little goes a long way. Grocery Store Search: It's found in the juice aisle; store it in the fridge after you open it.

RICE VINEGAR

Rice vinegar is made from fermented rice, and tends to have a lighter taste than other vinegars. My favourite brand is Marukan. It comes either seasoned with sugar and salt, or sugar- and sodium-free, which is the type I use.

ROASTED RED PEPPERS

If you need roasted red peppers for a recipe, either go to the grocery store and buy a 370 mL (12 oz) jar of flame-roasted whole peppers (in Canada, I buy Unico), or roast or grill your own (see page 25).

ROSEMARY

Fresh rosemary, touted for its extremely powerful antioxidant powers, is widely available year round, and it really does taste better than dried. Adding it to marinades can reduce the formation of carcinogens when barbecuing, frying, or roasting meat and fish.

But are the green pointy things leaves or needles? I have researched and researched, and the terms appear to be interchangeable. Whatever you prefer to call them, remove the green pointy things from the stalk before using. You can use the stalks as mini-skewers for mushrooms, or just throw them in your composter or green bin.

SALSA

Bottled salsa tends to be very high in sodium; the deli variety, not so much. I use Garden Fresh Gourmet Jack's Special Medium Salsa, which contains only 150 mg of sodium per 2 tbsp (30 mL). Grocery Store Search: Not surprisingly, it's available in the deli department.

SHALLOTS

These members of the allium family are shaped like garlic cloves, but are a lot bigger. (See photo on page 15.) With a taste somewhere between a garlic clove and an onion, these powerful little flavour enhancers are a must-have in your pantry. Store firm, dry shallots in a cool, dry place for up to one month.

When it comes to shallots, size matters. Use the wrong size hinges and your door may fall off; use the wrong size shallot and your recipe won't have the same flavour. But whatever the size, if a recipe calls for one shallot, use the entire head. When you cut it open, you will usually find two buds.

SKIM MILK POWDER

I find that adding skim milk powder to a smoothie adds extra protein and calcium, and it makes the drink thicker.

SOY BEVERAGE

Soy doesn't come from a cow, a goat, or a sheep, so its "milk" is officially called a beverage. It's all a matter of taste when you choose a soy beverage, but whichever brand you choose, be sure to shake the container well before pouring.

Since I like foods to be as "back to nature" as possible, I prefer Natur-a's fortified organic unsweetened soy beverage. Grocery Store Search: Natur-a is available in a Tetra Pak in the canned milk section or, in larger grocery stores, in a carton in the refrigerated section alongside the regular milk.

SOY SAUCE

All soy sauces are not created equally. I like Kikkoman's lower-sodium soy sauce because it is made with real soy beans that have been naturally fermented. It has all the flavour of regular soy sauce but 37% less sodium.

SPLENDA

If you are a person living with diabetes, feel free to use Splenda whenever a recipe says "or sweetener of your choice." The total amount of carbs in the recipe will be lower. For every 1 tbsp (15 mL) honey that you replace with granular Splenda, reduce the amount of carbs by 16 g. For every 1 tbsp (15 mL) granulated sugar you replace with granular Splenda, reduce the amount of carbs by 12 g.

SUGAR: DARK BROWN V. LIGHT BROWN

Why do I use dark brown sugar instead of light brown sugar? Dark brown sugar (or in BC, "Best Brown Sugar") has a slightly stronger taste and when you aren't adding salt you need ingredients that aren't wusses. So I pick dark brown—not to be confused with turbinado, demerara, or muscovado. When measuring any type of brown sugar, always pack it well into a dry measuring cup or spoon.

WASABI

Wasabi comes in two forms: a dry powder and a paste. A fabulous, out-of-body-experience condiment, it's the tiny, green cone-shaped blob on a sushi plate. It's potent and adds the perfect little bit of zip to salads, rice and barley dishes, and salmon. Grocery Store Search: Look in the Asian section or fresh sushi department of most major grocery stores.

For Anyone Who Missed Grade 8 Home Ec

Here's a roundup of some of the cooking terms I use in this book.

BLANCH

A culinary term meaning to plunge something, usually vegetables, briefly into boiling water, then into cold water to stop the cooking process. This will intensify the colour and slightly cook the food. I use this method when preparing asparagus and some leafy greens.

CHIFFONADE

According to *The Food Lover's Companion* by Sharon Tyler Herbst, *chiffonade* literally means made of rags. *That* sounds appealing. In chef-speak it means to roll up leaves (of kale, mustard greens, collards, or basil), then slice them into very thin strips. A chiffonade can be used as an ingredient or a garnish. Chiffonade of basil looks like gorgeous green threads.

DIVIDED

This term appears in a recipe when an ingredient isn't used all at once. For example, "3 cups (750 mL) fresh blueberries, divided," will tell you ahead of time, hopefully before you dump all the blueberries in the blender and whirl them beyond recognition, that you are going to be using only some of them in this step and the rest in another part of the recipe.

JULIENNE

Another culinary term meaning to slice as thinly as possible — think matchstick size. I like to julienne sweet red peppers to use as a garnish or to add to a salad.

RESERVE

Reserving something when you are cooking isn't quite the same thing as reserving a table at a restaurant. To reserve, in cookbook lingo, means to set aside because you are going to use it again, soon. I usually say "set aside," but every so often "reserve" sounds more glamorous.

SAUTÉ

Sauté is the French word for toss or jump, so if the food in the frying pan, saucepan, or whatever you are sautéing in is just sitting there, you aren't sautéing. Julia Child will roll over in her grave if you aren't sautéing correctly. Do not offend the Divine Ms. C.

SCRAPE THE BOWL

Maybe it was something my Grade 8 home economics teacher said, or maybe it was my mom, but I always really scrape a bowl clean when I am making cookies, cakes, muffins, or anything that sticks to the bowl. If you want to get the amount of cookies I say the recipe makes, scrape that bowl. Use a rubber spatula for a perfect scrape.

SIMMER

What does simmering look like anyway? It's when the surface of a liquid that's cooking is being broken up by little bubbles all over, not just at the edges. This may explain why, when you made something that needed to be simmered, it took an extra 45 minutes to cook.

ZEST

The outer layer of the peel of citrus fruit is where most of the flavour lies. To capture it for recipes, use a Microplane grater (see page 8) to remove a very thin layer from the peel, leaving the bitter white pith behind.

Keeping It Safe

- The number-one rule for food safety in the kitchen is wash your hands *with soap* before and after handling any food. Rinsing them briefly under the tap doesn't cut it. Count to 20 or sing "Happy Birthday" to yourself to ensure you lather for long enough.
- Keep your cooking area clean, and wash cutting boards, dishes, utensils (including knives), and countertops with hot soapy water after you finish prepping one type of food, and always before you proceed with another type of ingredient.
- Don't forget to clean your sink daily, and immediately after there has been any raw meat, fish, or poultry in it.
- Keep a separate cutting board for raw meat, fish, and poultry, and wash it well in hot soapy water with a small amount of either bleach or a disinfectant soap afterwards.
- Health Canada recommends combining 1 tsp (5 mL) bleach with 3 cups (750 mL) water in a spray bottle. It's a ton cheaper than buying expensive disinfectant cleaners.
- Wash dishcloths frequently.
- A safe fridge is one that runs at a temperature of 40°F (4°C) or below. Clean out your fridge often, at the bare minimum once a month. Toss out any scary-looking stuff, and wash all surfaces with hot soapy water.
- Always refrigerate food and leftovers within two hours of cooking, and remember you can't store leftovers forever. Most cooked food is okay in your *very cold* fridge up to three days. If you haven't seen the back of your fridge since Pierre Trudeau was prime minister, it's overcrowded. In this case, something refrigerated for three days is overstaying its welcome. You need cold air flowing around the food, not jammed up in the back somewhere.
- Smelling food to see if it's gone bad is risky. By the time bacteria starts to smell, the food will have been bad for quite some time. When in doubt, throw it out.
- Never, ever defrost food on the counter. Sure, your mom might have, but times are a-changin', so to be safe, defrost food in the fridge in a bowl, or in a clean sink of cold water, or in the microwave.
- Never, ever, *ever* place cooked food on the same plate that the raw version was on. I see people doing this at barbecues all the time, and it drives me crazy. Always place cooked foods on a clean plate, unless your idea of fun is visiting the ER with food poisoning.
- Always cook food to a safe internal temperature, and always check it with a food thermometer. These are the recommended internal temperatures from Health Canada:

- BEEF, PORK, VEAL, LAMB (pieces or whole cuts): 160°F (71°C)
- POULTRY (pieces): 165°F (74°C)
- POULTRY (whole): 185°F (85°C)
- GROUND MEAT: 160°F (71°C)

dry measuring cups

liquid measuring cup

packed brown sugar

Measuring for Newbie Cooks (And a Refresher for the Pros)

My favourite class in university was called "The Function of Ingredients."

This morning-long lab class was an up close and personal look at what each ingredient was responsible for in a recipe. It was very scientific, very interesting, oh, and I got an A-plus. At least, that's what I remember getting.

It was so neat to see a totally flat cake, a runny soufflé, or—my personal favourite—ice cream made with fillers that never actually melted. I learned that every ingredient had a function, whether it was to raise a cake or to keep a soufflé from falling or ice cream from melting.

But the most important thing I learned in that class was that baking is really all about science, and you need to measure accurately. If you don't, you're going to end up with something other than what the recipe creator (for the purposes of this book, that would be *moi*) had in mind.

MEASURING WET OR LIQUID INGREDIENTS

Use glass measuring cups for all liquids. Aside from the obvious choices like water, milk, and broth, the liquids in this book include oil, honey, and brown rice syrup.

Pour the liquid into the measuring cup at eye level. Why? Because an interesting thing happens when liquids cling to glass. The surface of the liquid dips and becomes U-shaped; this is called a meniscus. The correct measurement is when the lowest part of the meniscus (which is in the centre) lines up with the measurement you want.

MEASURING DRY INGREDIENTS

All dry ingredients—flour, sugar, wheat germ, etc.—need to be measured using dry measuring cups or spoons, which are usually made of metal or plastic.

Spoon the ingredient into the measuring cup, then level it off with the flat edge of a knife or spatula. If using a measuring spoon level it off with the flat edge of a knife or spatula.

Of course, there is an exception, because what are rules if they can't be broken? Brown sugar needs to be packed (not spooned) into the dry measuring cup or spoon. Think sandcastle and you'll be fine.

Canned pumpkin, grated cheese, yogurt, and salsa are all measured in dry measuring cups or spoons.

Handy How-Tos

DICE AND MINCE ONIONS

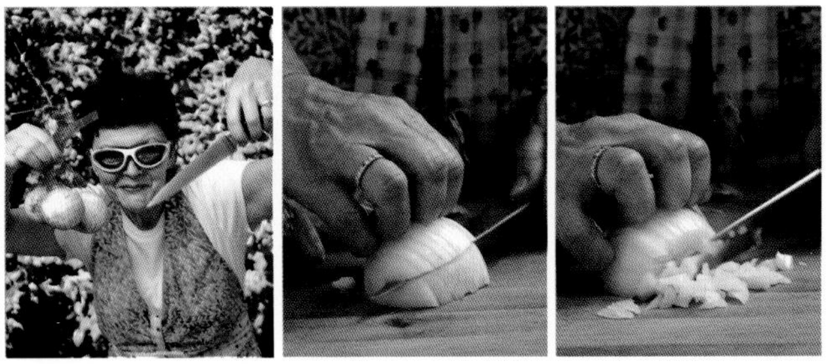

Here's a nifty chef's trick that makes prepping onions a breeze. (To avoid crying, try wearing onion goggles.)

1 Peel the onion, leaving its root end intact.

2 Cut the onion in half from the top to the root.

3 Lay one onion half, flat side down, on your cutting board.

4 Holding the onion by the root end, make several parallel cuts from the top to the root end, leaving the root end intact. The closer together the cuts, the finer the chopped pieces will be.

5 Still holding the onion half by its root end, make two or three cuts through the onion parallel to the cutting board, again not cutting through the root end.

6 Cut crosswise down through the onion half, from the top to the root end.

7 Repeat with the other onion half. Voilà: a diced or minced onion.

PEEL GINGER

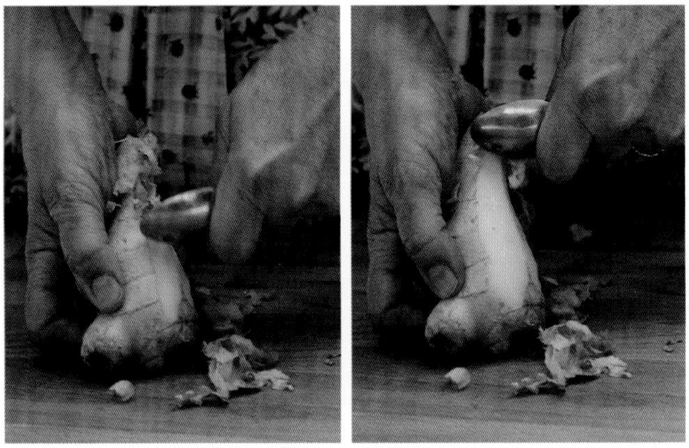

Fresh ginger adds a fabulous spicy flavour, but getting the peel off without cutting off the flesh is always challenging. A spoon to the rescue. Yes, a spoon, and a small, dull one at that. Here's what you do:

1 Hold the ginger root firmly in one hand.

2 Hold the spoon with the other hand and use the edge to scrape off the peel, even over the knobs and bumps. I am left-handed and I find it easier to scrape the peel off toward me, but see which direction works best for you.

3 Voilà! Peeled ginger root with hardly any waste.

CLEAN LEEKS

These heroes of the onion world grow in sandy soil. They can be very gritty if you don't clean them really well.

1. Check out where the dark green top attaches to the bottom white part. There is a horizontal-looking seam. Cut off the green part just above that. Throw the tops in your composter or green bin.
2. Cut off the roots at the other end.
3. Make a horizontal cut from the top to the bottom, slicing halfway through. Discard the outer leaf.
4. Turn on the tap and let the water run through the leek, fanning out the layers.
5. Check for any sand or grit, and run under the tap once more to be sure.
6. Let drain standing upright, then use as needed.

PIT OLIVES

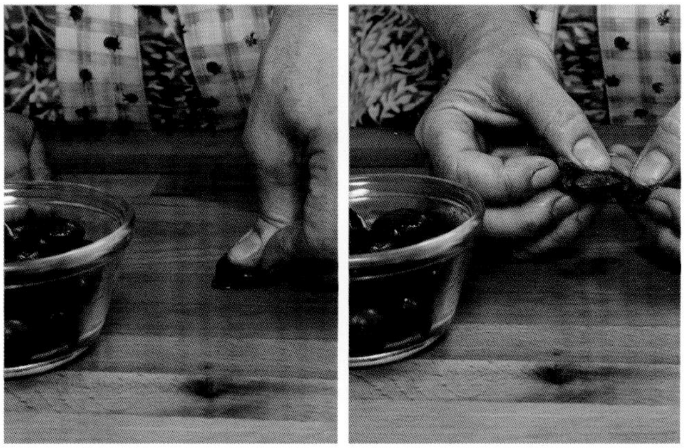

Before you reach for a cherry pitter or try cutting the little gems up with a knife, try this easy method:

1. Place an olive on a cutting board.
2. Press lightly with your thumb (the olive should split in half).
3. Pull out the pit (too cool).

(My apologies to aesthetically minded chefs; I know the olives don't look as pretty, but it sure is easier to do.)

CUT AND SEGMENT AN ORANGE OR GRAPEFRUIT

One of the first things I learned in my UBC class "The Function of Ingredients" was how to segment citrus fruit. Yes, it looks pretty, and yes, it takes some practice, but I have a newer, less finicky way that I use instead of that very careful, chef-approved method. (Note to all chefs: skip this blasphemous section.)

1. First of all you need a great knife. Use a sharp chef's knife.
2. Wash and dry the orange or grapefruit.
3. Cut a thin slice off the bottom and the top of the fruit.
4. Place the now flat bottom onto the cutting board so that it doesn't roll around and cause you to accidentally lose a finger.
5. Using that wonderfully sharp knife, and cutting from the top all the way to the bottom, slice off the peel and as much of the white part of the peel as possible. (It's called the pith, in case you ever get this as a question on *Jeopardy!*.)
6. Now for the unorthodox part (chefs, if you didn't heed the warning, please forgive me): cut the fruit in half horizontally, through the fattest part.
7. Using that brilliant knife and rotating the fruit as you go, cut one half into small bite-sized pieces, working your way to the core. Discard any seeds.
8. Do the other half and voilà, an orange or grapefruit worth plating.

PEEL AND CUT A MANGO

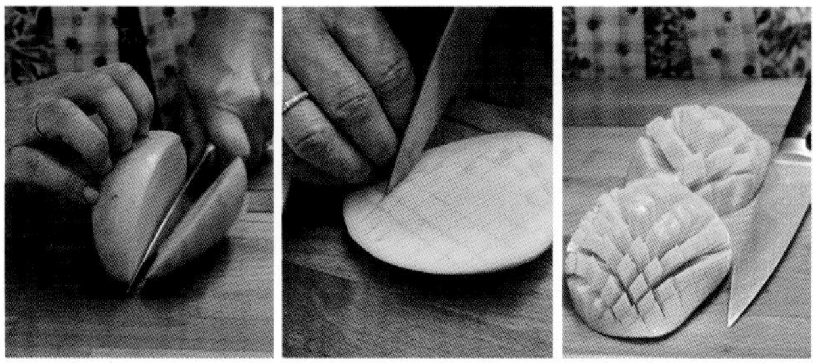

First of all, you need a really ripe mango, as that ensures it will be loaded with flavour and nutrition. Haden mangoes are the most commonly found variety. Look for a heavy mango that is golden yellow with red mottling and has a bit of give to it. Keep a ripened mango in the fridge for up to four days. To ripen a green mango, store it in a paper bag on the counter until the skin turns golden yellow and the fruit has some give when pressed.

The Ataulfo is another variety of mango that has made its way to North America. Slightly smaller than most other mangoes, it is a deep golden yellow when ripe, with a very velvety smooth texture.

I've seen at least three different techniques for preparing a mango but this is the method I use:

1. Wash and dry the mango.
2. The pit of a mango is thin, so guesstimate about 1 inch (2.5 cm) on either side of the middle of the mango.
3. Holding the mango on its edge, slice as close as possible to where you think the pit is. You should just miss the pit, or you fail the mango-cutting portion of this book.
4. Cut off the other side.
5. Using the tip of the knife, score a crosshatch pattern in the cut side of each slice, stopping just short of the peel.
6. Turn the slices inside out (they should look a bit like a porcupine). Slice off the mango cubes.
7. Peel the remaining piece of mango and cut any flesh from the pit. Or, standing over the sink, nibble around the pit and enjoy.

REMOVE THYME/ROSEMARY LEAVES FROM STEMS

When you use fresh thyme or rosemary, the easiest way to get the leaves off of the woody stem is to hold the top of the stem between the index finger and thumb of one hand. Drag the index finger and thumb of your other hand down the stem to the base. The leaves should just fly off, hopefully onto the counter.

SAUTÉ

I always cook over medium heat. There are two reasons for this:

- When you add a fat to a hot pan and it starts to smoke, you have broken down the fatty acid chain. In so doing, the goodness of that fat goes out the window. To protect the health benefits of extra virgin olive oil I cook over medium heat. Even though heart-healthy canola oil has a higher smoke point than extra virgin olive oil and can be used to stir-fry, I still like to cook over medium heat when using canola, unless I am stir-frying.
- I use non-stick skillets. The care instructions always tell you to cook over medium heat. I'm just following the rules.

CUT AND PIT AN AVOCADO

Packed with heart-healthy monounsaturated fat, avocados are a tasty addition to salads and dips. And they're easy to prep.

1. Cut the avocado in half lengthwise.
2. To remove the pit, cradle the half containing the pit, cut side up, in the palm of your hand and whack the pit with the blade of a sharp knife, which should then embed itself in the pit. Twist slightly and remove the pit. (If you're not going to use the entire avocado at once, save the pit to put back in the remaining half, in order to help it keep longer.)
3. Either scoop out the avocado flesh from each half of the peel using a spoon, or slice or chop the flesh inside the peel using the tip of a knife, then remove the flesh with a spoon.

ROAST RED PEPPERS

Wash and dry very ripe sweet red peppers. Cut them in half and remove the seeds. Either roast them in a 400°F (200°C) oven for about 30 minutes, or barbecue over medium-high heat, turning often, for 20 minutes, until the skins blacken. When cool enough to handle, remove the blackened skins.

1

Apples: *The Perfect Fruit*

The old adage "an apple a day keeps the doctor away" may in fact be right on the money. Recent research points out that a daily apple with the peel on may keep the heart surgeon and the oncologist away as well.

What I want to know is, who coined that phrase? I've searched the Internet, the library, everywhere, and the only thing I've dug up is that it was a Welsh saying. Did a Welsh country doctor happen to notice that everyone who didn't eat an apple was in his office regularly? Email me (mairlyn@mairlynsmith.com) if you know anything about this food mystery.

GOOD FOR YOU

Researchers from Cornell University reviewed the most recent literature regarding the health benefits of apples and concluded that, based on these epidemiological studies, it appears that apples may reduce the risk of cancer, heart disease, asthma, and type 2 diabetes when compared with other fruits and vegetables, and other sources of good-for-you flavonoids.

The peel, the peel, eat the peel! The apple's peel is loaded with flavonoids, antioxidants that appear to reduce your chances of developing heart disease and some cancers, specifically breast, colon, and lung cancers.

In a laboratory breast cancer study, published in *Nutrition and Cancer* (May 2010), researchers looked at the effects of apple peel extract on breast cancer cell growth. The results showed that the extract reduced the growth of the cancer cells.

BUY IT, STORE IT

If you are buying loose apples, rather than those packed in a plastic bag, pick firm apples that are bruise-, wrinkle-, and brown-spot-free. Think young supermodel: tight, flawless skin.

Don't be throwing your carefully selected apples into your grocery cart. They bruise, so be gentle. Treat them like you would eggs.

Yes, most TV cooking shows have a gorgeous bowl of apples on the counter, but that lovely fruit will turn soft and mushy fairly quickly, so store them in a plastic bag in the crisper of your fridge. They will keep their crisp, juicy selves that way for at least one month.

My dad always wiped an apple clean on the sleeve of his shirt, but it's better to scrub them well under cold running water before eating them. You never know who's been touching your apples.

FALL / WINTER
KID FRIENDLY

Pan-Fried Rutabaga and Apples

Most people think that rutabagas are turnips. Just to clarify, rutabagas are big and purple / brown in colour. The vegetable that's small and pale yellow with a ring of purple / pink at the top—that would be a turnip. They may look different, but what they have in common is they're both members of the cruciferous family of disease-lowering vegetables.

MAKES ABOUT 3 CUPS (750 ML) | ONE SERVING = ½ CUP (125 ML)

INGREDIENTS

½ medium rutabaga (10 oz/300 g), peeled
2 Empire or Gala apples, scrubbed
1 tbsp (15 mL) extra virgin olive oil
1 tbsp (15 mL) finely chopped crystallized ginger (see page 13)
¼ cup (60 mL) natural apple juice (see page 12)

1 Cut the rutabaga into ¼-inch (6 mm) slices. Set aside.

2 Cut the apples into quarters and remove their cores. Cut each quarter into 5 thin wedges. Set aside.

3 Heat a large non-stick skillet over medium heat. Add the oil then the rutabaga. Cook the rutabaga slices until golden brown on both sides, 3 to 5 minutes.

4 Add the apples and ginger to the skillet, and toss well. Stir in the apple juice. Reduce the heat to low, and simmer, covered, until the rutabaga is tender, about 5 minutes.

5 Remove the lid, increase the heat to medium, and continue cooking until most of the juices have evaporated, about 3 minutes.

PER SERVING: 81 CALORIES, 2.6 G TOTAL FAT, 0 G SATURATED FAT, 0 G TRANS FAT, 8 MG SODIUM, 15.4 G CARBOHYDRATE, 2 G FIBRE, 11.7 G SUGARS, 1 G PROTEIN

DIABETES FOOD CHOICE VALUES PER SERVING: 1 CARBOHYDRATE, ½ FAT

LOCAL BOUNTY

Local Canadian apples arrive in stores and markets around the middle of September, and thanks to cold storage, are available right through to the end of February. Choose from McIntosh, Red Delicious, Empire, Crispin, Royal Gala, Idared, Spartan, Cortland, Honeycrisp, Ambrosia, or the new kid on the apple block, the Red Prince, just to name eleven. Check out your local farmers market at the end of September to get an up close and intimate look at what your local farmers are growing. Each variety of apple tastes different, so mix 'em up and try to eat at least one every single day.

Apple-Cheddar Soup

It has been proven time and again that the family that eats together stays together. Kids who sit down at the family dinner table and share a meal do better in school and are less likely to get into trouble during those tumultuous teen years.

I believe that we need to take it to the next level and get our family members into the kitchen to help us cook. The act of preparing a meal together is a great way to bond. Teenaged boys will actually *talk when they are engaged in an activity. When my son, Andrew, cooks with me in the kitchen, I get a lot more than a grunted "Fine" when I ask how his day went.*

Cooking with kids can be a challenge, but if you think that's difficult, just wait until one of your teenaged kids comes home at 3:00 a.m. wearing their sweatshirt inside out and backwards.

Aside from learning how to cook, kids get so much more from spending time cooking. From learning teamwork, the dying art of conversation, and how to follow directions, to reading, math, and science skills, and broadening their food repertoire—it's all there in the kitchen.

Choose age-appropriate tasks for your kids. Andrew was my official salad greens washer when he was three years old, and yes, the kitchen got soaked. But when he served me a Mother's Day breakfast of French toast and tea when he was six, all those wet floors were but a dim memory.

If your kids are helping you, it's a great idea to prep all the ingredients first. I Mairlyn-ized this recipe from one on the Ontario Apple Growers' website (onapples.com).

MAKES 8 CUPS (2 L) | ONE SERVING = 2 CUPS (500 ML)

INGREDIENTS

1 tbsp (15 mL) extra virgin olive oil
1 cup (250 mL) thinly sliced leeks (see page 23)
3 McIntosh apples, scrubbed, cored, and coarsely chopped
1 cup (250 mL) chopped unpeeled and scrubbed carrots
1 cup (250 mL) chopped celery
1 tbsp (15 mL) finely chopped fresh rosemary (see page 25)
1 tbsp (15 mL) finely chopped fresh thyme (see page 25)
½ tsp (2.5 mL) cracked black pepper
2 cups (500 mL) natural apple juice (see sidebar)
2 cups (500 mL) lightly packed shredded extra-old cheddar
1 cup (250 mL) evaporated fat-free milk (see page 13)

1 Heat a large saucepan over medium heat. Add the oil then the leeks, and sauté for 5 minutes.

2 Add the apples, carrots, celery, rosemary, thyme, and pepper. Cook, stirring often, until the vegetables begin to soften, about 10 minutes.

3 Add the apple juice and 2 cups (500 mL) water, and bring to a boil. Reduce the heat to a simmer and cook, covered, until the vegetables are very tender, 20 to 25 minutes.

4 Use a hand-held immersion blender (see page 8) to purée the soup in the saucepan until smooth. (Or purée the soup in a blender, about 2 cups / 500 mL at a time, until smooth.)

5 Whisk in the shredded cheddar over medium heat until melted. Gently whisk in the milk and heat through but do not boil. Ladle into soup bowls. (If making this soup in advance, omit the cheese and milk and refrigerate the soup in an airtight container for up to 2 days, or freeze it for up to 3 months. To serve, thaw, then reheat the soup, whisk in the cheese, and add the milk before serving.)

PER SERVING: 407 CALORIES, 23.4 G TOTAL FAT, 12 G SATURATED FAT, 0.7 G TRANS FAT, 447 MG SODIUM, 37.7 G CARBOHYDRATE, 4 G FIBRE, 26.8 G SUGARS, 15 G PROTEIN

DIABETES FOOD CHOICE VALUES PER SERVING: 2½ CARBOHYDRATE, 2 MEAT AND ALTERNATIVES, 3½ FAT

TO JUICE OR NOT TO JUICE?

Commercial apple juice doesn't have the same nutritional moxie as freshly made juice, although the natural "cloudy" apple juice (which includes the peel) available in some stores is a better choice than the clear variety. (See page 12 for more on natural apple juice.) Try making your own using a powerful blender (see page 8 for my fave) that liquefies the apple while keeping the fibre and all the antioxidants present and accounted for. Remember to scrub the apples, then cut them into quarters, and remove the core/seeds before juicing.

PICTURED ON PAGE 121
FALL / WINTER
KID FRIENDLY

Apple-Date Muffins

When I started working on this recipe I was going for a muffin that had more than just applesauce in it. I wanted to use whole apples, and get most of the sweetness from antioxidant-rich dates.

The first attempt worked, but then I decided to up the nutrient ante, so I played with ground flaxseed, walnuts, and oat bran. As you'll see, sometimes playing with your food pays off. These whole-grain muffins contain omega-3 fatty acids, are a good source of both insoluble and soluble fibre, and taste fabulous.

My reality tester, Michale, of Los Angeles, wanted everyone to know that these muffins don't look like your everyday, run-of-the-mill muffin with a smooth, rounded top. So, please don't judge this muffin by its lid.

You'll need a blender for this recipe.

MAKES 12 MUFFINS | ONE SERVING = 1 MUFFIN

INGREDIENTS

1 to 2 Idared or Gala apples, scrubbed and patted dry
1 cup (250 mL) dates (see page 12)
1 cup (250 mL) natural apple juice (see page 12)
1 omega-3 egg (see page 13)
1/4 cup (60 mL) packed dark brown sugar
3/4 cup (185 mL) oat bran
1 cup (250 mL) whole wheat flour
3/4 cup (185 mL) ground flaxseed (see page 13)
1/4 cup (60 mL) chopped walnuts
1/4 cup (60 mL) wheat bran
2 tbsp (30 mL) wheat germ
2 tbsp (30 mL) cinnamon
1 tsp (5 mL) baking powder
1 tsp (5 mL) baking soda
pinch each of ground cloves and grated nutmeg

1 Preheat the oven to 400°F (200°C). Line a 12-cup muffin pan with paper liners.

2 Cut 1 apple into quarters and remove the core. Chop the apple into 1/2-inch (1 cm) cubes (about the size of a macaroni noodle). You should have 2 cups (500 mL); if you don't, use the second apple. (Eat any extras.) Set the chopped apple aside.

3 In a blender, process the dates and apple juice until almost puréed. Add 1 cup (250 mL) chopped apple, the egg, and brown sugar, and process until the mixture is well blended and you can't really tell there was ever apples or dates in it. Add the oat bran, and pulse a couple of times. Let the mixture stand in the blender for 5 minutes.

4 Whisk together the whole wheat flour, flaxseed, walnuts, wheat bran, wheat germ, cinnamon, baking powder, baking soda, cloves, and nutmeg in a large bowl.

5 Add the remaining chopped apple to the flour mixture and toss to coat the apple pieces.

6 Pulse the blended date mixture a couple of times, then add to the flour mixture and stir well.

7 Divide the batter evenly among the muffin cups (I use a ¼-cup / 60 mL ice-cream scoop with a release lever). Bake until a toothpick comes out clean, 20 to 25 minutes. Let the muffins cool in the pan on a wire rack for 5 minutes. Remove the muffins and let them cool completely on the wire rack. (Store the muffins in an airtight container for up to 2 days, or freeze them for up to 2 months.)

PER MUFFIN: 185 CALORIES, 5.8 G TOTAL FAT, 0.7 G SATURATED FAT, 0 G TRANS FAT, 146 MG SODIUM, 32.7 G CARBOHYDRATE, 6 G FIBRE, 7.7 G SUGARS, 4 G PROTEIN

DIABETES FOOD CHOICE VALUES PER SERVING: 2 CARBOHYDRATE, 1 FAT

MAIN EVENT OR AN INGREDIENT?

Apples are really versatile. Most of us think of them as a sweet dessert or a snack but you can use them as an ingredient by adding grated apples to a pancake recipe, or chopped apples to a salad or soup that needs a little sweetness. And yes, there is always apple pie. But I couldn't bring myself to include a recipe for one, since pies contain way too many calories and too much fat and sugar. So, here's the deal: have a slice as a treat at someone else's house or when you go to a restaurant. You don't have to say, "Bye-bye, pie," just have it very occasionally. And say "Hello, whole apple" more often.

Apple Chips

I adapted this recipe from one on the Ontario Apple Growers' website (onapples.com). The first time I made it, I was getting ready for a visit from our friends and fellow actors, Jill and Larry, who were coming over to watch the Golden Globe Awards with us. The house was filled with the aroma of apple and cinnamon while these chips cooked in the oven. While they were cooling, I thought I'd better try just one to make sure they were as good as they smelled, and the next thing I knew, I'd eaten all of them. So when Jill and Larry arrived for pre-awards snacks, we had nothing to offer them. Okay, I opened a bottle of Champagne and served it with goat cheese while the aroma of apple chips lingered in the air.

MAKES ABOUT 2 CUPS (500 ML) | ONE SERVING = ¼ CUP (60 ML)

INGREDIENTS

2 Gala, Idared, or Empire apples, scrubbed and patted dry
2 tsp (10 mL) granulated sugar
1 tsp (5 mL) cinnamon

1 Position the oven racks in the bottom and top thirds of the oven. Preheat the oven to 200°F (95°C). Line two 13- × 9-inch (33 × 23 cm) rimmed baking sheets with parchment paper.

2 Cut the apples vertically into very thin slices using a mandoline (see page 11) or a sharp knife, stopping and turning each apple when you reach the core. You want the slices to look like potato chips. Arrange the slices in a single layer on the prepared baking sheets.

3 Stir together the sugar and cinnamon in a small bowl. With your fingers, sprinkle the sugar mixture evenly over the apple slices.

4 Bake the apple slices for about 1 hour. Switch the positions of the baking sheets and bake until the slices are crisp, about 1 hour more.

5 Remove the baking sheets from the oven and let the apple chips cool on the baking sheets on wire racks.

6 Gently peel the apple chips off the paper and store them in an airtight container for up to 3 days.

KID ZONE

This is also a great recipe to make with your kids. Depending on how old they are, get them to wash the apples, arrange the slices on the prepared baking sheets, and sprinkle them with the cinnamon-sugar. You can do the slicing.

FLU FIGHTER

To reduce your chances of getting the flu, wash your hands regularly and eat an apple every day. Lab studies show that the peel contains the antioxidant quercetin, which may bolster your immune system. So scrub your apples well and eat that antioxidant-rich peel.

PER SERVING: 32 CALORIES, 0 G TOTAL FAT, 0 G SATURATED FAT, 0 G TRANS FAT, 1 MG SODIUM, 8.4 G CARBOHYDRATE, 1.1 G FIBRE, 6.4 G SUGARS, 0 G PROTEIN

DIABETES FOOD CHOICE VALUES PER SERVING: ½ CARBOHYDRATE

2

Asparagus:
Green, Pointy, and Powerful

In ancient times, if you had a toothache or a bee sting, or weren't doing a great job in the *amour* department, the cure-all was a great big plate of asparagus. The history books never say what people *did* with the asparagus, but I am assuming they ate it.

I become euphoric when I make my first local asparagus sighting. Those green pointy spears make me dizzy thinking of all the culinary possibilities. Asparagus is fabulous steamed, roasted, grilled, or added to an omelette (try my Spring Mushroom Omelette for Two on page 248), a salad, or a sandwich. Personally, I love my asparagus naked — no accessories, just the flavour of fresh local asparagus all by itself.

GOOD FOR YOU

Asparagus scores an A-plus in the nutrient department. It's a rich source of rutin, a bioflavonoid that strengthens blood vessel walls, and glutathione, an antioxidant believed to have cancer-fighting properties.

Asparagus is also an excellent source of folate, and contains potassium, vitamins A and C, selenium, and manganese. Weighing in with 2 grams of fibre and only 20 calories per half cup (125 mL), the mighty little green stalk is Herculean when it comes to nutrition.

BUY IT, STORE IT

Look for bright green stalks that are crisp and straight and have tightly closed, compact tips. Avoid spears with partially opened or wilted tips. Remove the rubber bands as soon as you can; they cut off the water flow in the spears and actually speed up rotting.

If you want the best bang for your nutritional loonie, wrap the bottom of the stalks in a damp paper towel, place the bunch in a plastic bag, and refrigerate. (Or stand them upright in a jug of fresh water covered with a plastic bag in the fridge.) Use within two days.

Asparagus is usually bundled in 1 lb (500 g) bunches; figure on one bunch serving four people. Wash asparagus really well under cold running water to get rid of any grit.

You can either snap off the thick, woody end of the asparagus where it breaks naturally, or guesstimate where the thick part ends and the tender part begins, and cut off the thicker part with a knife.

Asparagus Salad

Have you ever seen asparagus spears growing in a field? They look like rows of little green soldiers standing at attention, ready to do battle. Good thing for us that they're fighting for our good health.

For fans of raw asparagus, this recipe is just as good using uncooked asparagus. And it's even quicker to make!

MAKES ABOUT 4 CUPS (1 L) | ONE SERVING = ½ CUP (125 ML)

INGREDIENTS

1 lb (500 g) fresh asparagus, washed and trimmed
1 tbsp (15 mL) extra virgin olive oil
1 tbsp (15 mL) white wine vinegar
½ tsp (2.5 mL) grainy Dijon mustard
Cracked black pepper to taste
½ large sweet red pepper, seeded and diced
One 6 oz (170 mL) jar marinated artichoke hearts, well drained and coarsely chopped
2 tbsp (30 mL) finely chopped parsley

1 Steam the asparagus until it's tender-crisp, going heavy on the "crisp" part, about 3 minutes. Don't overcook it; grey-green, droopy spears of overcooked asparagus are a sin in the culinary world. Immediately, plunge the asparagus into a clean sink of cold water to stop the cooking. Drain the asparagus in a colander.

2 Whisk together the oil, vinegar, Dijon, and pepper in a large bowl. Add the red pepper, artichoke hearts, and parsley, and toss well.

3 Cut the asparagus into 1-inch (2.5 cm) pieces, keeping the tips intact. Add the asparagus to the bowl and toss gently. For the best flavour, cover the salad and refrigerate it for a couple of hours, although it's still great if you eat it right away.

PER SERVING: 40 CALORIES, 1.7 G TOTAL FAT, 0 G SATURATED FAT, 0 G TRANS FAT, 40 MG SODIUM, 5.1 G CARBOHYDRATE, 2 G FIBRE, 1.8 G SUGARS, 2 G PROTEIN

DIABETES FOOD CHOICE VALUES PER SERVING: ½ MEAT AND ALTERNATIVES, 1 EXTRA

SULPHUR AND THE HUMAN EXPERIENCE

Ever wonder why, after you've eaten asparagus, your urine may have a pungent smell? It's the sulphur compounds in the asparagus that cause this weird odour. I have read various opinions on and scientific explanations of this phenomenon. Apparently we all produce the skunky smell but only 40% of us can detect it.

Spring Asparagus and Shrimp with Lemon Pasta

If you time it right, this quick and easy dinner will be ready in the time it takes the pasta to cook. While you're waiting for the pasta water to boil and the shrimp to thaw, prep the veggies, and you'll be done in minutes.

If you've just decided to make this dish and the shrimp are frozen, remove them from the bag and place them in a clean sink of cold water, and they should be thawed by the time you need them. Drain well before tossing into the skillet.

You can easily turn this dish into a vegetarian entrée by skipping the shrimp and sprinkling each serving with 2 tbsp (30 mL) pine nuts or chopped walnuts.

MAKES 4 SERVINGS
ONE SERVING = ABOUT 2½ OZ SHRIMP AND ½ CUP (125 ML) PASTA

INGREDIENTS

3 large cloves garlic
One 1 lb (454 g) package frozen, uncooked extra-large shrimp (26 to 30 per bag), thawed
½ lb (250 g) fresh asparagus
4 oz (125 g) 100% whole-grain spaghettini
2 lemons
1 tbsp (15 mL) extra virgin olive oil
3 large shallots, diced
8 kalamata olives, pitted and chopped (see page 23)
1 tbsp (15 mL) capers, drained and rinsed (see page 12)
½ tsp (2.5 mL) red pepper flakes
1 tsp (5 mL) honey (optional)
Finely chopped parsley for garnish

1 Mince the garlic and set aside.

2 Wash your hands. Peel and devein the shrimp, leaving their tails on. Wash your hands again. Bring a large pot of water to a boil.

3 Meanwhile, wash the asparagus well and trim off the woody parts. Cut each asparagus spear into 4 pieces, keeping the tips intact.

4 By now, the water should be boiling. Add the pasta to the pot and bring the water back to a boil. Cook until the pasta is al dente (see sidebar), 7 to 9 minutes.

5 While the pasta is cooking, wash and dry the lemons. Using a Microplane grater, remove the zest from 1 lemon (you should have about 1 tbsp / 15 mL). With your palm, roll both lemons on the counter (this makes them yield more juice), then cut them in half and squeeze out the juice (you should have ½ cup / 125 mL).

6 Heat a large skillet over medium-low heat. Add the oil then the shallots, and sauté until golden brown, 3 to 5 minutes.

7 Increase the heat to medium. Add the asparagus and garlic, and sauté for 1 minute. By now the pasta should be ready. If it is, drain it well and set aside. Don't even think of rinsing it.

8 Back to the skillet. Add the shrimp, olives, capers, and red pepper flakes to the skillet, and sauté until the shrimp are pink and firm, about 3 minutes. Scrape the contents of the skillet into a clean bowl, cover it, and set aside.

9 Add the lemon juice to the now-empty skillet and bring to a boil over medium heat. Stir to scrape up any browned bits from the bottom of the skillet, and boil until the liquid has reduced by about one-quarter. (In chef-speak, you are deglazing the skillet.) Have a taste, and if it is too acidic, add honey, stirring to dissolve.

10 Add the drained pasta and lemon zest to the skillet, and toss well to coat. To serve, spoon the cooked pasta into 4 pasta bowls and top each with one-quarter of the shrimp mixture. Sprinkle with parsley before serving.

PER SERVING: 270 CALORIES, 6.9 G TOTAL FAT, 1.6 G SATURATED FAT, 0 G TRANS FAT, 412 MG SODIUM, 31.8 G CARBOHYDRATE, 4 G FIBRE, 2.6 G SUGARS, 27 G PROTEIN

DIABETES FOOD CHOICE VALUES PER SERVING: 2 CARBOHYDRATE, 3 MEAT AND ALTERNATIVES

PASTA 101

Use lots of water to boil pasta and don't add any oil. Bring the water to a full, rolling boil, add the pasta, and give it a stir to prevent it from sticking to the bottom of the pot. Bring the water back to a boil, then begin timing. When it's al dente (see below), drain but never rinse. Rinsing does two evil things: it rinses off nutrients, and it rinses off the starch that helps sauce stick to it.

So, what does "al dente" mean? It literally translates as "to the tooth," which in culinary parlance means "don't cook the living daylights out of it." Pasta should have some kind of texture. A lot of people cook it until it's mushy, which is a huge no-no. Read the package and follow the directions.

Chilled Asparagus with Mairlyn's World-Famous Lime Sauce

I created my World-Famous Lime Sauce back in my catering days as an accompaniment to cold cooked asparagus or cold poached salmon. It always got raves. Once I catered an event where there were umpteen dishes and the most popular item was this lime sauce.

I never wanted to give my secret away, not because it was so unique, but because it was so darned easy, and I was trying to be an oh-so-cool, chef-y type. Well, I'm over trying to be cool, so here it is, back by popular demand.

MAKES 1 LB (500 G) ASPARAGUS AND ABOUT ⅓ CUP (80 ML) SAUCE
ONE SERVING = ABOUT 5 ASPARAGUS SPEARS AND 1 HEAPING TBSP (20 ML) SAUCE

1 Using a Microplane grater (see page 8), remove the zest from the lime and set aside. With your palm, roll the lime on the counter (this makes the lime yield more juice), then cut in half and squeeze out 2 tbsp (30 mL) juice. Set aside.

2 Steam the asparagus until it is tender-crisp, going heavy on the "crisp" part, about 3 minutes. Don't overcook it. They shouldn't be droopy when you hold them perpendicular to the floor; it's such a sad little posture.

3 Immediately, plunge the asparagus into a clean sink of cold water to stop the cooking. Drain the asparagus in a colander. Place on a paper-towel-lined plate and refrigerate, covered, until serving time. (The asparagus will stay fresh for up to 2 days in the fridge.)

4 Just before serving, whisk together the mayonnaise, lime zest, and juice. Arrange the asparagus on 4 individual plates, or a large serving platter, and drizzle the sauce over the tips of the spears.

PER SERVING: 56 CALORIES, 2.7 G TOTAL FAT, 0 G SATURATED FAT, 0 G TRANS FAT, 81 MG SODIUM, 7.2 G CARBOHYDRATE, 3 G FIBRE, 2.5 G SUGARS, 3 G PROTEIN

DIABETES FOOD CHOICE VALUES PER SERVING: ½ MEAT AND ALTERNATIVES, ½ FAT, 1 EXTRA

INGREDIENTS

1 lime, scrubbed well and dried

1 lb (500 g) fresh asparagus, washed and trimmed

2 tbsp plus 2 tsp (40 mL) low-fat mayonnaise

ASPARAGUS ETIQUETTE

According to Emily Post, as long as the spears aren't droopy and don't have any type of sauce on them, you can pick asparagus up with your fingers. But, if the hostess is eating hers with a knife and fork, follow her lead.

HOW TO GRILL ASPARAGUS

Choose medium-thick asparagus spears, wash them well, and trim off the woody ends. Toss the spears in canola oil and place on the grill over medium heat, arranging the spears at right angles to the grates or they'll fall through. Grill for 6 to 8 minutes, turning often, until tender-crisp. Serve with a squirt of fresh lime or lemon juice.

THE BIG M (AND I DON'T MEAN FRANK MAHOVLICH)

(WARNING: THE FOLLOWING MAY CONTAIN LANGUAGE UNSUITABLE FOR MALES.)

Menopause. Medically defined as the ceasing of the menses, it's the time in your life when you wave bye-bye to your monthly visitor and hello to temporary insanity.

It's the only time in your life when you can say, "I want to stab you in the eye with an ice pick," then, in the next breath, "I love you so much. I can't believe I said that. I'm so sorry." And that's to your mechanic.

It's when your hormones are giving you the business and unfortunately so are your kids. To paraphrase a Bette Davis quote, aging isn't for wimps. And neither is menopause.

I had read that your menopause is often similar to the one your mother experienced. And I thought, dear God, I'm screwed. My mother was a total nutbag during the change.

So I hunkered down and prepared for the worst. And it never happened. I wasn't any crabbier than normal; my son told me I'd always been crabby, so he didn't notice a marked spike. I didn't have a lot of hot flashes or night sweats. Not once did I fantasize about axe-murdering my letter carrier. I really didn't have a terrible time.

Okay, occasionally I wanted to leave the country, live under an assumed name, and marry a rich man who would only want to see me for lavish dinners on Mondays and Fridays.

And if the truth be known, I did go through a chocolate phase during which I ate a lot of the elixir of the gods. I'm talking a small city's worth of chocolate. I ate so much that some days I realized that I'd forgotten to eat anything but chocolate, and the best part was I didn't care.

And then ... um ... ah ... eh ... I totally forget where I was going with this one. Oh, well, apparently all menopausal women experience lapses in memory. Great, I'm not alone.

So, all in all, it hasn't been all that bad for the past eight years. Sure, my body, and especially my skin, seems to be aiming for my feet, but inside, I am a goddess. Eating healthily, exercising, and working on stress management helps. There aren't any studies to prove this, so far, but I believe that what I've been eating, combined with my active lifestyle, has rewarded me with an easier menopause. So, here's some sage advice from an old broad: women in your twenties and thirties, the sooner you jump on board the health train, the better.

3

Beans, Beans: *The Musical Fruit!*

First of all, let's set the record straight. Are beans legumes, or are legumes beans?

High-five yourself if you knew that beans are legumes. Beans (not the green kind, the dried kind), lentils, and split dried peas are all part of the legume family.

GOOD FOR YOU

Beans are touted as one of the best nutritional all-stars, with the Mayo Clinic rating them one of its Top Ten foods. All the members of the legume family are treasure troves of vitamins, minerals, fibre, protein, and antioxidants, plus they're diabetes-friendly. Their low glycemic index rating helps keep insulin levels riding on a nice even keel, with no crazy storms to topple your pancreas.

Legumes also keep your colon and your heart happy with two types of fibre: insoluble and soluble. The first keeps everything moving through your intestines, the second helps absorb cholesterol in your blood stream then shows it the emergency exit. But Canadians don't eat enough legumes, which leads us to . . .

FEAR OF FARTING

(Warning: if you're sensitive about any mention of gas, you're better off skipping this next bit; I wouldn't want to offend you.)

We all know that wonderful childhood ditty "Beans, beans, the musical fruit / The more you eat the more you toot!" Well, here's a news flash: the lyrics are wrong. First of all beans aren't a fruit, they're a legume, and second, the more you eat, the *less* you'll toot. Let me explain.

Our gastrointestinal tracts are uniquely designed to digest what we eat on a regular basis. Your intestinal flora, as they're called in the gastro biz, produce an environment that helps digest what you just ate. So if you eat a lot of meat, you can digest that no problem. If you haven't had a bean since your Grade 6 field trip, then "Houston, we have a problem."

On the other hand, big bean eaters are relatively unscathed when they eat beans. But give them a steak, maybe twice a year, and all I can say is, "Wow, scary!"

Basically your body gets used to what you eat and becomes more efficient at digesting it. It takes about two weeks of eating beans every day to start to see toot reduction, so hang in there because your heart will thank you, even though your neighbours won't.

If you're in your fifties or a Mel Brooks fan you've probably seen the movie *Blazing Saddles,* with its famous campfire scene that every guy I've ever met, dated, or married loves. The first time I saw it, my date actually fell out of his seat into the aisle of the movie theatre. Most men think farts are funny; women, not so much.

We all have flatulence episodes. In fact, each and every one of us averages *14* episodes a day. You probably had one while you were reading this. I know most of my female friends claim never to have passed wind, but let's face it, they're fibbing. Everyone has the toots at some time or other. It is one of the main reasons I exercise. All that moving around helps gas exit my body, usually in the open air while I am walking my dog.

Yes, I know it's impolite to pass a little toot in public but so is burping, spitting, and picking your schnozz. We've all heard belches, witnessed a spit, and caught someone exploring the inner regions of their nostrils. But let one little badly timed fluff go, and you become the village idiot.

Lighten up, people. I'm with Shrek: "Better out than in." Just be discreet.

YEAR ROUND
KID FRIENDLY

Black Bean Tortilla Chip Soup

Traditional Mexican tortilla soup usually contains chicken, plus all the bells and whistles—avocado, cilantro, and tortilla chips—normally found in this quick and easy dinner. I decided to replace the chicken with antioxidant-rich black beans, to up the nutrient level. My soup still has that unique tortilla soup flavour but in a heart-healthier version.

If you're an organized cook and prep the green onions, cilantro, avocado, and lime while the soup is simmering, you can have this on the table in 15 minutes.

MAKES 8 CUPS (2 L) | ONE SERVING = 2 CUPS (500 ML)

INGREDIENTS

- 3 cups (750 mL) lower-sodium chicken or vegetable broth (see page 7)
- One 19 oz (540 mL) can diced tomatoes
- One 19 oz (540 mL) can black beans, drained and rinsed
- 1 cup (250 mL) frozen corn kernels (no need to thaw)
- 1/4 cup (60 mL) mild, medium, or hot fresh salsa (from the deli)
- 1 tbsp (15 mL) hot sauce (or to taste)
- 1 cup (250 mL) thinly sliced green onions (about 5)
- 1 cup (250 mL) chopped fresh cilantro
- 1 ripe avocado, peeled, pitted, and thinly sliced (see page 25)
- 1 lime, scrubbed well and cut into quarters
- 40 unsalted whole-grain corn tortilla chips

1 Heat the broth in a large saucepan over medium-high heat. When it comes to a boil, add the tomatoes, black beans, corn, salsa, and hot sauce. Bring the broth back to a boil. Reduce the heat to a simmer and cook, covered, for 5 minutes. Stir and remove from the heat.

2 Ladle the soup into 4 deep soup bowls. Sprinkle each portion with the green onions, cilantro, and avocado, dividing evenly. Squeeze a lime quarter over each bowl. Crumble 10 tortilla chips into each bowl and stir gently.

PER SERVING: 420 CALORIES, 13.4 G TOTAL FAT, 1.9 G SATURATED FAT, 0 G TRANS FAT, 526 MG SODIUM, 64.5 G CARBOHYDRATE, 13 G FIBRE, 11.8 G SUGARS, 15 G PROTEIN

DIABETES FOOD CHOICE VALUES PER SERVING: 3½ CARBOHYDRATE, 1 MEAT AND ALTERNATIVES, 2 FAT

GIVE IT A TWIST

If you make this in the summer during local corn season, cook fresh ears of corn (my favourite way is to grill them) and cut the kernels from the ears. Two medium ears of corn yield about 1 cup (250 mL) kernels.

Spicy Red Lentil Soup

Lentils are extremely high in disease-reducing antioxidants. Factor in the garlic and onions, plus the tomatoes and beta-carotene-rich apricots, then throw in the power of turmeric to reduce your chances of developing Alzheimer's, and you have a bowl of soup that's a powerhouse. If you forget where the remote is tonight, have another bowl.

MAKES 8 CUPS (2 L) | ONE SERVING = 2 CUPS (500 ML)

INGREDIENTS

- 4 large cloves garlic
- 1 tsp (5 mL) turmeric
- 1 tsp (5 mL) ground cumin
- 1 tsp (5 mL) cinnamon
- 1 tsp (5 mL) cracked black pepper
- ¼ tsp (1 mL) ground allspice
- 2 tbsp (30 mL) extra virgin olive oil
- 2 onions, diced
- 1 cup (250 mL) chopped celery (about 3 stalks)
- 1 tsp (5 mL) finely grated fresh ginger
- 4 cups (1 L) lower-sodium chicken or vegetable broth (see page 7)
- One 28 oz (796 mL) can diced tomatoes
- 1 cup (250 mL) dried red lentils, rinsed and drained
- 8 dried apricots, coarsely chopped

1 Mince the garlic and set aside. Mix together the turmeric, cumin, cinnamon, black pepper, and allspice in a small bowl. Set aside.

2 Heat a large saucepan over medium heat. Add the oil, then the onions and celery, and sauté until golden brown, about 5 minutes.

3 Add the garlic, ginger, and spice mixture, and sauté for 1 minute.

4 Add the broth, tomatoes, lentils, apricots, and 1 cup (250 mL) water, and bring to a boil. Reduce the heat to a simmer and cook, covered and stirring occasionally, until the lentils are tender, 35 to 40 minutes. Serve. (Refrigerate any leftovers in an airtight container for up to 2 days.)

PER SERVING: 249 CALORIES, 3.3 G TOTAL FAT, 1.4 G SATURATED FAT, 0 G TRANS FAT, 465 MG SODIUM, 42.9 G CARBOHYDRATE, 8 G FIBRE, 15.2 G SUGARS, 15 G PROTEIN

DIABETES FOOD CHOICE VALUES PER SERVING: 2½ CARBOHYDRATE, 1 MEAT AND ALTERNATIVES

WHAT IS . . . ?

Red lentils are smaller and cook faster than their green and brown cousins. Find them with the dried beans in your local grocery store.

Roasted Red Pepper and Chickpea Salad

This main-course salad, which is a spin on one in Ultimate Foods for Ultimate Health ... and don't forget the chocolate!, *is great to take on a picnic or to a potluck summer dinner. It's unique, tastes like summer, and is loaded with cancer-fighting ingredients like garlic, shallots, oregano, and parsley. Plus it boasts heart-healthy ingredients like chickpeas and red peppers. Basically this is jam-packed with healthy ingredients, and will surprise your taste buds with every bite.*

Artichokes are considered to be among the top ten antioxidant-rich foods, right below blueberries. You can buy canned plain artichoke hearts in most large grocery stores; find them with the canned vegetables (just don't use the marinated ones that come in a jar).

MAKES 5 CUPS (1.25 L) | ONE SERVING = 1 CUP (250 ML)

INGREDIENTS

3 cloves garlic
3 whole roasted sweet red peppers (see page 25)
One 19 oz (540 mL) can chickpeas, drained and rinsed
One 14 oz (398 mL) can artichoke hearts, drained and rinsed
1/3 cup (80 mL) finely chopped parsley
2 tbsp (30 mL) capers, drained and rinsed (see page 12)
2 tsp (10 mL) chopped fresh oregano
1 large shallot, diced
1/4 cup (60 mL) red wine vinegar
2 tbsp (30 mL) extra virgin olive oil

1 Mince the garlic and set aside.

2 If using bottled roasted peppers, drain them well and chop into pieces roughly the same size as the chickpeas. If using fresh roasted peppers, remove their seeds, then chop the peppers. Put into a large salad bowl and add the chickpeas.

3 Cut the artichokes into quarters and add them to the bowl. Add the parsley, capers, and oregano.

4 Whisk together the garlic, shallot, vinegar, and oil in a small bowl. Add the dressing to the salad and toss well. Refrigerate the salad, covered, for at least 2 hours before serving. (The salad will keep for up to 24 hours in the fridge.)

ENDORSEMENT

Even my bean-challenged sister, Kathleen, gives this one two thumbs up!

PER SERVING: 195 CALORIES, 7.1 G TOTAL FAT, 1.0 G SATURATED FAT, 0 G TRANS FAT, 291 MG SODIUM, 25.4 G CARBOHYDRATE, 5 G FIBRE, 3.5 G SUGARS, 7 G PROTEIN

DIABETES FOOD CHOICE VALUES PER SERVING: 1½ CARBOHYDRATE, ½ MEAT AND ALTERNATIVES, 1 FAT

SPRING / SUMMER / FALL
KID FRIENDLY

Mixed Bean Salad

This family-friendly bean salad makes a quick and easy lunch or dinner. Get your kids involved by having them wash the veggies and parsley, then spin the parsley dry in a salad spinner so you can chop it.

MAKES 5 CUPS (1.25 L) | ONE SERVING = 1 CUP (250 ML)

1 Mince the garlic and set aside.

2 Drain the sun-dried tomatoes on a paper towel to absorb any excess oil. Chop them finely.

3 Toss together the sun-dried tomatoes, beans, celery, sweet pepper, grape tomatoes, green onions, and parsley in a large salad bowl.

4 Whisk together the vinegar, oil, and garlic in a small bowl. Add the dressing to the salad and toss well. Season with pepper to taste.

PER SERVING: 179 CALORIES, 4.9 G TOTAL FAT, 0.6 G SATURATED FAT, 0 G TRANS FAT, 245 MG SODIUM, 27.1 G CARBOHYDRATE, 8 G FIBRE, 2.5 G SUGARS, 9 G PROTEIN

DIABETES FOOD CHOICE VALUES PER SERVING: 1½ CARBOHYDRATE, 1 MEAT AND ALTERNATIVES, ½ FAT

INGREDIENTS

3 cloves garlic

2 tbsp (30 mL) drained sun-dried tomatoes in oil

One 19 oz (540 mL) can mixed beans, drained and rinsed

2 stalks celery, diced

1 large sweet orange pepper, seeded and diced

1 cup (250 mL) grape tomatoes, cut in half

½ cup (125 mL) thinly sliced green onions or snipped fresh chives

½ cup (125 mL) chopped parsley

2 tbsp (30 mL) apple cider vinegar (see page 12)

1 tbsp (15 mL) extra virgin olive oil

Cracked black pepper to taste

QUICK TIP

During the hot summer months, keep a can of mixed beans in your fridge. Whenever you want to make this recipe, the beans are cold and ready to go. Just open, drain and rinse, and toss with the other ingredients.

GIVE IT A TWIST

Reality tester Orla, in Abbotsford, BC, suggests using balsamic vinegar instead of apple cider vinegar for a zippier salad.

Nutrition-Packed Curried Lentils with Spinach

(From Ultimate Foods for Ultimate Health ... and don't forget the chocolate! *by Liz Pearson and Mairlyn Smith)*

Curry gets its flavour from a blend of many spices. Coriander, ginger, chili, pepper, cinnamon, turmeric, cloves, cardamom, cumin, and nutmeg are just 10 of them. But you only need a couple, plus a good curry powder, to make a great curry. To read more on one of my favourite spice blends see the opposite page.

This meatless curry is so packed with good stuff, it needs no accompaniment.

MAKES 5 CUPS (1.25 L) | ONE SERVING = 1¼ CUPS (310 ML)

INGREDIENTS

4 cloves garlic
1 tbsp (15 mL) curry powder
1 tsp (5 mL) ground cumin
1 tsp (5 mL) ground coriander
¼ tsp (1 mL) turmeric
4 tsp (20 mL) extra virgin olive oil
1 onion, diced
One 28 oz (796 mL) can diced tomatoes
One 19 oz (540 mL) can lentils, drained and rinsed
4 cups (1 L) baby spinach

1 Mince the garlic and set aside. Mix together the curry powder, cumin, coriander, and turmeric in a small bowl. Set aside.

2 Heat a large saucepan over medium heat. Add the olive oil then the onion, and sauté for 2 minutes. Add the spice mixture. Cook for 1 minute, stirring constantly.

3 Stir in the tomatoes and lentils and bring to a boil. Reduce the heat to a simmer and cook, covered, for 15 minutes, stirring occasionally.

4 Increase the heat to medium and add the spinach and garlic. Cook, stirring, until the spinach has wilted.

PER SERVING: 209 CALORIES, 5.5 G TOTAL FAT, 0.7 G SATURATED FAT, 0 G TRANS FAT, 403 MG SODIUM, 31.0 G CARBOHYDRATE, 7 G FIBRE, 7.7 G SUGARS, 10 G PROTEIN

DIABETES FOOD CHOICE VALUES PER SERVING: 1½ CARBOHYDRATE, 1 MEAT AND ALTERNATIVES, ½ FAT

I'M A SPICE GIRL

Curry is one of those words that, depending on where you live, can mean a number of different things. Curry in India means a sauce, while in the UK it means any type of savoury South Asian food. Here in Canada, most of us think it's a single spice that grows on a tree somewhere in Asia, which would be totally incorrect.

Curry is a magical blend of spices that changes depending on the location and the chef who creates it. Curries vary from hot, like vindaloo and Madras, to mild kormas, or sweet garam masalas. You could probably say, without really exaggerating, that there are as many recipes for curry as there are families living in South Asia. It's unique and fabulous everywhere you go.

In Canada, most of us use ready-made curry powder instead of mixing or blending our own. Commercial curry powders usually contain a lot of turmeric, which not only gives the powder its rich golden yellow colour, but may also benefit the health of my second-favourite organ, the brain.

Curcumin, the active ingredient in turmeric, may ease inflammation. In South Asian medicine, turmeric has been used for thousands of years to treat arthritis and other ailments. Some research suggests that the anti-inflammatory properties turmeric displays may help in the battle against rheumatoid arthritis, heart disease, Alzheimer's, and perhaps cancer. Lab research suggests that curcumin may slow the spread of cancer and may cause cancer cells to die. However, all the evidence to date, while encouraging, is still far from conclusive. But that doesn't stop me from using turmeric at least twice a week in South Asian–style cooking.

Before you start sprinkling turmeric on everything you eat, be warned: it may be a spice, but it sure doesn't taste like cinnamon. Turmeric can be added to curry recipes, chilies, soups, and other savoury dishes, but needs to be cooked in some fat first. When I use it, I usually add it to sautéed onions and cook it for about 1 minute, stirring constantly, before adding my other ingredients.

Chickpeas with Sweet Potatoes à la Garam Masala

This recipe uses garam masala, a sweeter curry blend, with some extra South Asian spices thrown in just to make your palate sing. If you don't love spicy, omit the black pepper and red pepper flakes.

In either case, serve this with Thickened Yogurt (page 272) to tone down the heat.

MAKES 6 CUPS (1.5 L) | ONE SERVING = 1 CUP (250 ML)

1 Mince the garlic and set aside. Mix together the garam masala, cumin, cinnamon, coriander, black pepper, turmeric, and red pepper flakes in a small bowl. Set aside.

2 Peel the sweet potatoes and cut them into pieces a little larger than the chickpeas (you should have close to 4 cups / 1 L).

3 Heat a medium saucepan over medium heat. Add the oil, then the onions, and sauté until golden brown, about 5 minutes.

4 Add the sweet potato and sauté for 3 minutes. Add the spice mixture, garlic, and ginger, and sauté for 1 minute. The aroma will be amazing.

5 Stir in the chicken broth, making sure you scrape up all the little browned bits stuck to the bottom of the saucepan. This helps add more flavour and will prevent the curry from burning later on in the cooking process. Bring to a boil. Reduce the heat to a simmer and cook, covered, until the sweet potatoes are starting to soften, about 10 minutes.

6 Add the chickpeas, and bring back to a boil. Reduce the heat to a simmer and cook, covered, for 10 minutes. Remove the lid and stir. Simmer, uncovered, until the sweet potatoes are tender, about 10 minutes. Serve garnished with the chopped cilantro.

PER SERVING: 207 CALORIES, 4.2 G TOTAL FAT, 0.4 G SATURATED FAT, 0 G TRANS FAT, 255 MG SODIUM, 34.6 G CARBOHYDRATE, 8 G FIBRE, 4.6 G SUGARS, 9 G PROTEIN

DIABETES FOOD CHOICE VALUES PER SERVING: 2 CARBOHYDRATE, ½ MEAT AND ALTERNATIVES, ½ FAT

INGREDIENTS

4 cloves garlic
1 tbsp (15 mL) finely grated fresh ginger
2 tsp (10 mL) garam masala
1 tsp (5 mL) ground cumin
1 tsp (5 mL) cinnamon
1 tsp (5 mL) ground coriander
1 tsp (5 mL) cracked black pepper
1 tsp (5 mL) turmeric
¼ tsp (1 mL) red pepper flakes (optional)
2 large sweet potatoes (see below)
1 tbsp (15 mL) canola oil
2 onions, diced
1 cup (250 mL) lower-sodium chicken or vegetable broth (see page 7)
One 19 oz (540 mL) can chickpeas, drained and rinsed
½ cup (125 mL) chopped fresh cilantro, for garnish

HEALTH BITE

If the sweet potatoes are new and young, with thin skins, skip peeling them and just scrub really well before chopping.

Family-Style Meatless Chili

Heart-healthy, antioxidant-rich beans teamed with lentils, onions, red pepper, spices, and tomatoes, all topped with healthy fats from the avocado and a little bit of cheese for kids old and young—this is a recipe for health. I love making a big batch of this chili to use three different ways (see sidebar).

This isn't a spicy chili so it's the perfect kid-friendly dinner. If you want to give it a kick, add some hot sauce at the table.

MAKES 8 CUPS (2 L) | ONE SERVING = 1 CUP (250 ML)

CHILI

- 6 large cloves garlic
- One 19 oz (540 mL) can black beans
- One 19 oz (540 mL) can red kidney beans
- One 19 oz (540 mL) can lentils
- 1 tbsp (15 mL) canola oil
- 2 onions, diced
- 2 cups (500 mL) frozen corn kernels, thawed (or see sidebar page 48)
- 1 tbsp (15 mL) chili powder
- 1 tbsp (15 mL) dried oregano leaves
- 2 tsp (10 mL) ground coriander
- 2 tsp (10 mL) ground cumin
- 1 tsp (5 mL) dried basil leaves
- 1/4 to 1/2 tsp (1 to 2.5 mL) cracked black pepper
- 1 whole roasted sweet red pepper (see page 25)
- One 28 oz (796 mL) can diced tomatoes
- 1 tbsp (15 mL) Worcestershire sauce

TOPPINGS (PER SERVING)

- 2 tbsp (30 mL) chopped fresh cilantro
- 2 tbsp (30 mL) chopped avocado (1/8 avocado; see page 25)
- 1 tbsp (15 mL) shredded cheese of your choice (optional)

1 For the chili, mince the garlic and set aside.

2 Tip the cans of beans and lentils into a large colander set in a clean sink. Rinse them under cold running water until the water runs clear. Set aside to drain.

3 Heat a large saucepan over medium heat. Add the oil, then the onions, and sauté until golden brown, about 5 minutes.

4 Add the corn and sauté until the onions and corn turn a darker golden brown, 5 to 8 minutes. This step adds a really fabulous flavour.

5 While you're waiting for the onions and corn to do their thing, mix together the chili powder, oregano, coriander, cumin, basil, and black pepper in a small bowl. Set aside. If using a bottled roasted pepper, drain and chop the pepper. If using a fresh roasted pepper, remove the seeds, then chop the pepper.

6 When the onions and corn are the right colour, add the red pepper and garlic, and sauté for 30 seconds.

7 Add the spice mixture and sauté for about 30 seconds. You should be able to smell some fabulous aromas.

8 Stir in the tomatoes, making sure you scrape up all the little browned bits stuck to the bottom of the saucepan to prevent the chili from burning. Add the beans and lentils and Worcestershire sauce. The chili will look really thick but don't worry; as it cooks it will become more liquid.

9 Bring to a boil. Reduce the heat to a simmer and cook, covered, for at least 30 minutes, stirring occasionally. If you're not in a hurry, simmer the chili for another 15 to 30 minutes; the flavour will be even better. Best of all, simmer the chili for a total of 60 to 75 minutes, then let cool and refrigerate overnight.

10 Serve the chili in deep bowls, and sprinkle each portion with the cilantro, avocado, and cheese (if using).

PER SERVING: 282 CALORIES, 5.9 G TOTAL FAT, 0.7 G SATURATED FAT, 0 G TRANS FAT, 299 MG SODIUM, 46.9 G CARBOHYDRATE, 12 G FIBRE, 7.4 G SUGARS, 14 G PROTEIN

DIABETES FOOD CHOICE VALUES PER SERVING: 2½ CARBOHYDRATE, 1 MEAT AND ALTERNATIVES, ½ FAT

GIVE IT A TWIST

If you aren't in the "I love cilantro" camp, substitute either fresh parsley or basil. The recipe needs the sweetness of herbs as a finishing touch.

GLAM IT UP

You can dress up Family-Style Meatless Chili three different ways:

1 Nachos for One: On a large plate spoon 1 cup (250 mL) hot Family-Style Meatless Chili over 10 unsalted whole-grain tortilla chips. Top with 2 tbsp (30 mL) light sour cream, 2 tbsp (30 mL) mild, medium, or hot fresh salsa (from the deli), and ¼ cup (60 mL) diced avocado (see page 25). Dig in.

2 Use the chili to fill Mexican Jacket Potatoes (page 60).

3 Use the chili in Quickie Quesadilla for One (page 62).

YEAR ROUND
KID FRIENDLY

Mexican Jacket Potatoes

For my son Andrew's sixteenth birthday, I cashed in all my travel points and we flew to London, England, for a mother-and-son adventure. I figured he was still young enough to want to spend some time with me, before his high school life got too busy and it wasn't cool anymore to be seen with his mom.

We walked what seemed like 3,000 km that week and did *London, everything from Speaker's Corner to afternoon tea, and many visits to Lillywhites, a sports shop where my son spent most of his money. The trip was an "awesome" experience for both of us.*

The only thing my points didn't cover was food, and eating in London was fairly expensive, until we discovered shops selling "jacket potatoes."

Jacket potatoes are baked potatoes served with an assortment of toppings, from shredded cheese and sour cream to tuna sauce with dill. We tried many different toppings but our favourite was regular canned beans sprinkled with cheese.

When we got home, I started experimenting and ended up with what has become a house specialty. If you're really pushed for time, just open a can of baked beans in tomato sauce and substitute them for the chili.

MAKES 4 SERVINGS | ONE SERVING = ONE POTATO (TWO HALVES)

INGREDIENTS

4 small Russet or other baking potatoes
2 cups (500 mL) Family-Style Meatless Chili (page 58)
½ cup (125 mL) mild, medium, or hot fresh salsa (from the deli)
¼ cup (60 mL) shredded extra-old cheddar cheese
½ cup (125 mL) chopped fresh cilantro (optional)
½ cup (125 mL) thinly sliced green onions
¼ cup (60 mL) light sour cream
Hot sauce (optional)

1 If not using a microwave to bake the potatoes, preheat the oven to 350°F (180°C).

2 Scrub the potatoes well and pierce them in several places with a fork. Bake the potatoes in a conventional oven until tender, 1 to 1½ hours, or microwave them on high until tender, 12 to 20 minutes.

3 Reheat the chili in a medium saucepan over medium-low heat, until piping hot.

4 Cut the potatoes in half, cutting almost but not quite through the skin on the other side. Squeeze the potatoes gently to open them up. You are making a potato receptacle; okay, a bowl. Put the potatoes on 4 plates.

5 Spoon ½ cup (125 mL) chili onto each potato. Top each one with salsa, dividing evenly. Sprinkle each one evenly with shredded cheese, then the cilantro (if using) and green onions. Top each one with sour cream, dividing evenly, and sprinkle with hot sauce (if using).

PER SERVING: 335 CALORIES, 7.3 G TOTAL FAT, 2.9 G SATURATED FAT, 0 G TRANS FAT, 351 MG SODIUM, 57 G CARBOHYDRATE, 9 G FIBRE, 6.7 G SUGARS, 13 G PROTEIN

DIABETES FOOD CHOICE VALUES PER SERVING: 3 CARBOHYDRATE, ½ MEAT AND ALTERNATIVES, 1 FAT

BEANO, THE TOOT REDUCER

Beano, a type of capsule sold in drugstores, contains the enzyme needed to digest the gas-producing sugars in legumes. If you're concerned about gas, read the instructions and take some Beano.

Quickie Quesadilla for One

More than one of you? Just multiply all the ingredients by however many people you want to feed. Better yet, get your kids to do the math. Who knew that multiplication would come in so handy?

This is great teenager food. Teach your kids how to make them and they'll be whipping up weekend lunches in no time.

MAKES 1 SERVING

INGREDIENTS

1 large trans-fat-free 100% whole-grain whole wheat tortilla

½ cup (125 mL) Family-Style Meatless Chili (page 58)

2 tbsp (30 mL) shredded light Monterey Jack cheese or your cheese of choice

2 tbsp (30 mL) mild, medium, or hot fresh salsa (from the deli)

1 tbsp (15 mL) chopped fresh cilantro (optional)

1 tbsp (15 mL) light sour cream (optional)

1 If you are making more than one serving, preheat the oven to 200°F (95°C).

2 Heat a large skillet over medium-low heat. Place the tortilla flat in the skillet. Spoon the chili over half of the tortilla, then sprinkle with the cheese.

3 Fold the tortilla in half and press down gently. Cook until the cheese melts and the tortilla is golden brown on the underside, about 3 minutes.

4 Carefully flip the tortilla and cook it on the other side until golden brown, about 3 minutes. Remove the tortilla from the skillet and cut it in half. Place in oven to keep warm if making additional quesadillas. Serve with the salsa, and cilantro and sour cream (if using).

PER SERVING: 355 CALORIES, 9.2 TOTAL FAT, 2.2 G SATURATED FAT, 0 G TRANS FAT, 604 MG SODIUM, 55.5 G CARBOHYDRATE, 9 G FIBRE, 4.8 G SUGARS, 15 G PROTEIN

DIABETES FOOD CHOICE VALUES PER SERVING: 3 CARBOHYDRATE, 1 MEAT AND ALTERNATIVES, 1 FAT

MAKE IT EASY

For convenience I use canned beans. Draining and rinsing them under cold running water until the water runs clear reduces their sodium levels by about 40%. (Or buy low-sodium canned beans and drain and rinse them to reduce the sodium levels even further.) If you have the time and the inclination, cook your own beans from scratch, and my blessings to you.

YEAR ROUND
KID FRIENDLY

South-of-the-Border Roll-Ups

Most kids love Mexican food. Cash in on that, and serve up a whole-grain, heart-healthy, Canadian version of an enchilada.

MAKES 8 ROLL-UPS | ONE SERVING = 1 ROLL-UP

INGREDIENTS

3 large roasted sweet red peppers (see page 25)
1 cup (250 mL) light ricotta cheese
1 cup (250 mL) shredded light Monterey Jack cheese, divided
One 19 oz (540 mL) can black beans, drained and rinsed
1 tbsp (15 mL) chili powder
1 tsp (5 mL) ground cumin
8 small trans-fat-free 100% whole-grain whole wheat tortillas
1 cup (250 mL) frozen corn kernels, thawed and drained
1 cup (250 mL) mild, medium, or hot fresh salsa (from the deli)

1 Preheat the oven to 400°F (200°C). Line a 13- × 9-inch (3.5 L) baking dish with wet parchment paper (see page 11).

2 If using bottled roasted peppers, drain, then coarsely chop them. If using fresh roasted peppers, remove the seeds, then coarsely chop the peppers. Set aside.

3 Using a large spoon, mix together the ricotta and ¾ cup (185 mL) Monterey Jack cheese in a medium bowl. Reserve the extra ¼ cup (60 mL) cheese; no nibbling.

4 In a food processor, briefly process the black beans, chili powder, and cumin. Don't purée the mixture; you want some of the beans to remain whole. If you don't have a food processor, use a potato masher.

5 Lay 1 tortilla on the counter. Spread evenly with ¼ cup (60 mL) bean paste, spreading right to the edges. Spread evenly with ¼ cup (60 mL) cheese mixture, spreading right to the edges. Sprinkle with 1 heaping tbsp (20 mL) corn. Top with one-eighth of the roasted peppers.

6 Roll up the tortilla tightly and place it, seam side down, in the prepared dish. Repeat with the remaining tortillas and filling.

7 Pour the salsa over the top of the rolled-up tortillas, spreading it out evenly with a spoon. Sprinkle with the reserved cheese.

8 Bake, uncovered, until bubbly, about 40 minutes. Now, here's the tricky part: you have to let the dish sit for 10 minutes before you cut it up or I guarantee the roll-ups will fall apart.

HOW TO

When my partner, Scott, makes this dish, he has everything he needs on the counter before he even starts cooking and assembling. Works for him, but you need a lot of counter space.

PER SERVING: 273 CALORIES, 7.7 G TOTAL FAT, 3.8 G SATURATED FAT, 0 G TRANS FAT, 583 MG SODIUM, 35.2 G CARBOHYDRATE, 7 G FIBRE, 6 G SUGARS, 17 G PROTEIN

DIABETES FOOD CHOICE VALUES PER SERVING: 2 CARBOHYDRATE, 1 MEAT AND ALTERNATIVES, 1 FAT

GONE GROCERY SHOPPING

I hate shopping for clothes. I think it's because I have an hourglass figure.

If I were five foot ten, it wouldn't be too tough dressing the bigger parts of my body, but at five foot three, in a lot of outfits I tend to look like a sack of potatoes. It is discouraging to say the least. Bathing-suit shopping? I'd rather go over Niagara Falls in a barrel.

Which leaves grocery shopping as my only excursion into retail therapy.

I love shopping for food, which could explain why nothing fits me when I go shopping for clothes. Hmm, light-bulb moment. Anyway, after many years of shopping when everyone in town plus their five kids are in the store, I have a couple of tips to help you survive a grocery expedition:

- Pick a store that's close to where you live and that you love. Shopping at the same store will save time in the long run. Whenever I dash into a new store to pick up one thing, I usually spend ages trying to find it. Case in point: while I was creating the Chocolate Mousse (page 278), I needed more silken tofu. I was on my way to an appointment in a different neck of the woods, saw a big grocery store, and I thought I'd just dash in, pick it up, and be on my way. Well, 20 minutes later, I had three chocolate bars and a bag of onions, but no silken tofu. When I finally found someone who worked in the store, they told me they didn't carry it. Moral of the story: I was late for my appointment; the chocolate melted in the car; and I now hate that big grocery store.
- Plan your weekly groceries around store specials. You'll save money and won't end up making the same thing week in, week out.
- Write a list. Sure, trying to remember what you need for the week is a great memory exercise, but driving back to the store because you forgot the eggs and you're making omelettes for dinner is a waste of gas. Write a list, and remember to take it with you, along with your reusable bags.
- Unless you love people crashing into your buggy, never shop on the weekend, unless it's really early on Sunday morning, or Halloween. The best shopping trip I had was Halloween night at 7:00 p.m. I needed a couple of ingredients so I left my partner at home to hand out treats while I shopped. There wasn't a soul in my store. It was awesome — slightly freaky, but incredibly enjoyable.
- If someone does bump your cart do *not* ram theirs back. Just be a good Canadian and say, "I'm sorry." (Explanation for non-Canadian readers: Canadians say sorry even when it isn't their fault. We are incredibly polite, which certain countries think is actually a bad case of low self-esteem, but no, we really *are* incredibly polite.)
- My favourite time to shop is early on either Wednesday or Friday. On Wednesday there are still specials but no crowds; Friday has new specials, great selection, and not too many people.
- Never, ever shop when you're hungry. You'll buy stuff you wouldn't normally. I still have a bag of rice crackers covered in seaweed in my pantry that I bought during a low-blood-sugar moment.
- Never, ever take a small, tired, crabby child shopping when all you've had is a large Tim Hortons coffee. This spells *disaster*. Been there, done that. Shop after naps and snacks.
- Watch the cash register. If the price is wrong, the law says it's free. Yes, *free*. But this only pertains to items under $10, so don't try to scam them on a new patio set. For example, if you

buy three bottles of natural apple juice and the cashier rings them in at $4.50 and the price is actually $3.25, the first one is free, and you should be charged $3.25 each for the second and third bottles.

- Don't go driving around looking for who-knows-what after you've packed your precious groceries in the trunk. Perishable foods should go in the fridge or freezer as soon as possible. Drive straight home and put the cold stuff into the fridge right away. Keeping cold foods cold and hot foods hot is an important food safety rule that we tend to forget about. In the heat of the summer, carry a thermal shopping bag or a cooler in the car so that ice cream or salmon won't spoil on the way home. In the middle of January in Winnipeg, you can drive around for days and the ice cream will never melt. August in Ottawa? Break out the cooler.

4

Berries:
Antioxidants to the Rescue!

Berries and me, we go way back. We had raspberry canes in our backyard, our neighbours grew blueberries, and once I went strawberry picking with my brother in the Fraser Valley in BC. Once.

There I was in my cute little strawberry-picking outfit, hoping to meet the man of my dreams. I was 18 years old and my mission in life was to find a boyfriend; the picking part was just a device to attract guys. It all made great sense in my hormone-crazed teenage brain.

Those strawberries were ripe and delicious and by the end of the day I had eaten most of my profits and had extreme heatstroke. The only guy who'd spoken to me was my brother, who kept nagging, "Stop eating all the strawberries."

In hindsight it might have been one of the wisest things my brother ever said to me.

The next day an allergic reaction kicked in (eating an entire flat of strawberries can do that) and I spent most of the day covered in hives and sitting on the loo.

I made a whopping $1.50 and learned a fabulous life lesson: always pack a lunch.

GOOD FOR YOU

With all their culinary possibilities, ripe, T-shirt-staining berries are a nutritional grand slam. Having your clothes wrecked is worth it. Those vibrant colours that can stain your outfit come with a huge nutrient curriculum vitae. All berries are loaded with vitamins, minerals, fibre, and disease-lowering antioxidants, so try to eat them every day.

Free radicals. No; they're not a band from the '60s, they're the evil compounds in your body that attack healthy cells, causing damage that can adversely affect your long-term health. Free radicals can damage LDL cholesterol, making that already *bad* cholesterol *worse*. They can even damage your DNA. The antioxidants in berries can neutralize cell-damaging free radicals and send them on their way.

HEALTH BITE

In epidemiological and clinical studies, eating berries has been associated with heart health.

BUY IT, STORE IT

If they're perfectly ripe when you buy them, strawberries, raspberries, and blackberries will keep for one to two days in the fridge; blueberries (if they're completely dry) can be refrigerated for up to ten days.

To freeze berries for longer storage, sort through them, discarding any mushy or mouldy ones. Rinse and drain well in a colander. Remove any stems. Let dry on paper towels or tea towels, then spread out on baking sheets. Freeze for 24 hours.

The next day, tip the frozen berries into freezer bags or plastic containers, remove as much air as possible, date the bags or containers, and store them in the freezer for those winter months when the only fresh berries are from who-knows-where.

Don't wash fresh berries until just before you use them, and never soak them. I repeat, never soak them. Sure they float, but soaking makes them water-logged. Rinse them, and drain well in a colander. Let dry on paper towels or tea towels and use right away.

Berries taste better when they aren't really cold right out of the fridge. So, for the best hit of flavour, after washing and drying them, let them sit at room temperature for about 30 minutes to one hour before serving.

IN SEASON

Berry season in Canada starts with strawberries in June and ends with blackberries in the early fall. Depending on the weather and global warming, here's what to expect when:

STRAWBERRIES: mid-June to mid-July

EVERBEARING STRAWBERRIES: mid-June to September

RASPBERRIES: mid-July to mid-September

BLUEBERRIES: early to mid-July to the end of September

SASKATOON BERRIES: July

BLACKBERRIES: late August to the end of September

Strawberry Lassi

Lassis are a popular South Asian yogurt drink that can be either sweet or sour. I like the taste of tart plain yogurt, but most people prefer a sweeter version.

The sweetness of this lassi depends on how ripe and sweet your strawberries are. Give it a taste. Not sweet enough? Add a little honey or your favourite sweetener.

MAKES 3 CUPS (750 ML) | ONE SERVING = 1½ CUPS (375 ML)

INGREDIENTS

2 cups (500 mL) fresh strawberries, rinsed, and hulled
2 tbsp (30 mL) lightly packed fresh mint
½ cup (125 mL) non-fat plain yogurt
1 cup (250 mL) ice cubes (about 4)

1 Whirl all the ingredients together in a blender. Pour into two glasses, dividing evenly.

GIVE IT A TWIST

Feeling exotic? Add a pinch each of ground cardamom and cinnamon.

PER SERVING: 82 CALORIES, 0.5 G TOTAL FAT, 0 G SATURATED FAT, 0 G TRANS FAT, 41 MG SODIUM, 17.2 G CARBOHYDRATE, 4 G FIBRE, 9.6 G SUGARS, 4 G PROTEIN

DIABETES FOOD CHOICE VALUES PER SERVING: 1 CARBOHYDRATE

Strawberries: One Hull of a Berry

Strawberries—the only fruit that shows off its seeds on the outside—are the warm-up act for berry season. Sometime in June these ripe, juicy red bundles of flavour start showing up at local farmers markets and grocery stores.

Strawberries are an excellent source of vitamin C (1 cup / 250 mL provides 149% of your daily requirement) and are a good source of folate. They're also packed with antioxidants. Two in particular, quercetin and kaempferol, may help keep bad LDL cholesterol from oxidizing and damaging artery walls.

Strawberries also contain ellagic acid, also found in raspberries, blackberries, cranberries, grapes, cherries, walnuts, pecans, and Brazil nuts. In lab and animal studies, ellagic acid has shown promise as an anticarcinogen. All this, and only 50 calories per cup (250 mL).

Buy It, Store It

Choose the perfect basket filled with shiny, dark red berries with fresh, bright green tops. Once a strawberry is picked, it stops ripening. Size doesn't determine sweetness. The strawberries' flavour has more to do with the variety, weather, and their degree of ripeness when they're picked.

Strawberries like to be eaten as soon as possible after picking. And they aren't swimmers, so don't float them in your sink. Just before you need them, leave their green caps on and gently rinse them under cold running water.

Drain the strawberries, then spread them out on a clean tea towel or paper towels to completely dry. Only then hull them (chef-speak for removing the green caps). Voilà—they're ready to eat.

Chocolate Pancakes with Strawberry Sauce

Fresh strawberries are so perfect all they need is something to sit on. What better cushion for ripe, delicious strawberries than chocolate-chip-studded pancakes?

These are quick and easy to make, especially if you use my unorthodox pancake method (see sidebar).

MAKES EIGHTEEN 4-INCH (10 CM) PANCAKES | ONE SERVING = 4 PANCAKES

1 Preheat the oven to 200°F (95°C).

2 Whisk together the milk, egg, and oil in a medium bowl.

3 Whisk in the flour, cocoa powder, wheat germ, sugar, baking powder, and cinnamon. Stir in the chocolate chips. Let the batter sit while you heat the skillet (the batter will get a little thicker).

4 Heat a large non-stick skillet over medium heat. Grease the skillet lightly with canola oil or spray lightly with baking spray.

5 Stir the batter well. Why? Because chocolate chips sink, so, unless you want the last couple of pancakes to be laden with the little morsels, stirring is crucial.

6 Spoon 2 tbsp (30 mL) batter into the skillet, swirling the batter with the back of a spoon to make a 4-inch (10 cm) pancake. Repeat to form 2 or 3 more pancakes in the skillet. Cook until bubbles form on top of the pancakes and the undersides are dark chocolate brown. Flip the pancakes and cook on the other side until the undersides are dark chocolate brown. Remove the pancakes from the skillet and keep warm in the oven on an ovenproof plate until all the pancakes are cooked.

7 Serve the pancakes with the strawberry sauce (recipe follows) or, if you are pressed for time, simply top the pancakes with sliced fresh strawberries.

PER SERVING (WITHOUT STRAWBERRY SAUCE) 257 CALORIES, 9.5 G TOTAL FAT, 3.3 G SATURATED FAT, 0 G TRANS FAT, 288 MG SODIUM, 35 G CARBOHYDRATE, 4 G FIBRE, 11.2 G SUGARS, 9 G PROTEIN

DIABETES FOOD CHOICE VALUES PER SERVING (WITHOUT STRAWBERRY SAUCE): 2 CARBOHYDRATE, ½ MEAT AND ALTERNATIVES, 1½ FAT

INGREDIENTS

1¼ cups (310 mL) skim milk or fortified organic soy beverage
1 omega-3 egg (see page 13)
1 tbsp (15 mL) canola oil
1 cup (250 mL) whole wheat flour
¼ cup (60 mL) natural cocoa powder (see page 12)
1 tbsp (15 mL) wheat germ
1 tbsp (15 mL) granulated sugar
1 tbsp (15 mL) baking powder
1 tbsp (15 mL) cinnamon
¼ cup (60 mL) chocolate chips with at least 60% cocoa mass
Canola oil or non-stick baking spray
Strawberry Sauce (recipe follows)

MY NEW, IMPROVED, UNORTHODOX PANCAKE METHOD

The conventional method of making pancakes: dry ingredients in one bowl, wet in another; add wet to dry and mix. I always thought this meant one extra bowl to wash so, when I make pancakes, I just add the dry ingredients to the wet, all in one bowl. In the world of home economics, I'm a troublemaker or a trendsetter, depending on which side of the fence you're on.

Strawberry Sauce

I prefer to sweeten this sauce with honey (if the strawberries need it), but Splenda works well if you'd rather use it.

MAKES ABOUT 2½ CUPS (625 ML) | ONE SERVING = ½ CUP (125 ML)

1 Hull the strawberries (remove their green caps). Put the strawberries in a blender or food processor.

2 Add the lemon juice and whirl together. (If you don't have a blender or food processor, use a potato masher.) I think chunky looks better but if you want a really smooth sauce, go crazy with the On button. Depending on the sweetness of the berries, you may or may not have to add honey or sweetener. If you do, add and whirl. Serve the strawberry sauce drizzled over the chocolate pancakes.

PER SERVING (WITHOUT HONEY) 40 CALORIES, 0.4 G TOTAL FAT, 0 G SATURATED FAT, 0 G TRANS FAT, 2 MG SODIUM, 9.6 G CARBOHYDRATE, 3 G FIBRE, 5.8 G SUGARS, 1 G PROTEIN

DIABETES FOOD CHOICE VALUES PER SERVING (WITHOUT HONEY) ½ CARBOHYDRATE

INGREDIENTS

4 cups (1 L) fresh strawberries, rinsed and dried
1 tbsp (15 mL) fresh lemon juice
Honey, or your choice of sweetener to taste

GIVE IT A TWIST

Substitute raspberries for strawberries. Or make the sauce in the winter using frozen berries.

Raspberries: The Berry That Tastes Too Good to Be Good for You

I have a confession to make. I am a raspberry thief. My neighbour's raspberry canes made their way into my garden and I am keeping them. Raspberries throw out underground runners that can travel for what seems like miles. One year the plants were in my neighbour's garden, the next year in mine.

As soon as they're ripe, I'm out there first thing in the morning picking the antioxidant-rich, sweet berries to pop into my cereal bowl.

Buy It, Store It

Raspberries are extremely delicate. It's best to pick your own or buy them from a farmers stand or market. I always buy them last when I'm at my farmers market and put them in the fridge as soon as I get home.

Do not wash raspberries until just before you are going to use them, and never, ever soak them. This is grounds for a felony conviction in the Foodie Supreme Court. Rinse and drain them well in a colander. Let them dry on paper towels or tea towels and use them right away.

Fresh-from-the-Vine Red Raspberry Salad Dressing

This is a great alternative to bottled raspberry salad dressing. It's quick and easy to make, and any leftovers will keep in your fridge for up to two days.

MAKES 10 TBSP (150 ML) | ONE SERVING = 1 TBSP (15 ML)

1 Whirl all the ingredients in a blender until smooth. (Or use a hand-held immersion blender to whirl the ingredients together in a medium bowl until smooth.)

2 Serve over a baby spinach or romaine salad, and feel free to scatter your salad with extra raspberries before serving.

PER SERVING: 25 CALORIES, 1.6 G TOTAL FAT, 0 G SATURATED FAT, 0 G TRANS FAT, 51 MG SODIUM, 2.5 G CARBOHYDRATE, 0 G FIBRE, 2 G SUGARS, 0 G PROTEIN

DIABETES FOOD CHOICE VALUES PER SERVING: ½ FAT, 1 EXTRA

INGREDIENTS

½ cup (125 mL) fresh raspberries, rinsed and drained

1 tsp (5 mL) honey, or your choice of sweetener to taste

2 tbsp (30 mL) balsamic vinegar

2 tbsp (30 mL) 100% pure pomegranate juice

1 tbsp (15 mL) canola oil

2 tsp (10 mL) Dijon mustard

CANADIAN, EH?

Raspberries are Canadian through and through. About 94% of all the raspberries sold in Canada during raspberry season come from Abbotsford, BC, the Raspberry Capital of Canada.

GIVE IT A TWIST

For another savoury way with raspberries, try my Raspberry Salsa on page 319.

Raspberries with Orange-Flavoured "Cream"

I first created this recipe as a Christmas breakfast idea for an article I wrote for alive *magazine. It combines thawed frozen raspberries with a decadent-tasting, orange-flavoured "cream" made with thickened yogurt, sometimes called yogurt cheese. Of course, in the summer, make this with fresh raspberries.*

Plain yogurt tends to be quite tart, so feel free to substitute a low-fat vanilla yogurt and omit the honey. And make sure you use a yogurt that doesn't have any thickeners or gelatin in it (check the label). Or use plain 0% fat Greek-style yogurt and skip Step One.

MAKES 6 SERVINGS | ONE SERVING = ½ CUP (125 ML)

INGREDIENTS

- 2 cups (500 mL) low-fat plain yogurt, or 1½ cups/375 mL plain 0% fat Greek-style yogurt
- ¼ cup (60 mL) frozen orange juice concentrate, thawed (see page 13)
- 2 tbsp (30 mL) honey, or your choice of sweetener to taste
- 6 cups (1.5 L) frozen unsweetened raspberries, thawed

1 If using low-fat plain yogurt, set a wire-mesh strainer over a bowl. Line the strainer with a large paper coffee filter or a piece of cheesecloth. Place the yogurt in the lined strainer, cover, and let sit in the fridge for 6 to 12 hours to drain. (If you're using plain 0% fat Greek-style yogurt, you can skip this step.)

2 The next day, remove the drained yogurt from the fridge, discard the liquid, and place the yogurt in a medium bowl. Stir in the orange juice concentrate and honey.

3 Divide the thawed raspberries evenly among 6 small bowls. Top with the yogurt mixture, dividing evenly.

HEALTH BITE

A 1-cup (250 mL) serving of raspberries provides 34% of your daily requirement for fibre, and they sure taste a lot better than downing a commercial fibre drink!

PER SERVING: 150 CALORIES, 1.5 G TOTAL FAT, 0.5 G SATURATED FAT, 0 G TRANS FAT, 52 MG SODIUM, 31.5 G CARBOHYDRATE, 9 G FIBRE, 19 G SUGARS, 5 G PROTEIN

DIABETES FOOD CHOICE VALUES PER SERVING: 1½ CARBOHYDRATE, ½ MEAT AND ALTERNATIVES

Raspberries with Mango

This combination of fresh ripe raspberries and beta-carotene-rich mango, plus a hint of fresh lime, is a winner. A light, fruity dessert, it tastes better if you let it marinate in the fridge for up to 4 hours.

If you need a hint of summer in the middle of winter, make this with frozen unsweetened raspberries and mango.

MAKES ABOUT 4 CUPS (1 L) | ONE SERVING = 1 CUP (250 ML)

INGREDIENTS

1 lime, scrubbed well and dried

2 tbsp (30 mL) honey, or sweetener of your choice to taste

2 cups (500 mL) fresh or frozen raspberries

2 ripe mangoes (see below), or 2 cups (500 mL) frozen mango chunks

1 Using a Microplane grater (see page 8), remove the zest from the lime. Set aside. With your palm, roll the lime on the counter, then cut in half and squeeze out 2 tbsp (30 mL) juice.

2 Whisk together the lime juice and honey in a medium bowl.

3 If using fresh raspberries, rinse them under cold running water. Drain well and pat dry on paper towels.

4 If using fresh mango, peel and chop the mangoes (see page 24), discarding the pits.

5 Gently toss together the raspberries, mango, and honey mixture in a large bowl. Sprinkle with the lime zest.

6 If using fresh fruit, refrigerate the dessert for up to 4 hours for the flavours to blend before serving. If using frozen fruit, leave the bowl on the counter until the fruit has thawed, then serve.

CULINARY WARNING

Don't even think about making this with a fresh mango unless it's a ripe and juicy one.

PER SERVING: 128 CALORIES, 0.4 G TOTAL FAT, 0 G SATURATED FAT, 0 G TRANS FAT, 1 MG SODIUM, 31.4 G CARBOHYDRATE, 6 G FIBRE, 24.5 G SUGARS, 2 G PROTEIN

DIABETES FOOD CHOICE VALUES PER SERVING: 2 CARBOHYDRATE

Blueberry and Tomato Summer Salad for One

There is a week or so around the middle of August when both fresh local blueberries and summer tomatoes hit their peak. That's the only time to make this salad.

The recipe's easily multiplied to serve two, three, four, or more. I think it looks prettiest when I plate the salad, which is chef-speak for preparing each salad on its own plate.

MAKES 1 SERVING

INGREDIENTS

- 1 cup (250 mL) lightly packed baby arugula
- 1 to 2 really ripe summer tomatoes, washed and dried
- 1/4 cup (60 mL) fresh blueberries, rinsed and dried
- 2 tbsp (30 mL) crumbled goat's milk feta cheese (see page 14)
- 2 tsp (10 mL) extra virgin olive oil
- 1 tsp (5 mL) balsamic vinegar

1 Place the arugula in a clean sink of cold water. Swish it well to make sure there isn't any sand or dirt clinging to it. Spin-dry in a salad spinner or pat dry with a clean tea towel.

2 Pile the arugula on a large white plate. (Okay, any colour will do, but it looks spectacular on an oversized white plate. My friend Jill calls my large white plates my "restaurant plates.")

3 Using a serrated knife, slice the tomato(es) into ½-inch (1 cm) slices. Arrange the tomato slices artistically on top of the arugula.

4 Sprinkle the blueberries, then the feta, overtop the tomatoes. Drizzle with the oil and vinegar. Garnish with fresh basil, if desired.

GIVE IT A TWIST

Skip the arugula and just use heirloom tomatoes as shown here. Heirlooms are plants grown from heritage seeds that produce fruit that may be too fragile to make it to a commercial market. Fragile the tomatoes may be, but they're also way more flavourful. I get my heirlooms all summer long at my local farmers market. (For tips on shopping at a farmers market, see page 222.)

PER SERVING: 226 CALORIES, 16.6 G TOTAL FAT, 6.3 G SATURATED FAT, 0 G TRANS FAT, 359 MG SODIUM, 14.5 G CARBOHYDRATE, 3 G FIBRE, 8.6 G SUGARS, 8 G PROTEIN

DIABETES FOOD CHOICE VALUES PER SERVING: 1 CARBOHYDRATE, 1 MEAT AND ALTERNATIVES, 3 FAT

SUMMER
KID FRIENDLY

Blueberry-Quinoa Salad

The combination of whole-grain, protein-rich quinoa and amazing blueberries makes this dish a gift for your brain and your heart.

Prep the quinoa the night before and store it in the fridge so it's fresh and really cold when you make the salad the next day.

MAKES ABOUT 4 CUPS (1 L) | ONE SERVING = 1 CUP (250 ML)

1 For the blueberry-quinoa salad, the night before you plan to serve it, rinse the quinoa in a fine wire-mesh strainer under cold running water to get rid of any bitter resins.

2 Place the quinoa in a medium saucepan, add 1 cup (250 mL) water, and bring to a boil. Reduce the heat to a simmer and cook, covered, until the quinoa is translucent and all the water has been absorbed, 18 to 20 minutes. Remove the saucepan from the heat, fluff the quinoa with a fork, and let stand for 10 minutes. Let cool, then place in a bowl, cover, and refrigerate overnight.

3 The next day, tip the quinoa into a large salad bowl. Add the fresh blueberries, parsley, green onions, dried blueberries (if using), and olives.

4 For the orange dressing, whisk together the orange zest, orange juice, oil, vinegar, cinnamon, and ginger (if using) in a small bowl.

5 Add the dressing to the salad and toss well.

PER SERVING: 174 CALORIES, 5.5 G TOTAL FAT, 0.6 G SATURATED FAT, 0 G TRANS FAT, 63 MG SODIUM, 28.7 G CARBOHYDRATE, 6 G FIBRE, 8.6 G SUGARS, 4 G PROTEIN

DIABETES FOOD CHOICE VALUES PER SERVING: 1½ CARBOHYDRATE, 1 FAT

PER SERVING (WITH DRIED BLUEBERRIES) 198 CALORIES, 5.5 G TOTAL FAT, 0.6 G SATURATED FAT, 0 G TRANS FAT, 65 MG SODIUM, 34.5 G CARBOHYDRATE, 7 G FIBRE, 13.9 G SUGARS, 5 G PROTEIN

DIABETES FOOD CHOICE VALUES PER SERVING (WITH DRIED BLUEBERRIES): 2 CARBOHYDRATES, 1 FAT

BLUEBERRY-QUINOA SALAD

- ½ cup (125 mL) whole-grain quinoa (see page 152)
- 2 cups (500 mL) fresh blueberries, rinsed and dried
- 1 cup (250 mL) finely chopped parsley
- ¼ cup (60 mL) chopped green onions
- ¼ cup (60 mL) dried blueberries (optional)
- 4 large pimento-stuffed green olives, diced

ORANGE DRESSING

- 1 tsp (5 mL) orange zest
- 2 tbsp (30 mL) fresh orange juice
- 1 tbsp (15 mL) extra virgin olive oil
- 1 tbsp (15 mL) apple cider vinegar (see page 12)
- ¼ tsp (1 mL) cinnamon
- 1 tsp (5 mL) finely grated fresh ginger (optional)

GIVE IT A TWIST

When Canadian blueberries aren't in season, use frozen berries instead of fresh. Add them straight from the freezer, then leave the salad on the counter for 1 hour before serving to let the blueberries thaw. The salad will turn a really neat shade of purple.

Blueberry Trifle

Here is a deliciously decadent summer dessert that tastes fattening, but isn't. Best of all, you get to buy an angel food cake. (If you're a real food purist, then go ahead and bake the cake from scratch.) You'll need about half of a 283-gram angel food cake. In the winter, use frozen blueberries.

I Mairlyn-ized this recipe from the BC Blueberry Council's website (bcblueberry.com).

MAKES 6 SERVINGS | ONE SERVING = ONE GLASSFUL

INGREDIENTS

2 cups (500 mL) fresh blueberries, rinsed and dried, divided
¼ cup (60 mL) granulated sugar, or your choice of sweetener to taste, divided
1½ tsp (7.5 mL) cornstarch
1 lemon, scrubbed well and dried
4 oz (125 g) light cream cheese, at room temperature (see below)
2 tbsp (30 mL) frozen orange juice concentrate, thawed (see page 13)
¾ cup (185 mL) non-fat or low-fat plain yogurt
Half 10 oz (283 g) angel food cake, cut into ½-inch (1 cm) cubes

1 Combine ½ cup (125 mL) blueberries, 2 tbsp (30 mL) sugar, the cornstarch, and ¾ cup (185 mL) water in a small saucepan. Stir until the cornstarch has dissolved.

2 Bring to a boil over medium heat, then cook, stirring, until the sauce has thickened and the berries have popped, 3 to 5 minutes. Remove the saucepan from the heat and stir in 1 cup (250 mL) blueberries. Set aside to cool.

3 Using a Microplane grater (see page 8), remove 1 tsp (5 mL) zest from the lemon and set aside.

4 Beat the cream cheese in a small bowl until smooth. Add the remaining 2 tbsp (30 mL) sugar and the orange juice concentrate. Continue beating until smooth. Gently beat in the yogurt and lemon zest.

5 Get out 6 martini glasses, or any other show-stopping glasses you have. Divide half of the cake cubes among the glasses. Top with about 2 tbsp (30 mL) blueberry sauce and about 2 tbsp (30 mL) cream cheese mixture. Repeat the layers once.

6 Make sure the remaining ½ cup (125 mL) blueberries are really dry. If not, roll them gently between paper towels. Garnish each glass with blueberries, dividing evenly. Refrigerate for at least 1 hour before serving.

PER SERVING: 190 CALORIES, 3.2 G TOTAL FAT, 2.1 G SATURATED FAT, 0 G TRANS FAT, 302 MG SODIUM, 36.1 G CARBOHYDRATE, 2 G FIBRE, 18.1 G SUGARS, 5 G PROTEIN

DIABETES FOOD CHOICE VALUES PER SERVING: 2½ CARBOHYDRATE, ½ FAT

QUICK TIP

In Canada, most plain cream cheese is sold in 250-gram packages. For this recipe, you need half a package.

GIVE IT A TWIST

Serve this trifle in a 4-cup (1 L) glass bowl. Arrange half of the cake in the base of the bowl, then top with half the blueberry sauce and half the yogurt mixture; repeat the layers once. Garnish with remaining ½ cup (125 mL) berries. Cover and refrigerate for 2 hours.

Blueberries: A Mighty Little Purple Berry

Just when you think the blueberry news couldn't get any better, it does. This superfruit may slow down the aging process by reducing cell damage to both your heart and brain, two of my favourite organs. Baby boomers and beyond: take notes, there'll be a test.

- Blueberries are loaded with a powerful, disease-fighting antioxidant called anthocyanin.
- Eating blueberries on a regular basis may reduce the buildup of LDL ("bad") cholesterol that contributes to cardiovascular disease and stroke.
- Blueberries are high in fibre and are an excellent source of vitamin C and manganese.
- Eating blueberries regularly may slow down age-related declines in memory skills.

Time for the test (and you thought I was kidding). Cover the information above—no cheating—and answer the following question: where are your car keys?

If you can't remember, perhaps you should be eating more blueberries.

Buy It, Store It

Look for firm, plump, intensely dark-coloured berries with a silvery bloom. Don't buy wet-looking berries that have lost this bloom; they will get mouldy quickly.

Store them in the fridge for up to ten days and wash just before you're going to eat them. Keep them dry until you need them for sprinkling on cereal, adding to yogurt, or using in your favourite recipe.

SUMMER
KID FRIENDLY

Frosted Blueberry-Banana Soup

I had never been a fan of cold summer soups until I moved to hot, humid Toronto. Now I totally get why you'd want to eat one.

This fruit soup is like a smoothie in a bowl. Cold, refreshing, and mildly sweet, it's become a part of my summer dinner repertoire.

I adapted the recipe from the BC Blueberry Council's website (bcblueberry.com).

MAKES ABOUT 4 CUPS (1 L) | ONE SERVING = 1 CUP (250 ML)

INGREDIENTS

3 cups (750 mL) fresh blueberries, divided
1½ cups (375 mL) ice cubes
4 chunks frozen ripe banana (see below)
½ cup (125 mL) skim milk
½ cup (125 mL) non-fat plain yogurt
2 tbsp (30 mL) honey, or your choice of sweetener to taste
1 tsp (5 mL) lemon zest
1 tsp (5 mL) fresh lemon juice

1 Rinse the blueberries well under cold running water, then drain well. Spread the blueberries out on paper towels to dry. Sort through the blueberries and remove any stems.

2 In a blender, combine 2 cups (500 mL) blueberries, the ice, banana, milk, yogurt, honey, and lemon zest and juice. Whirl until smooth.

3 Ladle the soup into 4 soup bowls, dividing evenly. Sprinkle the rest of the blueberries overtop each serving, using ¼ cup (60 mL) per bowl. Serve right away before it melts.

PER SERVING: 135 CALORIES, 0.6 G TOTAL FAT, 0 G SATURATED FAT, 0 G TRANS FAT, 36 MG SODIUM, 31.9 G CARBOHYDRATE, 3 G FIBRE, 23.6 G SUGARS, 3 G PROTEIN

DIABETES FOOD CHOICE VALUES PER SERVING: 2 CARBOHYDRATE

HOW TO

When bananas get too ripe to eat, peel and then cut each banana into four chunks, pack in freezer bags, then store in the freezer. Frozen banana chunks are great for smoothies, too.

HEALTH BITE

Blueberries contain anthocyanin, a naturally occurring compound that is responsible for the purple or blue colour in fruits, berries, vegetables, and plants. Anthocyanin-rich foods act as an anti-inflammatory and help keep your blood vessels healthy. Packing both nutrition and flavour, blueberries are a win-win all around.

Turkey Breast with Cranberries and Rosemary

This recipe is totally yummy. It's a little sweet, a little tart, and a whole lot fabulous. Easy enough to make any old weeknight, it also has that company-quality zing that makes it great to serve to guests.

Reality tester Barb H. of Markham, Ontario, suggests serving this with peas and mashed potatoes.

You'll need a skillet with a lid for this recipe.

MAKES 4 SERVINGS | ONE SERVING = ONE PLATEFUL

INGREDIENTS

¼ cup (60 mL) lower-sodium chicken broth (see page 7)
2 tbsp (30 mL) frozen orange juice concentrate, thawed (see page 13)
1 lb (500 g) skinless, boneless turkey breast
1 tbsp (15 mL) extra virgin olive oil
4 large shallots, thinly sliced
½ cup (125 mL) fresh or frozen cranberries
¼ cup (60 mL) dried cranberries
1 tbsp (15 mL) finely chopped fresh rosemary (see page 25)

1 Whisk together the chicken broth and orange juice concentrate in a small bowl. Set aside.

2 Wash your hands. Slice the turkey breast into 4 even-sized pieces. (There is probably a technical term for this but my menopausal brain doesn't care. They should look like four chunks of turkey.) Set aside. Wash your hands and cutting board really well. (I keep a separate cutting board to use for raw meat and fish.)

3 Heat a medium skillet over medium heat. Add the oil, then the shallots, and sauté until the shallots start to soften, about 2 minutes.

4 Add the turkey pieces to the skillet and cook until browned on both sides, about 5 minutes. Stir the shallots occasionally to prevent them from burning.

5 Add the fresh and dried cranberries to the skillet. Pour the chicken broth mixture over the top and sprinkle with the rosemary.

6 Bring to a boil. Reduce the heat to a simmer and cook, covered, until the turkey is no longer pink inside and a meat thermometer inserted into each piece of turkey registers 165°F (74°C), about 20 minutes.

7 Place a piece of turkey on each of 4 plates and spoon the sauce over the top, dividing evenly.

PER SERVING: 247 CALORIES, 4.8 G TOTAL FAT, 0.8 G SATURATED FAT, 0 G TRANS FAT, 58 MG SODIUM, 19 G CARBOHYDRATE, 1 G FIBRE, 10.4 G SUGARS, 34 G PROTEIN

DIABETES FOOD CHOICE VALUES PER SERVING: 1 CARBOHYDRATE, 5 MEAT AND ALTERNATIVES

HEALTH BITE

Cranberries contain polyphenols, antioxidants known for their cancer-fighting properties. Cranberries may help prevent urinary tract infections and heart and gum diseases.

BUY IT, STORE IT

Never buy shrivelled cranberries; they won't plump up no matter what you do. Pick firm, plump, bright crimson berries. Use fresh cranberries within four weeks or freeze them for up to six months. If using frozen cranberries in a recipe, don't thaw them first.

Blackberry and Green Bean Salad for Two

My parents have blackberry brambles growing around their summer place, and the year I was lucky enough to be home when the berries were ripe was heaven.

Blackberries and green beans are in season at the same time, which just goes to show that Mother Nature knows a thing or two about combining flavours.

MAKES 2 SERVINGS | ONE SERVING = ONE PLATEFUL

BLACKBERRY AND GREEN BEAN SALAD

1 cup (250 mL) fresh blackberries

4 large romaine lettuce leaves, washed and dried

1 cup (250 mL) cold cooked green beans

BALSAMIC DRESSING

1½ tbsp (22.5 mL) balsamic vinegar

2 tsp (10 mL) extra virgin olive oil

1 tsp (5 mL) grainy Dijon mustard

1 For the salad, rinse the blackberries under cold running water. Drain them and spread out on paper towels or a clean tea towel to absorb as much water as possible.

2 Tear the romaine lettuce into bite-sized pieces and place in a large bowl. Cut the green beans into 1-inch (2.5 cm) pieces and add to the bowl.

3 For the balsamic dressing, whisk together vinegar, oil, and mustard in a small bowl. Pour the dressing over the salad, and toss well. Add the blackberries and toss gently.

PER SERVING: 126 CALORIES, 5.6 G TOTAL FAT, 0.7 G SATURATED FAT, 0 G TRANS FAT, 176 MG SODIUM, 17.9 G CARBOHYDRATE, 8 G FIBRE, 40.5 G SUGARS, 4 G PROTEIN

DIABETES FOOD CHOICE VALUES PER SERVING: ½ CARBOHYDRATE, ½ MEAT AND ALTERNATIVES, 1 FAT

GIVE ME A CLUE

If you're ever on *Jeopardy!*, the answer to "Raspberries and this berry have the most fibre of all berries" is "What are blackberries?" They both pack 8 grams of fibre in just 1 cup (250 mL).

Blackberries: The Fibre-Full Berry

Not to be too much of a West Coast snob or anything, but the blackberries in and around Vancouver are really huge and juicy, unlike the ones I get in Ontario. It has a lot to do with the Vancouver R-word: *rain*. Ontario just doesn't get as much liquid love.

Buy It, Store It

Blackberries are especially sensitive to the bumps and grinds that go along with shipping, so if you are lucky enough to have a blackberry plant (a.k.a. bramble) of your own, I am pea-green with envy. The second-best place to get your blackberries is at your local farmers market. Eat them ASAP—they really hate visiting your fridge.

Fantastic Frozen Yogurt

This has become a classic among the followers of Ultimate Foods. *It's a cinch to make and fabulous to eat. It contains no added fillers or weird ingredients, just pure berries and yogurt. Play around with the combinations or be a purist and use just one type of berry. I'm always trying new yogurts, so use your favourite low-fat or non-fat brand.*

You need a food processor for this recipe. I've tried it in a blender but it doesn't work very well. (See page 8 to read why a food processor needs to be one of your kitchen must-haves.)

You can eat this all year round, but for me, it's a summer treat.

MAKES 2 CUPS (500 ML) | ONE SERVING = ½ CUP (125 ML)

1 In a food processor, pulse the frozen berries and yogurt until smooth. It's going to be noisy but it's totally worth it.

2 Serve right away. Too cinchy.

PER SERVING: 98 CALORIES, 1.2 G TOTAL FAT, 0.5 G SATURATED FAT, 0 G TRANS FAT, 34 MG SODIUM, 20.8 G CARBOHYDRATE, 3 G FIBRE, 15.3 G SUGARS, 2 G PROTEIN

DIABETES FOOD CHOICE VALUES PER SERVING: 1 CARBOHYDRATE

INGREDIENTS

2 cups (500 mL) frozen unsweetened berries or peeled, cubed fruit (see below)

1 cup (250 mL) low-fat or non-fat vanilla yogurt

GIVE IT A TWIST

Try other flavours in your frozen yogurt, or invent your own combos by mixing and matching different berries and fruit. Use 2 cups (500 mL) total of any or all of the following:

- frozen raspberries
- frozen blueberries
- frozen mixed berries
- frozen mango cubes
- frozen pineapple cubes

HEALTH BITE

The healthiest version of frozen yogurt is this homemade version. All of the good-for-you bacteria is still present and accounted for, unlike commercial brands.

5

Broccoli, Brussels Sprouts, Cabbage, and Cauliflower: *The Cruciferous Family of Superheroes*

You've heard the name bandied around, but who are the members of the elite Cruciferous Family anyway?

Ladies and gentlemen, put your hands together for broccoli, Brussels sprouts, cabbages, cauliflower, kale, turnips, and rutabagas, too. Yes, they are lean, mean fighting machines. A special unit of tactical fighters. And boy, oh boy, do you need them in your diet.

GOOD FOR YOU

According to the American Institute for Cancer Research, several compounds found in these veggies—*glucosinolate, crambene, indole-3-carbinol,* and especially *isothiocyanate*—have been linked to a reduction in cancer risk. Laboratory studies suggest that these compounds have the ability to stop the growth of cancer cells in various cell, tissue, and animal models, including tumours of the breast, lung, colon, liver, endometrium, and cervix.

If that isn't reason enough to eat your fill of these potent warriors, throw these stats into the fray: the antioxidants in cruciferous vegetables cause cancer cells to self-destruct. Anything that can talk an evil precancerous cell into throwing itself under a bus makes it onto my "Healthiest Veggies in Town" list.

Here are some of my faves from this potent family. Make sure you recruit these veggies into your personal army of disease-risk-lowering foods.

Broccoli 101

The most popular of the cruciferous vegetables, broccoli is the Sidney Crosby of the family, a gold-medal winner and a superstar. As well as containing antioxidants, broccoli is an excellent source of vitamin C and folate, and is a source of fibre, vitamin A, and potassium. Broccoli is delicious in stir-fries and salads, roasted or raw.

To steam broccoli, place it in a steamer basket in a large saucepan with a lid. Add about 1 inch (2.5 cm) of cold water to the saucepan. Cover and bring to a boil over medium-high heat. Steam for 4 to 8 minutes until broccoli is tender-crisp (time will vary according to the size of the florets).

Buy It, Store It

Look for firm broccoli that has a deep colour. The little buds on the heads of the stalks should be tight and so dark as to be almost deep green-purple in colour. Choose bunches with slender stalks. Store broccoli in either an open or a perforated bag in your crisper for up to five days.

Before using, wash broccoli well under cold running water, then drain and remove the outer leaves. Cut off a small amount of the bottom of the stalks, then cut into florets using as much of the tender stalk as possible.

Broccoli with Peanut Sauce

If you love peanut sauce, this version is so yummy you'll to want to lick your plate. Garlic warning: if you're hoping to get kissed tonight, make sure you eat this with your loved one.

MAKES ABOUT 4 CUPS (1 L) STEAMED BROCCOLI AND ¾ CUP PLUS 2 TBSP (215 ML) PEANUT SAUCE
ONE SERVING = ½ CUP (125 ML) BROCCOLI AND 1 TBSP (15 ML) PEANUT SAUCE

1 Mince the garlic and set aside.

2 Whisk together the peanut butter and boiling water in a medium bowl until smooth. Whisk in the soy sauce and vinegar. Stir in the ginger, red pepper flakes, and garlic, and set aside. (The sauce will keep for up to 24 hours in the fridge.)

3 Cut the broccoli florets from the stalks, using as much of the stalk as you like. (You can save the stalks for Chili-Roasted Broccoli Stalks, page 100.) Steam the broccoli (see Broccoli 101, facing page) until tender-crisp.

4 To serve, drizzle each serving of steamed broccoli (½ cup / 125 mL) with 1 tbsp (15 mL) peanut sauce. (If you prefer, heat the sauce by gently simmering it in a small saucepan, or microwaving it on low for 10 to 15 seconds.)

PER SERVING: 45 CALORIES, 2.5 G TOTAL FAT, 0.3 G SATURATED FAT, 0 G TRANS FAT, 99 MG SODIUM, 4.5 G CARBOHYDRATE, 1 G FIBRE, 0.8 G SUGARS, 3 G PROTEIN

DIABETES FOOD CHOICE VALUES PER SERVING: ½ MEAT AND ALTERNATIVES, ½ FAT, 1 EXTRA

INGREDIENTS

5 cloves garlic
¼ cup (60 mL) natural peanut butter (see page 14)
2 tbsp (30 mL) boiling water
2 tbsp (30 mL) lower-sodium soy sauce (see page 17)
2 tbsp (30 mL) rice vinegar (see page 16)
1 tbsp (15 mL) finely grated fresh ginger
¼ to ½ tsp (1 to 2.5 mL) red pepper flakes
1 lb (500 g) broccoli (1 large bunch)

LOVE THAT SAUCE?

Just in case you want to put my peanut sauce on every vegetable you ever eat, here's its nutrient breakdown:

Per tbsp (15 mL): 29 calories, 2.3 g total fat, 0.3 g saturated fat, 0 g trans fat, 83 mg sodium, 1.5 g carbohydrate, 0.3 g fibre, 0 g sugars, 1 g protein
Diabetes Food Choice Values per tbsp (15 mL): ½ Carbohydrate, ½ Meat and Alternatives, ½ Fat

YEAR ROUND
KID FRIENDLY

Stir-Fried Broccoli and Chicken

My mission was to create an Asian-flavoured stir-fry that doesn't require a ton of prep; that is quick and easy to cook, nutrient dense, and kid friendly; and that tastes great. Mission accomplished.

This goes well with ½ cup (125 mL) cooked brown rice or barley per person.

MAKES 4 SERVINGS | ONE SERVING = ONE PLATEFUL

SAUCE

- 6 tbsp (90 mL) lower-sodium chicken broth (see page 7)
- 1 tbsp (15 mL) lower-sodium soy sauce (see page 17)
- 1 tbsp (15 mL) Thai-style chili sauce (see page 12)
- 2 tsp (10 mL) hot sauce (optional)
- 1½ tsp (7.5 mL) cornstarch

STIR-FRIED BROCCOLI AND CHICKEN

- 1 tbsp (15 mL) lower-sodium soy sauce (see page 17)
- 1 tbsp (15 mL) rice vinegar (see page 16)
- 1 tbsp (15 mL) hot sauce
- 14 oz (400 g) skinless, boneless chicken breast
- 1 lb (500 g) broccoli (1 large bunch)
- 1 large sweet red or orange pepper
- 1 bunch green onions (5 or 6)
- 1 tbsp (15 mL) canola oil

1 For the sauce, whisk together the chicken broth, soy sauce, chili sauce, hot sauce (if using), and cornstarch in a small bowl. Set aside.

2 For the stir-fry, whisk together the soy sauce, vinegar, and hot sauce in a medium bowl.

3 Wash your hands. Cut the chicken into thin strips. Add the chicken to the soy / vinegar / hot sauce mixture, and toss well. Set aside. Wash your hands and cutting board really well. (I keep a separate cutting board to use for raw meat and fish.)

4 Prep broccoli: Remove the stalks and save them for Chili-Roasted Broccoli Stalks (page 100). Cut the florets into 1-inch (2.5 cm) pieces and set aside.

5 Slice the sweet pepper into thin strips, discarding the seeds. Set aside. Cut the green onions into 1-inch (2.5 cm) pieces. Set aside.

6 Heat a large non-stick skillet over medium heat. Add the oil. Using a fork, remove the chicken from the marinade (discard marinade). Add the chicken to the skillet and stir-fry until it is no longer pink inside, 3 to 5 minutes. Using a slotted spoon, remove the chicken from the skillet. Place the chicken in a clean bowl, cover, and set aside.

7 Add the broccoli florets to the skillet and stir-fry until the broccoli starts to turn a darker green, 3 to 4 minutes. Add the sweet pepper and stir-fry until just tender-crisp, 2 to 3 minutes.

8 Add the cooked chicken (plus any juices in the bowl) and the green onions to the skillet, and stir-fry for 2 minutes. Whisk the sauce and add to the skillet. Stir-fry until the sauce comes to a boil and thickens slightly, about 1 minute. Divide the stir-fry evenly among 4 plates.

PER SERVING: 230 CALORIES, 5.8 G TOTAL FAT, 0.8 G SATURATED FAT, 0 G TRANS FAT, 461 MG SODIUM, 17.9 G CARBOHYDRATE, 4 G FIBRE, 8.2 G SUGARS, 29 G PROTEIN

DIABETES FOOD CHOICE VALUES PER SERVING: 1 CARBOHYDRATE, 4 MEAT AND ALTERNATIVES

HEALTH BITE

One of the best ways to enjoy broccoli is to eat it raw. Try serving raw broccoli florets and pieces of stem with a dip made with half low-fat ranch or Caesar salad dressing and half low-fat plain yogurt.

Winter Brussels

I keep trying to persuade my family and friends to join the Brussels sprouts team, but it's a difficult mission.

This is the only way I can get my partner, Scott, to even look at a Brussels sprout. Hopefully, you'll love them this way, too.

MAKES 2 CUPS (500 ML) | ONE SERVING = ½ CUP (125 ML)

INGREDIENTS

One 14 oz (300 g) package frozen Brussels sprouts (or 2 cups/500 mL fresh)
1 tsp (5 mL) canola oil
1 small shallot, minced
2 tbsp (30 mL) dried cranberries
1 tbsp (15 mL) pure maple syrup (see page 14)
1 tbsp (15 mL) balsamic vinegar

1 Cook the Brussels sprouts according to the package instructions (or steam fresh ones as described on the opposite page until tender-crisp).

2 While the sprouts are cooking, heat a medium skillet over medium heat. Add the oil, then the shallot, and sauté just until the shallot starts to turn golden brown, 3 to 5 minutes.

3 Add the cranberries and maple syrup to the skillet. If the sprouts aren't ready yet, remove the skillet from the heat.

4 When the Brussels sprouts are tender-crisp, add them to the skillet, tossing to coat with the maple syrup mixture. Drizzle the sprouts with the vinegar and toss again.

PER SERVING: 71 CALORIES, 1.4 G TOTAL FAT, 0 G SATURATED FAT, 0 G TRANS FAT, 48 MG SODIUM, 14.2 G CARBOHYDRATE, 2 G FIBRE, 8.1 G SUGARS, 2 G PROTEIN

DIABETES FOOD CHOICE VALUES PER SERVING: 1 CARBOHYDRATE, ½ FAT

Brussels Sprouts 101

"Hands up, who loves little baby cabbages?"

Whenever I ask this question at any of my talks, not many people put up their hands.

I never used to like them either. My mother cooked the living daylights out of Brussels sprouts, just like her mother. Granny used to say, "Okay, dinner is at 5:00 p.m. The roast went in at noon. It's 1:00 p.m, let's start the sprouts." Seriously, cooked for hours, they were grey-green blobs of what was once a vibrant green plant, sitting on your plate in a completely lifeless heap.

During my fourth year of university, in the Winter Vegetables lab, we cooked up the wee sprouts. To my shock and amazement, the Smith Family Food of Death was, in fact, a flavourful, vibrant, semi-firm green orb. Who knew they didn't taste of sulphur? Not me, or anyone else in my extended family — well, at least on my mom's side.

So I became a born-again Brussels sprouts eater. And like any reformed individual, I have made it my life's mission to convince anyone who will listen how great Brussels sprouts are. I love Brussels sprouts steamed and served with a tiny bit of non-hydrogenated margarine. At Christmas I go crazy and serve them with butter.

To steam fresh Brussels sprouts, place them in a steamer basket in a large saucepan with a lid. Add about 1 inch (2.5 cm) cold water to the saucepan. Cover and bring to a boil over medium-high heat. Steam for 5 to 8 minutes until the sprouts are tender-crisp (time will vary according to the size of the sprouts).

Buy It, Store It

Choose tiny Brussels sprouts; they'll be sweeter and less cabbagey tasting. They should be firm and a beautiful deep shade of green. Try to pick sprouts that are all the same size; that way they will take the same amount of time to cook.

Store Brussels sprouts in an open or perforated bag in your crisper and eat them ASAP. The longer they sit around, the stronger they'll taste. Oh, and the stronger they'll smell when you cook them.

Before using, trim away the outer leaves, wash the Brussels sprouts well under cold running water, and trim off a tiny bit of the woody bottoms. Either leave them whole if you're going to steam them, or cut them in half for stir-fries or if you're roasting them.

Brussels Sprouts and Broccoli Slaw

This is a great after-school or after-work snack. I created the recipe years ago for an article I wrote for alive *magazine. It's low in calories but high in flavour and fibre. Better still, it's a wonderful way to get yourself and your family eating Brussels sprouts and their cruciferous warrior buddy, broccoli, more often.*

To make your life easier, you really need a food processor to make this (see page 8 to find out why you need one). If you don't own one, either grate or thinly slice the veggies by hand (like we did for the picture), or run out and buy a food processor today.

MAKES 8 CUPS (2 L) | ONE SERVING = 1 CUP (250 ML)

BRUSSELS SPROUTS AND BROCCOLI SLAW

1 lb (500 g) broccoli (1 large bunch)
1 cup (250 mL) Brussels sprouts
½ medium red onion
1 large sweet red pepper, halved and seeded
1 large sweet orange pepper, halved and seeded
2 large unpeeled carrots, scrubbed

HONEY-DIJON DRESSING

½ cup (125 mL) apple cider vinegar (see page 12)
2 tbsp (30 mL) extra virgin olive oil
1 tsp (5 mL) grainy Dijon mustard
1 tsp (5 mL) honey

1 For the Brussels sprouts and broccoli slaw, fit a food processor with the thinnest slicing attachment, and thinly slice the broccoli, Brussels sprouts, red onion, and peppers. Place the sliced veggies in a large bowl. (If you don't have a food processor, very thinly slice the veggies with a large, sharp chef's knife.)

2 Fit the large grater attachment to the food processor, and grate the carrots. Add to the other veggies. (Use a box grater if you don't have a food processor. Now see why you need one?)

3 For the honey-Dijon dressing, whisk together the vinegar, oil, mustard, and honey in a small bowl.

4 Drizzle the dressing over the veggies and toss well. (The slaw will keep for up to 4 days in the fridge.)

PER SERVING: 83 CALORIES, 4 G TOTAL FAT, 0.5 G SATURATED FAT, 0 G TRANS FAT, 52 MG SODIUM, 11.3 G CARBOHYDRATE, 3 G FIBRE, 4.2 G SUGARS, 3 G PROTEIN

DIABETES FOOD CHOICE VALUES PER SERVING: ½ CARBOHYDRATE, ½ MEAT AND ALTERNATIVES, ½ FAT

Chili-Roasted Broccoli Stalks

For all of you who hate throwing away broccoli stalks, here's a recipe just for this vastly underappreciated part of the plant. Save the florets for salads or steaming, to serve as crudités, or to use in Stir-Fried Broccoli and Chicken (page 94) or Broccoli with Peanut Sauce (page 93).

MAKES ABOUT 2 CUPS (500 L) | ONE SERVING = ½ CUP (125 ML)

INGREDIENTS

3 cloves garlic
1 lb (500 g) broccoli (1 large bunch)
2 tbsp (30 mL) canola oil
2 tbsp (30 mL) chili powder
1 tsp (5 mL) dried oregano leaves
1 tsp (5 mL) dried basil leaves
½ tsp (1 mL) cracked black pepper

1 Preheat the oven to 400°F (200°C). Line an 11- × 7-inch (2 L) rimmed baking sheet with parchment paper or foil.

2 Mince the garlic and set aside.

3 Trim off a tiny bit from the end of the broccoli stalks, then cut the florets from the stalks, cutting as close to the florets as possible. (Save the florets in a plastic bag in the fridge and use in another recipe.)

4 Slice the broccoli stalks lengthwise into four equal strips. Thicker slices take longer to cook than really thin ones, but don't go crazy trying to get them even. Set the stalks aside.

5 Mix together the garlic, oil, chili powder, oregano, basil, pepper, and 1 tbsp (15 mL) water in a large bowl. Add the broccoli stalks and toss well with a rubber spatula.

6 Tip the broccoli onto the prepared baking sheet and arrange it in a single layer. If any of the spice mixture remains in the bowl, scrape it out and add it to the broccoli where it belongs.

7 Roast the broccoli until tender-crisp, 15 to 20 minutes (timing will depend on how thinly you sliced the broccoli).

QUICK TIP

If you love spicy, this is the recipe for you; there's a fair amount of heat in every bite.

PER SERVING: 122 CALORIES, 8.2 G TOTAL FAT, 0.7 G SATURATED FAT, 0 G TRANS FAT, 81 MG SODIUM, 11.5 G CARBOHYDRATE, 5 G FIBRE, 2.4 G SUGARS, 4 G PROTEIN

DIABETES FOOD CHOICE VALUES PER SERVING: ½ CARBOHYDRATE, ½ MEAT AND ALTERNATIVES, 1½ FAT

Coleslaw: The Master Recipe

At my house, we eat coleslaw all winter long. Depending on what I have in the fridge, the coleslaw is a little different each time I serve it.

Here's my master recipe for coleslaw, plus three ways to switch it up.

I make the dressing first, right in the bowl, then I add the cabbage and onion, plus any extra bells and whistles (see variations on page 103). You gotta love a one-bowler.

MAKES ABOUT 4 CUPS (1 L) | ONE SERVING = ½ CUP (125 ML)

INGREDIENTS

¼ cup (60 mL) apple cider vinegar (see page 12)

2 tsp (10 mL) canola oil

1 tsp (5 mL) honey

¼ medium red (it looks purple but it's called red) or green cabbage, thinly sliced (4 cups / 1 L)

¼ medium red onion, thinly sliced

1 Whisk together the vinegar, oil, and honey in a large salad bowl.

2 Add the cabbage and onion and toss well. Serve as is or make one of the variations listed on page 103.

PER SERVING: 27 CALORIES, 1.2 G TOTAL FAT, 0 G SATURATED FAT, 0 G TRANS FAT, 9 MG SODIUM, 4.1 G CARBOHYDRATE, 1 G FIBRE, 2.6 G SUGARS, 1 G PROTEIN

DIABETES FOOD CHOICE VALUES PER SERVING: 1 EXTRA

CONTINUED . . .

Cabbage 101

Cabbage was a boon for Canada's early settlers because it kept for a fairly long time in their root cellars. Come fall and winter, when fresh lettuces aren't necessarily local anymore, take a leaf from those settlers, and switch to cabbage salads or coleslaw.

Like the rest of the cruciferous family, cabbage is a good source of vitamin C, and a source of folate.

Buy It, Store It

Heavy may not be great if you're trying out for *Swan Lake*, but it's perfect if you're a cabbage. Hold up a couple to compare and go with the heaviest for its size. Look for firm cabbages without any wilting leaves.

Before using, remove the cabbage's outer leaves, then rinse the cabbage under cold running water.

Once cut, store cabbage in an open or perforated bag in the crisper for up to three weeks.

CONTINUED FROM PAGE 101

Blueberry Coleslaw

1 Add 1¼ cups (310 mL) slightly thawed frozen blueberries to the master recipe. Toss and serve at once (the salad turns blue if not served right away).

MAKES ABOUT 5 CUPS (1.25 L) | ONE SERVING = ½ CUP (125 ML)

PER SERVING: 32 CALORIES, 1.1 G TOTAL FAT, 0 G SATURATED FAT, 0 G TRANS FAT, 7 MG SODIUM, 5.8 G CARBOHYDRATE, 1 G FIBRE, 3.7 G SUGARS, 1 G PROTEIN

DIABETES FOOD CHOICE VALUES PER SERVING: 1 EXTRA

Apple Coleslaw

1 Add 2 apples, scrubbed well, cut into quarters, cored, and sliced thinly, and ¼ cup (60 mL) dried cranberries to the master recipe. Toss and serve.

MAKES ABOUT 6 CUPS (1.5 L) | ONE SERVING = ½ CUP (125 ML)

PER SERVING: 38 CALORIES, 0.9 G TOTAL FAT, 0 G SATURATED FAT, 0 G TRANS FAT, 6 MG SODIUM, 8.1 G CARBOHYDRATE, 1 G FIBRE, 5.8 G SUGARS, 1 G PROTEIN

DIABETES FOOD CHOICE VALUES PER SERVING: ½ CARBOHYDRATE

Citrus Coleslaw

1 Add 2 oranges, peeled and coarsely chopped (see page 24), and ¼ cup (60 mL) dried cranberries to the master recipe. Toss and serve.

MAKES ABOUT 6 CUPS (1.5 L) | ONE SERVING = ½ CUP (125 ML)

PER SERVING: 37 CALORIES, 0.9 G TOTAL FAT, 0 G SATURATED FAT, 0 G TRANS FAT, 6 MG SODIUM, 7.5 G CARBOHYDRATE, 1 G FIBRE, 5.5 G SUGARS, 1 G PROTEIN

DIABETES FOOD CHOICE VALUES PER SERVING: ½ CARBOHYDRATE

Cauliflower 101

This antioxidant-rich veggie can be steamed, stir-fried, roasted, or added to a favourite soup recipe. To protect the vitamin C, eat cauliflower raw or only lightly cooked.

To prepare cauliflower, simply cut off the outer leaves, wash the cauliflower well under cold running water, cut out the core, then break off the florets. Discard thick stems or cut them up to serve with a dip, or to use in soups or veggie stock.

To steam cauliflower florets, place them in a steamer basket in a large saucepan with a lid. Add about 1 inch (2.5 cm) cold water to the saucepan. Cover and bring to a boil over medium-high heat. Steam for 3 to 5 minutes until the florets are tender-crisp (time will vary according to the size of the florets).

Buy It, Store It

Look for intensely white, tight heads of cauliflower that are surrounded by fresh green leaves. Any brown spots? Keep looking.

Check out the purple and golden-orange cauliflowers, too. They have a similar flavour to the white variety, but if your kids are into colour, they may be tempted to try these brighter-looking varieties, especially if you serve the cauliflower raw with a dip.

Store whole cauliflower in an open or perforated bag in your crisper for up to five days.

YEAR ROUND
KID FRIENDLY

Cauliflower with Cheater Cheese Sauce

So how do you get your kids and other vegetable-challenged family members to eat more of Mother Nature's treats? Add sauces or dips. Seems to work on most of vegetable abstainers I've met.

Most cheese sauces require you to make a white sauce, then add cheese. My version skips the whole melting-fat-adding-flour-whisking-in-milk part, and goes right to the cheese. It's simple, and kids will love it.

MAKES ABOUT 2 CUPS (500 ML) STEAMED CAULIFLOWER AND 6 TBSP (90 ML) CHEESE SAUCE | ONE SERVING = ½ CUP (125 ML) CAULIFLOWER AND 1 TBSP (15 ML) CHEESE SAUCE

INGREDIENTS

½ cauliflower, divided into florets

CHEATER CHEESE SAUCE

2 tbsp (30 mL) light cream cheese
2 tbsp (30 mL) skim milk
½ cup (125 mL) shredded extra-old cheddar cheese

1 Steam the cauliflower florets (see Cauliflower 101, opposite page) until tender-crisp.

2 For the cheater cheese sauce, heat the cream cheese and milk in a small saucepan over medium-low heat. Whisk gently until smooth. Add the cheddar and reduce the heat to low. Whisk gently until the sauce is smooth. Remove the saucepan from the heat.

3 To serve, drizzle each serving of steamed cauliflower (½ cup / 125 mL) with 1 tbsp (15 mL) cheese sauce.

PER SERVING: 45 CALORIES, 2.4 G TOTAL FAT, 1.5 G SATURATED FAT, 0 G TRANS FAT, 75 MG SODIUM, 3.6 G CARBOHYDRATE, 1 G FIBRE, 1.9 G SUGARS, 3 G PROTEIN

DIABETES FOOD CHOICE VALUES PER SERVING: ½ MEAT AND ALTERNATIVES, ½ FAT, 1 EXTRA

LOVE THAT SAUCE?

Cheater cheese sauce goes well with all kinds of veggies, so here's its nutrient breakdown (without the cauliflower):

Per tbsp (15 mL): 31 calories, 2.3 g total fat, 1.5 g saturated fat, 0 g trans fat, 59 mg sodium, 0.8 g carbohydrate, 0 g fibre, 0.6 g sugars, 1.6 g protein
Diabetes Food Choice Values per tbsp (15 mL): ½ Fat

6

Carrots, Sweet Potatoes, Winter Squash, and Pumpkin: *Golden and Good for You*

My mom always told me that if I ate my carrots, I'd be able to see in the dark. Some of her other sayings ("You can't get blood from a turnip" is one) were totally off base, but when it comes to carrots, Mom was right on the money.

GOOD FOR YOU

Carrots contain beta-carotene, which our bodies convert into vitamin A. This vitamin is needed for cell growth and development, and for healthy skin, bones, teeth, nails, and vision. It also helps boost immunity.

Beta-carotene is also a powerful antioxidant that neutralizes free radicals, which are believed to lead to cancer. Beta-carotene is found in winter squash, peaches, mangoes, papayas, carrots, apricots, cantaloupes, muskmelons, and sweet potatoes.

It's also found in spinach, kale, and broccoli, but in this book, the green leafy guys get their very own chapter (see Greens: Nature's Perfect Colour, page 192), and broccoli stars in Broccoli, Brussels Sprouts, Cabbage, and Cauliflower: The Cruciferous Family of Superheroes on page 90.

Can't we just pop a beta-carotene supplement? Well, no. The American Heart Association, the American Cancer Society, the World Cancer Research Institute in association with the American Institute for Cancer Research, and the World Health Organization's International Agency for Research on Cancer all believe that we need to eat the foods rich in beta-carotene and not take a supplement.

So get out your pots and pans and let's start cooking up some recipes featuring carrots, sweet potatoes, winter squash, and pumpkin.

HEALTH BITE

Muskmelons, intensely flavoured melons that grow in some parts of Canada, and their milder version, cantaloupes, are also great sources of beta-carotene.

To prepare either melon, wash it well and cut off the thick peel. Chop the melon flesh, cover, and refrigerate for up to three days. Best eaten as is, ripe juicy muskmelon and cantaloupe are an excellent source of vitamin A and C, and are high in potassium.

SUMMER / FALL
KID FRIENDLY

Carrot-Raisin Salad

This recipe is a favourite of mine. I love the combination of spicy flavours from the mango chutney and the ginger, plus the sweetness of the carrots and raisins.

MAKES ABOUT 2 CUPS (500 ML), DEPENDING ON THE SIZE OF THE CARROTS
ONE SERVING = ½ CUP (125 ML)

INGREDIENTS

- 2 tbsp (30 mL) mango chutney (see below)
- 4 tsp (20 mL) low-fat mayonnaise
- 4 tsp (20 mL) low-fat plain yogurt
- 2 tsp (10 mL) finely grated fresh ginger
- 4 large unpeeled carrots, scrubbed and coarsely grated
- ¼ cup (60 mL) raisins

1 Whisk together the chutney, mayonnaise, yogurt, and ginger in a salad bowl.

2 Add the grated carrots and raisins to the bowl, and toss well. (Salad will keep fresh in the fridge for up to 2 days.)

PER SERVING: 95 CALORIES, 1.6 G TOTAL FAT, 0 G SATURATED FAT, 0 G TRANS FAT, 161 MG SODIUM, 21 G CARBOHYDRATE, 2 G FIBRE, 12.6 G SUGARS, 1 G PROTEIN

DIABETES FOOD CHOICE VALUES PER SERVING: 1½ CARBOHYDRATE, ½ FAT

WHAT IS . . . ?

A South Asian condiment, mango chutney has a bit of sweetness, a bit of tang, and a whole lot of yummy flavours. Grocery Store Search: It can be found in the Asian or South Asian section of most large grocery stores.

Pan-Fried and Oven-Finished Fall Vegetables

This crowd-pleasing dish is well worth the wait, and will fill your house with lovely aromas as it cooks.

MAKES ABOUT 5 CUPS (1.25 L) | ONE SERVING = ½ CUP (125 ML)

1 Preheat the oven to 350°F (180°C).

2 Hold a sharp knife at a 45-degree angle to one of the carrots and slice down through it. Reverse the angle and cut again. Hopefully the slice will look like a big fat triangle; if not, oh well. Just make sure all the pieces are about the same size. Repeat with the remaining carrots and the parsnips.

3 Heat a large ovenproof skillet (a cast iron one is perfect; see sidebar) over medium heat. Add the oil, then the carrots, parsnips, and shallots. Sauté for 5 minutes.

4 While the veggies are cooking, whisk together the vinegar and honey in a small bowl. Set aside.

5 When the veggies have been cooking for 5 minutes, remove the skillet from the heat. If your skillet isn't ovenproof, transfer the veggies to the prepared pan (see sidebar).

6 Drizzle veggies with the vinegar mixture. Sprinkle with the rosemary and pepper, and toss gently.

7 Transfer the skillet or pan to the oven and roast for 45 minutes. Remove from the oven and toss gently. Basically, you're basting the veggies.

8 Return the veggies to the oven and roast until they're tender, about 10 more minutes. (If you like really soft roasted veggies, cook them for an extra 20 minutes; it's your call.)

PER SERVING: 91 CALORIES, 3 G TOTAL FAT, 0.4 G SATURATED FAT, 0 G TRANS FAT, 37 MG SODIUM, 16.2 G CARBOHYDRATE, 2 G FIBRE, 4.8 G SUGARS, 1 G PROTEIN

DIABETES FOOD CHOICE VALUES PER SERVING: 1 CARBOHYDRATE, ½ FAT

INGREDIENTS

8 large shallots, cut in half lengthwise
4 unpeeled carrots, scrubbed
4 unpeeled parsnips, scrubbed
2 tbsp (30 mL) extra virgin olive oil
1 tbsp (15 mL) balsamic vinegar
1 tbsp (15 mL) honey
2 tbsp (30 mL) finely chopped fresh rosemary (see page 25)
1 tsp (5 mL) cracked black pepper

HOW TO

If you don't have an ovenproof skillet, use a regular large skillet to pan-fry the veggies. Transfer the sautéed mixture to an 11- x 7-inch (2 L) baking pan lined with dry parchment paper, and continue with Step 6.

MAKEOVERS

Reheat any leftover veggies in the microwave, then . . . toss them with cooked whole-grain pasta or brown rice, and serve with fish or poultry . . . or add them to a grilled sandwich.

Carrots and Parsnips 101

Half of your success in the kitchen is due to picking the best ingredients. So, choose firm-looking carrots and parsnips that are free of brown spots. For best flavour, select smaller vegetables that are about 9 to 10 inches (23 to 25 cm) long. Basically don't buy a carrot or parsnip that's bigger than your head. And if it looks shrivelled, don't buy it. Bottom line: don't buy any produce that doesn't look amazing.

Parsnips Rule!

I really ought to become the national spokesperson for parsnips—they're one of my favourite winter veggies. It kills me that most people think they're just an anemic-looking carrot. Okay, they are sort of a pale shade of cream but savvy marketers would call the colour something sexy like "Cosmic Corn Silk" or "Champagne Bubbles," not "a pale shade of cream."

My pitch for parsnips would go something like this: "Give your blood pressure a spa treatment with soothing potassium. Your body loves to keep all systems moving so don't be afraid to treat it to half a cup of nature's answer to 'Sneaking in the Fibre.' Let your heart sing as you make room for parsnips on your plate."

Okay, maybe a tad over the top, but parsnips need all the help they can get. They're an excellent source of folate, and a source of potassium, an important mineral that helps regulate blood pressure. If you need more pluses, one large parsnip provides a whopping six grams of fibre.

Sweet Potatoes 101

Colour is an indicator of beta-carotene, so you would be right as rain to guess that sweet potatoes are rich in this important antioxidant.

Sweet potatoes are full of vitamin C, fibre, potassium, and vitamin B6, which is essential for red-blood-cell metabolism and extremely important for both the nervous and immune systems to function efficiently.

In Canada, the darker variety of sweet potato is sometimes called a yam, which drives me insane. A yam is a hairy-coated white root vegetable from the tropics. Sweet potatoes have brown or tan peels, are orange or yellow on the inside, and are grown in North America. I've written many rants on this subject so I'll spare you here. But if you have a copy of *Ultimate Foods for Ultimate Health … and don't forget the chocolate!,* check out page 177.

Sweet Potato Soup

This family-friendly, nutrient-dense soup has great sweet potato flavour.

MAKES ABOUT 7 CUPS (1.75 L) | ONE SERVING = 1 CUP (250 ML)

1 Mince the garlic and set aside.

2 Heat a large saucepan over medium heat. Add the oil, then the onions, and sauté until the onions are a rich golden colour, 5 to 8 minutes. (This step really deepens the flavour of the soup.)

3 Add the garlic and sauté for 30 seconds. Add the sweet potatoes and sauté for 3 minutes, stirring often to prevent them from sticking.

4 Stir in the chicken broth and bring to a boil. Reduce heat to medium-low and simmer, covered, until the sweet potato is tender, 25 to 30 minutes. The time will depend on how large the sweet potatoes pieces are. In a hurry? Chop them the size of chickpeas.

5 Use a hand-held immersion blender (see page 8) to purée the soup in the saucepan until smooth. (Or purée the soup in a blender, about 2 cups/500 mL at a time, until smooth.) (If making the soup in advance, refrigerate the soup in an airtight container for up to 2 days, or freeze it for up to 3 months. To serve, thaw the soup, reheat, then continue with the next step.)

6 Whisk in the evaporated milk and heat through over medium heat but do not let boil. Ladle into soup bowl and sprinkle with pepper.

PER SERVING: 166 CALORIES, 2 G TOTAL FAT, 0.3 G SATURATED FAT, 0 G TRANS FAT, 180 MG SODIUM, 32.1 G CARBOHYDRATE, 4 G FIBRE, 11.9 G SUGARS, 6 G PROTEIN

DIABETES FOOD CHOICE VALUES PER SERVING: 2 CARBOHYDRATE, ½ FAT

INGREDIENTS

2 cloves garlic
1 tbsp (15 mL) extra virgin olive oil
2 onions, diced
6 cups (1.5 L) peeled, chopped sweet potatoes (about 6 large)
3 cups (750 mL) lower-sodium chicken broth (see page 7)
1 cup (250 mL) evaporated fat-free milk (see page 13)
Cracked black pepper to taste

GIVE IT A TWIST

If you want to kick things up a couple of notches, add some Thai-style chili sauce (see page 12) a little at a time until you reach your desired level of heat.

HEALTH BITE

For an extra hit of fibre, don't peel the sweet potatoes; just scrub them well before chopping.

Oven-Roasted Sweet Potatoes

If you're in a hurry, cut the sweet potatoes into small pieces so they'll roast more quickly.

MAKES ABOUT 4 CUPS (1 L) | ONE SERVING = ½ CUP (125 ML)

INGREDIENTS

¼ cup (60 mL) frozen orange juice concentrate, thawed (see page 13)
1 tbsp (15 mL) canola oil
2 tsp (10 mL) Dijon mustard
2 large sweet potatoes, scrubbed

1 Preheat the oven to 400°F (200°C). Line a 13- × 9-inch (3.5 L) metal baking pan with dry parchment paper.

2 Whisk together the orange juice concentrate, oil, and Dijon mustard in a large bowl.

3 Cut the sweet potatoes into quarters, then cut each quarter into 1-inch (2.5 cm) cubes, or smaller (see above).

4 Add the sweet potato to the bowl and toss with the orange juice mixture.

5 Tip the sweet potatoes into the prepared pan and spread them out in a single layer. If any of the orange juice mixture remains in the bowl, scrape it out onto the sweet potatoes where it belongs.

6 Roast the sweet potatoes in the oven until they're tender and slightly golden, 45 to 55 minutes.

PER SERVING: 127 CALORIES, 3.8 G TOTAL FAT, 0 G SATURATED FAT, 0 G TRANS FAT, 97 MG SODIUM, 21.3 G CARBOHYDRATE, 2 G FIBRE, 9.9 G SUGARS, 2 G PROTEIN

DIABETES FOOD CHOICE VALUES PER SERVING: 1½ CARBOHYDRATE, 1 FAT

Roasted Butternut Squash with Turmeric and Cracked Black Pepper

When I buy a butternut squash, I choose a fairly large one that has a long, thick neck. I use this seedless part for this recipe. And the end with the seeds? I use that a couple of days later in Roasted Butternut Squash with Cranberries (recipe follows). Two totally different recipes using the same vegetable. How cool is that? The combination of turmeric and cracked black pepper makes this favourite of mine spicy with a fabulous golden-orange colour. It's good for your brain, your immune system, your heart, and your taste buds.

MAKES ABOUT 2 CUPS (500 ML) | ONE SERVING = ½ CUP (125 ML)

INGREDIENTS

Neck end of 1 large butternut squash
2 tsp (10 mL) canola oil
1 tsp (5 mL) turmeric
½ tsp (2.5 mL) cracked black pepper

1 Preheat the oven to 350°F (180°C). Line an 8-inch (20 cm) square metal baking pan with wet parchment paper (see page 11).

2 Using a really sharp knife (as opposed to a sort-of sharp knife or worse, a dull knife), cut the thick peel off the butternut squash (or use a really good vegetable peeler).

3 Cut the neck end of the squash in half lengthwise. Place it flat side down on a cutting board and cut lengthwise into 1-inch (2.5 cm) slices. Cut each slice into 1-inch (2.5 cm) cubes as shown in the picture (page 117). Just try your best; it's okay if it doesn't look exactly the same.

4 Place the squash in a large bowl and toss with the oil. Add the turmeric and pepper, and toss until well coated.

5 Place the squash in the prepared pan, scraping any oil remaining in the bowl onto the squash where it belongs. Roast, uncovered, until tender and golden, 45 to 60 minutes.

PER SERVING: 57 CALORIES, 2.4 G TOTAL FAT, 0 G SATURATED FAT, 0 G TRANS FAT, 3 MG SODIUM, 9.2 G CARBOHYDRATE, 1 G FIBRE, 1.6 G SUGARS, 1 G PROTEIN

DIABETES FOOD CHOICE VALUES PER SERVING: ½ CARBOHYDRATE, ½ FAT

Roasted Butternut Squash with Cranberries

... and this is my squash recipe for the end with the seeds. The combination of the dried and the fresh cranberries gives this dish a great sweet-tart flavour.

MAKES 4 SERVINGS | ONE SERVING = ONE-QUARTER SQUASH

INGREDIENTS

- Bottom end of 1 butternut squash (the part with the seeds)
- 1 tbsp (15 mL) fresh or frozen cranberries
- 1 tbsp (15 mL) dried cranberries
- 1 tsp (5 mL) unsalted non-hydrogenated margarine
- 1/4 tsp (1 mL) cinnamon

1 Preheat the oven to 350°F (180°C). Line an 8-inch (20 cm) square metal baking pan with wet parchment paper (see page 11).

2 Cut the bottom end of the squash in half lengthwise. Scoop out the seeds. Cut each half in half. (Okay, I could have said, cut the squash into quarters, but the seeds would have been a mess—there is always a reason for my madness.) Pierce each quarter using a fork or a knife without going right through to the other side; we don't want any leakage.

3 Place the squash quarters in the prepared pan. Divide the fresh or frozen cranberries and the dried cranberries evenly among the 4 quarters.

4 Put 1/4 tsp (1 mL) margarine on top of each quarter. Yes, I know what you're thinking—it is a tiny amount. Use your fingers to sprinkle a little dusting of cinnamon overtop each squash quarter (or if your cinnamon bottle has holes in the top, just gently sprinkle with what amounts to about 1/4 tsp / 1 mL).

5 Roast the squash, uncovered, until tender, 40 to 50 minutes.

PER SERVING: 51 CALORIES, 1.1 G TOTAL FAT, 0 G SATURATED FAT, 0 G TRANS FAT, 16 MG SODIUM, 11.1 G CARBOHYDRATE, 1 G FIBRE, 3.3 G SUGARS, 1 G PROTEIN

DIABETES FOOD CHOICE VALUES PER SERVING: 1/2 CARBOHYDRATE

CRANBERRIES: NOT JUST A PRETTY SAUCE

Cranberries grow low to the ground in marshes. Because these hardy little gems float, when the berries are ripe, the marshes are flooded to make harvesting easier. Growers use water-reel harvesting machines to loosen the cranberries from the vines. The berries are corralled onto conveyer belts, then into waiting trucks that take them to packing plants, and finally they make it onto your Thanksgiving or Christmas table.

Top: Roasted Butternut Squash with Turmeric and Cracked Black Pepper (page 115)
Bottom: Roasted Butternut Squash with Cranberries (facing page)

Jamaican-Spiced Pumpkin Soup

This soup gets its Caribbean flavour from antioxidant-rich thyme, allspice, and cinnamon. It's a little bit of the islands, but my version isn't spicy hot. If you want a bit more kick, add some hot pepper sauce at the table.

MAKES ABOUT 7 CUPS (1.75 L) | ONE SERVING = 1½ CUPS (375 ML)

INGREDIENTS

2 tsp (10 mL) dried thyme leaves
1 tsp (5 mL) ground allspice
¼ tsp (1 mL) cinnamon
1 tbsp (15 mL) extra virgin olive oil
4 large shallots, diced
2 tbsp (30 mL) finely grated fresh ginger
3 cups (750 mL) lower-sodium chicken broth (see page 7)
One 28 oz (796 mL) can pure pumpkin purée (not pumpkin-pie filling; see page 16)
12 dried apricots, cut in half
One 13 oz (375 mL) can evaporated fat-free milk (see page 13)

1 Mix together the thyme, allspice, and cinnamon in a small bowl. Set aside.

2 Heat a large saucepan over medium heat. Add the oil, then the shallots, and sauté until the shallots are beginning to brown, about 3 minutes.

3 Add the ginger and the spice mixture, and sauté for 30 seconds. The aromas will hit you in the face.

4 Stir in the chicken broth, making sure you scrape up all the little browned bits stuck to the bottom of the saucepan. This will make the soup more flavourful and will prevent it from burning.

5 Whisk in the pumpkin, then stir in the dried apricots. Bring to a boil, stirring well. Reduce the heat to a simmer and cook, covered and stirring occasionally, until the shallots and apricots are soft, 30 to 45 minutes.

6 Use a hand-held immersion blender (see page 8) to purée the soup in the saucepan until smooth. (Or purée the soup in a blender, about 2 cups / 500 mL at a time, until smooth.)

7 Whisk in the evaporated milk and heat through over medium heat, but do not let boil. Ladle into soup bowls. (Omit the milk and refrigerate the soup in an airtight container for up to 2 days, or freeze it for up to 3 months. To serve, thaw the soup, then whisk in the milk and reheat the soup before serving.)

HEALTH BITE

I like to add dried apricots, a source of beta-carotene, to orange vegetable soups because they add extra colour and a bit of sweetness. This soup is mildly spicy but if you're looking for a non-spicy beta-carotene-rich soup check out the recipe for Carrot-Apricot Soup on page 312.

PER SERVING: 242 CALORIES, 3.2 G TOTAL FAT, 0.4 G SATURATED FAT, 0 G TRANS FAT, 205 MG SODIUM, 45.4 G CARBOHYDRATE, 4 G FIBRE, 26.2 G SUGARS, 11 G PROTEIN

DIABETES FOOD CHOICE VALUES PER SERVING: 3 CARBOHYDRATE, 1 MEAT AND ALTERNATIVES

Double-Chocolate Pumpkin Muffins

What's a chocolate muffin doing in the beta-carotene chapter? It's the pumpkin, which is one of the most important ingredients in this totally chocolatey-tasting whole-grain muffin, that puts it here.

Next time you have to send a treat to school, pack up these muffins and tell your kids they're chocolate cupcakes—they taste that good. Sometimes when you tell a kid there's pumpkin in something they just won't eat it, so I give you permission to omit that minor detail. (If you're sending these muffins to school, check the chocolate chips' label for any mention of peanuts, in case of allergies.)

I adapted this recipe from one in Ultimate Foods for Ultimate Health... and don't forget the chocolate!

MAKES 12 MUFFINS | ONE SERVING = 1 MUFFIN

INGREDIENTS

1 cup (250 mL) packed dark brown sugar
1 cup (250 mL) buttermilk
1 cup (250 mL) pure pumpkin purée (not pumpkin-pie filling; see page 16)
½ cup (125 mL) oat bran
1 omega-3 egg (see page 13)
1 cup (250 mL) whole wheat flour
¾ cup (185 mL) ground flaxseed (see page 13)
½ cup (125 mL) natural cocoa powder (see page 12)
¼ cup (60 mL) chocolate chips with at least 60% cocoa mass or chocolate chunks with at least 70% cocoa mass
2 tbsp (30 mL) wheat germ
2 tbsp (30 mL) cinnamon
1½ tsp (7.5 mL) baking powder
1 tsp (5 mL) baking soda

1 Preheat the oven to 400°F (200°C). Line a 12-cup muffin pan with paper liners.

2 Whisk together the brown sugar, buttermilk, pumpkin, oat bran, and egg in a medium bowl. Set aside.

3 Whisk together the flour, flaxseed, cocoa, chocolate chips, wheat germ, cinnamon, baking powder, and baking soda in a large bowl.

4 Add the sugar / pumpkin mixture to the flour mixture and mix until just combined.

5 Divide the batter evenly among the muffin cups (I use a ¼-cup / 60 mL ice-cream scoop with a release lever). Bake until a toothpick comes out clean, 20 to 25 minutes. Let the muffins cool in the pan on a wire rack for 5 minutes. Remove the muffins and let them cool completely on the wire rack. (Store the muffins in an airtight container for up to 2 days, or freeze for up to 2 months.)

PUMPKIN 101

Aside from making scary jack-o'-lanterns, pumpkins are a storehouse of nutrients, but only the ones that are too small for lanterns are good for eating.

PER MUFFIN: 190 CALORIES, 4.6 G TOTAL FAT, 1 G SATURATED FAT, 0 G TRANS FAT, 183 MG SODIUM, 35.6 G CARBOHYDRATE, 5 G FIBRE, 18.4 G SUGARS, 5 G PROTEIN

DIABETES FOOD CHOICE VALUES PER MUFFIN: 2 CARBOHYDRATE, 1 FAT

Top down: Apple-Date Muffins (page 32), Double-Chocolate Pumpkin Muffins (facing page), and Really, Really High-Fibre Banana Chocolate Chip Muffins (page 186)

7

Fish:
Get Your Omega-3s

I was raised on salmon. My mom packed me salmon sandwiches for my lunch at school, she packed salmon sandwiches in a picnic hamper when we ate at Stanley Park, and she packed salmon sandwiches whenever we went camping. I should have a PhD by now with all those brain-enhancing omega-3s running through my body.

GOOD FOR YOU

Evidence of the positive effects of eating fatty fish such as salmon, mackerel, sardines, anchovies, and herring continues to mount. These types of fish supply our bodies with valuable omega-3 fatty acids, which can help reduce our chances of developing heart disease, keep our brains working, reduce inflammation that can lead to arthritis, and protect our eyes from age-related diseases.

A study published in *Alzheimer's & Dementia: The Journal of the Alzheimer's Association* showed that, after two months of consuming supplemental omega-3 fatty acids, adults aged over 55 years who had age-related cognitive decline experienced an improvement in learning and memory function.

All fish is lower in saturated fat than meat. So, choosing fish over poultry or red meat is a great way to reduce the amount of total saturated fat in your diet. Practise moderation and limit your intake of all types of fish to two to four servings per week.

FISH PRIMER

Being a fish lover, I'm always surprised when people say they don't like fish. What? How can you *not* love fish?

I think people don't like fish because they buy the wrong kind. I didn't realize that until I cooked up some frozen fish from my local grocery store, and had one of those "oh, I get it" moments. The fish was grim. It was rubbery, dried out, and chewy all at the same time.

To help you navigate the fish department, here's how to find the best fish:

- Buy the freshest fish possible—if it's smelly, don't buy it. Fresh fish should smell clean and fresh like the ocean, not smelly and stale like low tide.
- Check to see that the flesh of the fish is firm to the touch. Gently press the flesh with your finger; if your finger leaves a hole, walk away—the fish is old.

- If you're buying a whole fish, its eyes should be bulging and clear. If they're sunken and cloudy, walk away.

- It's harder to tell how fresh frozen fish is. Most frozen fish should be the absolute freshest; the fish is usually flash-frozen very soon after being caught. Any deterioration usually has to do with fluctuating temperatures during storage. If there are ice crystals inside the package, the temperature of the freezer has gone up and down, and with it, the quality of the fish. Choose packages that are free of ice crystals.

- When choosing frozen seafood, don't buy seafood that has any freezer burn or looks dry.

- Always thaw frozen fish and seafood in the fridge before cooking it.

FISH HOW-TO

For any type of fish, whether whole or filleted, the rule of thumb when cooking it is to allow 10 minutes for each inch (2.5 cm) of thickness. Simply measure the fish at its thickest part, then time the cooking accordingly.

How can you tell when the fish is cooked? The flesh of the fish should look opaque and start to flake when prodded, there should be no raw-looking parts inside, and a meat thermometer inserted into each piece of fish should register 158°F (70°C). Overcooked fish falls apart easily, and is very dry and extremely chewy. Perfectly cooked fish should be tender and juicy, and melt in your mouth.

Why do all my recipes call for 13 oz (370 g) fish fillets? The dreaded shrinkage issue strikes again. A fillet that weighs 13 oz (370 g) will yield about 12 oz (340 g) of cooked fish.

HEALTH BITE

Methyl mercury causes damage to your central nervous system, heart, brain, and kidneys. How much damage is caused is related to how much of this toxic compound gets into your body. Due to certain manufacturing practices, mercury has become fairly common in the environment, with trace amounts of methyl mercury present in many varieties of seafood.

Health professionals, as well as Health Canada, recommend that women who are pregnant or who may become pregnant, nursing mothers, and small children avoid fish that may contain unsafe levels of methyl mercury.

These varieties include fresh or frozen tuna (including sushi tuna), shark, swordfish, marlin, orange roughy, tilefish, and escolar.

WHAT ABOUT CANNED TUNA?

The amount of methyl mercury present in fish is related to the size of the fish. The rule of thumb is the bigger the fish, the higher the concentration of the toxin. This is because the big guys eat the little guys, and the mercury builds up in their bodies.

Canned tuna is a popular seafood choice for many people. Choosing canned light tuna made from smaller varieties of fish, like skipjack and tongol, is a better decision. Limit the amount of canned albacore tuna you eat. Health Canada advises that women who are or who may become pregnant, or who are nursing, and children should limit their intake of canned tuna to one serving a week.

Since I am concerned about mercury toxicity, I like to err on the side of caution. So, I limit my consumption of canned light tuna to once a month, and have decided to skip albacore altogether.

SALMON: WILD V. FARMED

The first time I saw Atlantic farmed salmon in a fish store I thought the fish had been labelled incorrectly. Of course, I had to tell the fishmonger he'd made a mistake. When he told me that I was wrong and that it was Atlantic farmed salmon, not wild sockeye salmon, I still thought he was pulling a fast one. But it turned out he was right, and I was wrong.

For the newbies and the pros, here are the differences between these two varieties of salmon:

- Wild salmon is usually darker in colour than farmed salmon.
- Wild salmon has a stronger flavour than farmed salmon.
- Wild salmon has less fat than farmed salmon. In the wild, you have to swim hard or get eaten. All that swimming creates muscle, not fat. Atlantic farmed salmon aren't very active. There isn't much need for swimming quickly in a pen, and as a result the fish are fatter.

Concerned about farmed salmon? Don't eat the skin, or choose wild salmon. (We used both wild and farmed nutrient breakdowns in the following recipes to show the nutrient difference between the two varieties.)

YEAR ROUND
KID FRIENDLY

Take One Salmon Fillet

Here's a brilliant idea: cook a fillet of salmon any way you want —poached, grilled, or roasted—then drizzle it with one of four different sauces or toppings, and dinner's done.

Here are all the instructions you need to mix and match a good-for-you salmon feast.

Poached Salmon

The English language is so weird. You can "poach" a fish, as in go down to the river and steal one, or you can "poach" a fish, as in cook it gently in a bath of simmering liquid.

Note that, in culinary terms, poaching doesn't mean boiling the life out of a piece of fish. You want to cook the salmon gently so it's delicate, tender, and brimming with flavour. Boiling the fish will toughen up its proteins and leave you with a lump of pink rubber.

Serve the poached salmon hot, or refrigerate it and serve it cold the next day with any one of the sauces (recipes follow).

MAKES 4 SERVINGS (NUTRIENT BREAKDOWN PER SERVING FOLLOWS)
ONE SERVING = ONE PIECE OF FISH

INGREDIENTS

One 13 oz (370 g) skinless salmon fillet
2 cups (500 mL) water, fish stock, lower-sodium chicken broth (see page 7), or orange juice

1 Prepare the sauce of your choice (recipes follow). Set aside for the flavours to blend.

2 Wash your hands and cut the salmon into 4 even-sized pieces.

3 Bring the water or other liquid to a boil in a large skillet with a lid (or if you're lucky enough to own a fish poacher, use that).

4 When the liquid begins to boil, add the salmon pieces. The liquid should just cover the fillets. Wash your hands and cutting board really well. (I keep a separate cutting board to use for raw meat and fish.) Cover the skillet with a lid.

KEEPING IT GREEN

Certain species of fish are threatened due to overfishing or the destruction of their natural habitat. The sustainable fish you choose in the grocery store or in a restaurant will help protect these endangered populations.

For omega-3 health and sustainability, choose anchovies, herring, mackerel, sardines, or salmon.

For general health and sustainability, choose tilapia, catfish, or Arctic char. Many kinds of shrimp are sustainable too—for more info, visit www.oceanwise.ca.

5 Gently poach the salmon (there should be gently simmering bubbles all around the fish and at the edges of the skillet) until the pieces are opaque and start to flake when prodded, with no raw-looking parts inside, about 10 to 15 minutes (a meat thermometer inserted into each piece of salmon should register 158°F / 70°C).

6 Using a slotted spoon, carefully remove the salmon pieces and drain briefly on paper towels to absorb any excess liquid. Serve with the sauce of your choice.

Grilled Salmon

This is my favourite way to fix salmon in the summer. The fish cooks so quickly that it stays moist and juicy. To prevent it from sticking to the grill, pat the fish dry with paper towels before placing it on the preheated grill.

MAKES 4 SERVINGS (NUTRIENT BREAKDOWN PER SERVING FOLLOWS)
ONE SERVING = ONE PIECE OF FISH

INGREDIENTS

One 13 oz (370 g) skinless salmon fillet

MAKE IT EASY

For a quick and easy dinner, grill the salmon and serve it on a bed of mixed salad greens, then top with one of the sauces.

1 Preheat the barbecue to high. Prepare the sauce of your choice (recipes follow). Set aside for the flavours to blend.

2 Wash your hands. Cut the salmon into 4 even-sized pieces. Pat the salmon pieces dry with paper towels. Wash your hands and cutting board really well. (I keep a separate cutting board to use for raw meat and fish.)

3 Place the salmon on the grill, close the lid, and reduce the heat to medium. Grill until the salmon releases easily from the grill, 3 to 5 minutes. Flip the salmon over. Close the lid and cook until the pieces are opaque and start to flake when prodded, with no raw-looking parts inside, 3 to 5 minutes more, depending on the thickness of the fillets. Salmon needs to be *just* cooked; overcooking will dry it out. A meat thermometer inserted into each piece of fish should register 158°F (70°C). Serve with the sauce of your choice.

CONTINUED . . .

Roast Salmon

1 Preheat the oven to 425°F (220°C). Line an 8-inch (20 cm) square baking pan with parchment paper or spray the pan with oil.

2 Prepare the sauce of your choice (recipes follow). Set aside for the flavours to blend.

3 Wash your hands, and cut the salmon into 4 even-sized pieces. Place the salmon in the prepared pan. Wash your hands and cutting board really well. (I keep a separate cutting board to use for raw meat and fish.)

4 Roast the salmon, uncovered, until the pieces are opaque and start to flake when prodded, with no raw-looking parts inside, about 10 to 15 minutes depending on the thickness of the pieces (a meat thermometer inserted into each piece of salmon should register 158°F / 70°C). Serve with the sauce of your choice.

MAKES 4 SERVINGS | ONE SERVING = ONE PIECE OF FISH

PER SERVING (MADE WITH ATLANTIC FARMED SALMON AND WITHOUT SAUCE): 169 CALORIES, 10 G TOTAL FAT, 2.0 G SATURATED FAT, 0 G TRANS FAT, 54 MG SODIUM, 0 G CARBOHYDRATE, 0 G FIBRE, 0 G SUGARS, 18 G PROTEIN

DIABETES FOOD CHOICE VALUES PER SERVING (MADE WITH ATLANTIC FARMED SALMON AND WITHOUT SAUCE): 2½ MEAT AND ALTERNATIVES, ½ FAT

PER SERVING (MADE WITH WILD SOCKEYE SALMON AND WITHOUT SAUCE): 155 CALORIES, 7.9 G TOTAL FAT, 1.4 G SATURATED FAT, 0 G TRANS FAT, 43 MG SODIUM, 0 G CARBOHYDRATE, 0 G FIBRE, 0 G SUGARS, 20 G PROTEIN

DIABETES FOOD CHOICE VALUES PER SERVING (MADE WITH WILD SOCKEYE SALMON AND WITHOUT SAUCE): 3 MEAT AND ALTERNATIVES

INGREDIENTS

Canola oil or non-stick baking spray

One 13 oz (370 g) skinless salmon fillet

CAN'T GET ENOUGH SALMON?

For another way to serve salmon, check out the recipe for Grilled Salmon Fillets with Raspberry Salsa (page 319).

Sauces for Salmon × 4 (plus one topping)

Each of the following condiments for salmon is unique and easy to make, and tastes fabulous. You may never buy a bottled sauce again—at least, that's my dream.

Citrus Sauce

Put some zip into your salmon with this tangy sauce.

MAKES ABOUT 1/4 CUP (60 ML) | ONE SERVING = 1 TBSP (15 ML)

INGREDIENTS

- 2 tbsp (30 mL) frozen orange juice concentrate, thawed (see page 13)
- 1 tbsp (15 mL) lime zest
- 1 tbsp (15 mL) lemon zest
- 1 tsp (5 mL) finely chopped fresh ginger
- 1 tsp (5 mL) honey, or your choice of sweetener to taste

1 Mix together the orange juice concentrate, lime and lemon zest, ginger, and honey in a small bowl. Set aside until ready to serve. (Sauce can be covered and refrigerated for up to 2 days.)

2 Drizzle the sauce evenly over each serving of cooked salmon.

PER SERVING: 22 CALORIES, 0 G TOTAL FAT, 0 G SATURATED FAT, 0 G TRANS FAT, 0 MG SODIUM, 5.6 G CARBOHYDRATE, 0.4 G FIBRE, 5.1 G SUGARS, 0 G PROTEIN

DIABETES FOOD CHOICE VALUES PER SERVING: 1 EXTRA

Teriyaki Sauce

This sweet and spicy sauce complements cooked rice as well as salmon.

MAKES ABOUT 1/4 CUP (60 ML) | ONE SERVING = 1 TBSP (15 ML)

KID FRIENDLY

INGREDIENTS

- 2 cloves garlic
- 2 tbsp (30 mL) lower-sodium soy sauce (see page 17)
- 1 tbsp (15 mL) rice vinegar (see page 16)
- 1 tbsp (15 mL) honey, or your choice of sweetener to taste
- 1 tbsp (15 mL) finely chopped fresh ginger

1 Mince the garlic and set aside.

2 Mix together the soy sauce, vinegar, honey, ginger, and garlic in a small bowl. Set aside until ready to serve. (Sauce can be covered and refrigerated for up to 2 days.)

3 Drizzle the sauce evenly over each serving of cooked salmon.

PER SERVING: 25 CALORIES, 0 G TOTAL FAT, 0 G SATURATED FAT, 0 G TRANS FAT, 291 MG SODIUM, 5.7 G CARBOHYDRATE, 0 G FIBRE, 4.5 G SUGARS, 1 G PROTEIN

DIABETES FOOD CHOICE VALUES PER SERVING: 1/2 CARBOHYDRATE

Wasabi Sauce

Wasabi is a Japanese horseradish that can clear your sinuses and take your breath away, depending on how much you eat. Read more about it on page 17.

MAKES ABOUT 1/4 CUP (60 ML) | ONE SERVING = 1 TBSP (15 ML)

INGREDIENTS

1 clove garlic

1 tbsp (15 mL) honey, or your choice of sweetener to taste

2 tsp (10 mL) wasabi paste

2 tsp (10 mL) lower-sodium soy sauce (see page 17)

2 tsp (10 mL) rice vinegar (see page 16)

2 tsp (10 mL) finely chopped fresh ginger

1 Mince the garlic and set aside.

2 Mix together the honey, wasabi paste, soy sauce, vinegar, ginger, and garlic in a small bowl. Set aside until ready to serve. (Sauce can be covered and refrigerated for up to 2 days.)

3 Drizzle the sauce evenly over each serving of cooked salmon.

PER SERVING: 27 CALORIES, 0.5 G TOTAL FAT, 0 G SATURATED FAT, 0 G TRANS FAT, 150 MG SODIUM, 6.5 G CARBOHYDRATE, 0 G FIBRE, 5.9 G SUGARS, 0 G PROTEIN

DIABETES FOOD CHOICE VALUES PER SERVING: 1/2 CARBOHYDRATE

Dijon Sauce

This will please the mustard lovers in the crowd.

MAKES ABOUT 1/4 CUP (60 ML) | ONE SERVING = 1 TBSP (15 ML)

INGREDIENTS

1 clove garlic

1 tbsp (15 mL) grainy Dijon mustard

1 tbsp (15 mL) honey, or your choice of sweetener to taste

2 tsp (10 mL) lower-sodium soy sauce (see page 17)

2 tsp (10 mL) rice vinegar (see page 16)

2 tsp (10 mL) finely chopped fresh ginger

1 Mince the garlic and set aside.

2 Mix together the mustard, honey, soy sauce, vinegar, ginger, and garlic in a small bowl. Set aside until ready to serve. (Sauce can be covered and refrigerated for up to 2 days.)

3 Drizzle the sauce evenly over each serving of cooked salmon.

PER SERVING: 27 CALORIES, 0.4 G TOTAL FAT, 0 G SATURATED FAT, 0 G TRANS FAT, 184 MG SODIUM, 5 G CARBOHYDRATE, 0 G FIBRE, 4.4 G SUGARS, 1 G PROTEIN

DIABETES FOOD CHOICE VALUES PER SERVING: 1 EXTRA

CONTINUED . . .

purple basil

CONTINUED FROM PAGE 131

Olive and Herb Topping

The combination of olives and fresh herbs is a great complement to salmon. I used the purple basil in the picture.

MAKES ABOUT 1/4 CUP (60 ML) | ONE SERVING = 1 TBSP (15 ML)

INGREDIENTS

8 kalamata olives, pitted and coarsely chopped (see page 23)
2 tbsp (30 mL) fresh green or purple basil chiffonade (see page 18)
2 tbsp (30 mL) finely chopped parsley
1 tbsp (15 mL) finely chopped fresh oregano

1 Mix together the olives, basil, parsley, and oregano in a small bowl. Set aside until ready to serve. (Topping can be covered and refrigerated for up to 2 days.)

2 Spoon the topping evenly over each serving of cooked salmon.

PER SERVING: 19 CALORIES, 1.7 G TOTAL FAT, 0.2 G SATURATED FAT, 0 G TRANS FAT, 175 MG SODIUM, 1.1 G CARBOHYDRATE, 0.3 G FIBRE, 0 G SUGARS, 0 G PROTEIN

DIABETES FOOD CHOICE VALUES PER SERVING: 1/2 FAT, 1 EXTRA

Salmon Tacos

I had my first fish taco a couple of years ago at an outdoor fish stand overlooking the docks at Vancouver's Granville Island. The sun was shining, the harbour was busy, and the fish taco — a soft tortilla wrapped around grilled salmon, coleslaw, and avocado — was yummy. I wished I'd ordered two.

I bake the salmon in the oven for my version of salmon tacos, but feel free to barbecue it, if you prefer.

MAKES 4 SERVINGS | ONE SERVING = ONE TORTILLA

SALMON

One 13 oz (370 g) skinless salmon fillet
1 lime, scrubbed well and dried
1 tsp (5 mL) ancho chili powder or regular chili powder (see sidebar)

COLESLAW

3 tbsp (45 mL) apple cider vinegar (see page 12)
2 tbsp (30 mL) canola oil
4 cups (1 L) shredded green cabbage (about 1/4 small cabbage)
1 sweet red pepper, seeded and thinly sliced
1 orange, segmented and sliced (see page 24)
1/2 cup (125 mL) thinly sliced red onion (1/2 small onion)

TACOS

4 large trans-fat-free 100% whole-grain whole wheat tortillas
1 avocado, peeled, pitted, and chopped (see page 25)
1/2 cup (125 mL) chopped fresh cilantro (optional)
Hot pepper sauce (optional)

1 For the salmon, preheat the oven to 400°F (200°C). Line an 8-inch (20 cm) square metal baking pan with wet parchment paper (see page 11).

2 Using a Microplane grater (see page 8), remove the zest from the lime and set aside.

3 Wash your hands and cut the salmon into 4 even-sized pieces. Place the salmon in the prepared pan. Wash your hands and cutting board really well. (I keep a separate cutting board to use for raw meat and fish.)

4 Cut the lime in half and squeeze the juice over the salmon. Sprinkle the salmon with the chili powder. Bake, uncovered, until just cooked, 10 to 15 minutes.

5 While the salmon is cooking, make the coleslaw by whisking together the vinegar and oil in a large bowl.

6 Add the cabbage, red pepper, orange, red onion, and reserved grated lime zest. Toss until well combined. Set aside.

7 To assemble each taco, place 1 piece of the salmon on 1 tortilla. Spoon 1 cup (250 mL) coleslaw over the salmon. Top with 1 tbsp (15 mL) chopped avocado, 2 tbsp (30 mL) cilantro (if using), and a drizzle of hot pepper sauce (if using). Fold or roll up the tortillas and eat. It's messy, but that's part of the fun.

PER SERVING (MADE WITH ATLANTIC FARMED SALMON): 538 CALORIES, 27.8 G TOTAL FAT, 4.3 G SATURATED FAT, 0 G TRANS FAT, 423 MG SODIUM, 48.6 G CARBOHYDRATE, 9 G FIBRE, 9.9 G SUGARS, 27 G PROTEIN

DIABETES FOOD CHOICE VALUES PER SERVING (MADE WITH ATLANTIC FARMED SALMON): 2½ CARBOHYDRATE, 4 MEAT AND ALTERNATIVES, 3½ FAT

PER SERVING (MADE WITH WILD SOCKEYE SALMON): 525 CALORIES, 25.7 G TOTAL FAT, 3.7 G SATURATED FAT, 0 G TRANS FAT, 411 MG SODIUM, 48.6 G CARBOHYDRATE, 9 G FIBRE, 9.9 G SUGARS, 29 G PROTEIN

DIABETES FOOD CHOICE VALUES PER SERVING (MADE WITH WILD SOCKEYE SALMON): 2½ CARBOHYDRATE, 4 MEAT AND ALTERNATIVES, 3 FAT

WHAT IS . . . ?

Chili powder from the supermarket is usually a blend of dried chilies, cumin, coriander, oregano, garlic, and cloves. Ancho chili powder is made simply from ground ancho chilies, and has a spicier, purer taste. I like to use it for a different chili flavour, plus it goes really well with fresh lime juice.

Grilled Garlic Shrimp

This recipe needs six large cloves of garlic to get the right hit of flavour (see page 15 for a picture of a large clove of garlic). If the thought of peeling all that garlic seems daunting, check out frozen garlic, like Toppits Crushed Garlic Cubes, which is a much better choice than bottled. All you do is open the package and add the right amount. Grocery Store Search: Frozen garlic cubes are usually in the frozen foods section of your supermarket or in their own mini-freezer in the produce aisle.

MAKES 4 SERVINGS | ONE SERVING = ABOUT 5 SHRIMP

INGREDIENTS

6 large cloves garlic
1 lb (500 g) frozen, uncooked extra-large shrimp (16 to 20 per lb / 500 g), thawed
1 lemon, scrubbed well and dried
1 lime, scrubbed well and dried
1 tbsp (15 mL) canola oil
1/4 to 1/2 tsp (1 to 2.5 mL) red pepper flakes

1 Mince the garlic and set aside.

2 Wash your hands. Peel and devein the shrimp, leaving their tails on. Place the shrimp in a resealable plastic bag or in a shallow non-metallic baking dish. Set aside.

3 Wash your hands again. Using a Microplane grater (see page 8), remove 1 tsp (5 mL) zest from both the lemon and the lime. Set zest aside.

4 With your palm, roll the lemon and lime on the counter (this makes them yield more juice), then cut them in half and squeeze out 1/2 cup (125 mL) juice from the lemon and 3 tbsp (45 mL) juice from the lime.

5 Whisk together the lemon juice, lime juice, oil, red pepper flakes, and garlic in a small bowl.

6 Pour the lemon juice mixture over the shrimp in the bag. Gently press the air out of the bag and seal it. Turn the bag over once or twice to make sure the marinade coats of all the shrimp. (Or pour the marinade over the shrimp in the dish, stir to coat, then cover the dish.) Refrigerate the shrimp for 45 minutes to 1 hour. (Don't marinate the shrimp for longer or the acid from the citrus juices will start to cook the protein in the shrimp.)

CONTINUED ...

7 Remove the shrimp from the bag or dish, and discard the marinade. Place the shrimp on a plate and let sit at room temperature for 5 minutes.

8 Preheat the barbecue to medium. Either grill the shrimp directly on the barbecue or place them in a mesh grill basket, like in the picture. Grill, with the lid down, turning often, until pink and firm, 3 to 5 minutes.

9 Remove the shrimp from the grill and place on a clean plate. Sprinkle with reserved lemon and lime zest before serving. (Any leftover shrimp can be refrigerated for up to 2 days.)

PER SERVING: 97 CALORIES, 1.5 G TOTAL FAT, 1.2 G SATURATED FAT, 0 G TRANS FAT, 255 MG SODIUM, 0.4 G CARBOHYDRATE, 0 G FIBRE, 0.1 G SUGARS, 22 G PROTEIN

DIABETES FOOD CHOICE VALUES PER SERVING: 3 MEAT AND ALTERNATIVES

LOVELY LEFTOVERS

If you have any cooked shrimp left over, they taste great the next day served cold over a mixed green salad, drizzled with an oil and vinegar dressing.

CAN'T GET ENOUGH SHRIMP?

If you love shrimp, check out the recipe for Spring Asparagus and Shrimp with Lemon Pasta on page 40.

FOR THE LOVE OF HOME EC

In the early 1970s, every girl in my high school had to take Grade 8 home ec. The guys took shop. It was sexist, but it was normal back then — girls cooked and sewed, guys fixed stuff.

By Grade 10, some progressive thinking by the school board meant that guys were finally allowed into the home ec classes.

It was weird and exciting to have boys in our building. By the end of the first mixed class, I had a mad crush on a Grade 12 "hunk of burning love."

Lorne was a rough-and-tumble bad boy and I adored him. He wore a wallet chain hanging out of his rugged, ripped jeans, had long hair, and drove a hearse. The guy was hot! Every classroom had complete cooking units set up around the room and his unit was right beside mine. (And yes, I am well aware of the double meaning of that one!)

Anyway, one day we had a fire in our unit and Lorne saved us. No pot over the flames, no fire extinguisher; no, Lorne just walked over and blew it out. My hormones went mental. I was in love.

It was, like most of my early love affairs, one-sided. I never missed a class for an entire semester; I would sprint down the hall, into the classroom, and be there when Lorne arrived. I could always figure out how to wheedle my way over to his unit and offer some pearls of wisdom. And in the end, Lorne knew how to cook some stuff; not brilliantly, but he could cook. And I learned how to talk to older boys; not brilliantly, but I could talk.

Those classes were teaching us valuable life lessons. Getting along in a group and knowing your way around a kitchen are important skills that you can use every day of your life.

Home economics, or whatever you want to call a class that teaches food and nutrition, is no longer a mandatory element in education. As a result, we are seeing generations of people who know nothing about cooking. They barely know that the kitchen is the room with the stove.

They know how to order takeout, how to navigate a drive-through, and how to get a pizza delivered in 40 minutes or it's free, but how to make something from scratch is a total mystery.

And this is now affecting the health of our country.

In an editorial in *The Journal of the American Medical Association*, Alice Lichtenstein, a nutritional biochemist at Tufts University, and David Ludwig, a physician at Children's Hospital Boston, argued that mandatory home ec should be reincorporated into the classroom as a means of combating obesity. They suggest that teaching all kids to cook healthy foods will begin a domino effect on the health of the next generation.

Now, there's a concept. Let's educate our kids to eat better by making home ec mandatory again.

In our quest for healthier citizens, we need to combat the ever-increasing numbers of people suffering from type 2 diabetes and heart disease. We need to bring back home ec. It will take a while to see the results, but if we don't do something soon, it may be too late for many of us.

Petition your government to make food and nutrition a mandatory class in high schools. Chemistry, physics, and math may have expanded my brain, but learning about food and nutrition expanded my knowledge of health, and with it my chances of making healthier decisions all my life.

8

Grains:
Three Pluses in One Tiny Package

Hands up if you eat brown rice, pot barley, whole-grain wheat, whole-grain corn, kamut, spelt, buckwheat, wheat berries, whole oats, amaranth, or quinoa. If you said yes to at least three of them, you get a gold star.

Every time you choose a whole grain over a refined grain you're reducing your chances of developing heart disease, type 2 diabetes, and certain cancers.

GOOD FOR YOU

So, what's the big deal about whole grains? They're full of fibre, and loaded with vitamins, minerals, and antioxidants that help reduce the risk factors for many long-term diseases. If you're on the Low Carb Bus, avoiding whole grains and whole-grain cereals, ring the bell and ask the driver to let you off.

All grains are made up of three important parts: the bran, the germ, and the endosperm. Each of these parts contributes to your long-term health.

The *bran* is the outer layer of the grain and provides our bodies with fibre, B vitamins, and minerals.

The *germ* is the new growth of the plant and provides food for the seed. It provides both the seed and our bodies with B vitamins, vitamin E, minerals, and healthy fats.

The *endosperm* is the inner layer of the seed. It contains carbohydrate and protein, plus a small amount of vitamins and minerals, and its job is to supply energy.

Refine a grain and you lose the bran and the germ, plus it's bye-bye to most of the fibre and at least 80% of the disease-protecting antioxidants.

THE SKINNY ON WHOLE GRAINS

If eating whole grains for their flavour and health benefits isn't enough, how about for weight loss? A study out of Penn State University looked at 50 obese adults on a calorie-reduced diet. The group was divided in half. Both groups followed similar diets, with the exception of the grains they consumed. Half the group ate only whole grains, the other half only refined grains. In just 12 weeks, the whole-grain eaters had a greater decrease in abdominal fat, a.k.a. the evil belly fat. If you want to be wearing a smaller pair of pants, lower your caloric intake, add some exercise, and make your grains whole.

RICE? MAKE MINE BROWN

Brown rice is a staple in my house. I usually make a large pot of rice once a week (it will keep in the fridge for up to five days), then either reheat it to serve as a whole-grain side dish, or use it to create new recipes. For everything you've ever wanted to know about rice, visit the USA Rice Federation's website (riceinfo.com).

BROWN RICE PRIMER

- Brown rice is a great source of whole-grain carbs, which supply your body with energy. It's also an excellent source of manganese, which helps produce energy from protein and carbohydrates.
- Eating brown rice supports a healthy nervous system.
- Brown rice is a source of magnesium, a mineral that is necessary for healthy bones. One cup (250 mL) of brown rice supplies you with 17% of your recommended daily intake.
- Brown rice is a chameleon—it can be sweet or savoury, a main course, salad, side dish, or dessert.
- It's economical, costing about 10¢ per serving.
- Uncooked brown rice has a great shelf life and will keep for up to six months in the cupboard, or longer in the fridge or freezer.

BROWN RICE HOW-TO

To cook brown rice, you need a heavy-bottomed saucepan with a tight lid (picture a kangaroo wearing a tight hat and you're on the right track). Because brown rice triples in volume when it's cooked, the saucepan also needs to be large enough to hold the cooked rice.

1. For 3 cups (750 mL) cooked rice, add 2 ¼ cups (560 mL) cold water and 1 cup (250 mL) brown rice to the saucepan. Bring to a boil and stir once.
2. Cover with a tight-fitting lid and reduce the heat to a simmer. Never remove the lid or stir the rice while it's cooking. This will lengthen the cooking time and result in sticky, gummy rice, plus you may go to Culinary Purgatory.
3. Cook until tender and all the water has been absorbed, 45 to 50 minutes. To check for doneness, taste a grain of rice. If it's still hard, cook the rice for 4 to 5 more minutes.
4. Using a rice paddle (a shamoji; see page 11) or a flat spoon, scoop the rice from the bottom of the saucepan to the top to redistribute the moister rice at the bottom. I do 4 scooping turns. Remove the saucepan from the heat. Let sit, covered, for 10 minutes.

Or buy a rice cooker (see page 11 to find out why you need one) and call it a day.

YEAR ROUND
KID FRIENDLY

My All-Time Favourite Whole-Grain Side Dish

I cook this yummy combo of three of my favourite whole grains — brown rice, pot barley, and wheat berries — once a week. Often I make a double batch so I have 6 cups (1.5 L) cooked grains on hand to just heat and serve.

For a richer flavour, use 1 ½ cups (375 mL) lower-sodium chicken or vegetable broth (see page 7) instead of water.

MAKES 3 CUPS (750 ML) LIGHTLY PACKED | ONE SERVING = ½ CUP (125 ML)

INGREDIENTS

¼ cup (60 mL) pot barley
¼ cup (60 mL) wheat berries (see sidebar)
¼ cup (60 mL) long-grain brown rice

1 Place the barley and wheat berries in a wire-mesh strainer and rinse them under cold running water.

2 Mix together the barley, wheat berries, and brown rice in a medium saucepan.

3 Add 1 ½ cups (375 mL) water or broth and bring to a boil. Reduce the heat to a simmer and cook, covered, until tender, 45 to 55 minutes.

4 Using a shamoji (a rice paddle; see page 11) or a flat spoon, scoop the grains from the bottom of the saucepan to the top to redistribute the moister grains at the bottom. I do 4 scooping turns; this way all the grains will have the same fluffy consistency. Remove the saucepan from the heat. Let sit, covered, for 10 minutes.

PER SERVING (MADE WITH WATER): 80 CALORIES, 0.6 G TOTAL FAT, 0 G SATURATED FAT, 0 G TRANS FAT, 1 MG SODIUM, 17.1 G CARBOHYDRATE, 1.9 G FIBRE, 0.3 G SUGARS, 2 G PROTEIN

DIABETES FOOD CHOICE VALUES PER SERVING (MADE WITH WATER): 1 CARBOHYDRATE

WHAT IS . . . ?

Wheat berries are the whole wheat kernels before they are ground up into flour. Chewy and slightly nutty, they're a fabulous whole grain. Grocery Store Search: Look for them in larger grocery stores or in any health food store; Bob's Red Mill is the brand I buy, or try your bulk store.

Jambalaya

One of the most elusive fringe benefits of being a food writer is the press junket. I know fellow writers who've been to Italy, France, and Spain. Me? I got to jump on the subway once and go to a hotel in downtown Toronto to taste olive oil. But my luck changed in 2009 and I was invited to join a group of Canadian food writers on a trip to Louisiana.

For five days, we travelled around Cajun country, saw the French Quarter in New Orleans, and ate more fried food than I thought was humanly possible. I have no idea how any native Louisianian lives past 55 without triple-bypass surgery. Who knew you could deep-fry spinach?

My absolute favourite Louisiana moment was taking a cooking class from New Orleans icon Miss Poppy Tooker. Yes, that is her real, extremely cool name.

She prepared a jambalaya, a Louisiana rice dish that features spicy sausage, that was out of this world. Of course it wasn't all that healthy, what with the pork fat, cracklings, and smoked sausage, so I vowed to create a healthier version. For sure, I'd switch the white rice to brown, but I still wanted to create a mouth-watering comfort food with flavours from the Deep South.

After much experimenting, I ended up with a main dish that tastes fabulous but is admittedly not an authentic jambalaya. I think you really need to visit Louisiana for that. We just can't get ingredients like chaurice or andouille sausage, or tasso (Cajun ham) at our local grocery stores. So, with apologies to Miss Tooker, here is my Canadian version of a southern classic. Sure still tastes yummy, y'all.

MAKES 8 CUPS (2 L) | ONE SERVING = 1½ CUPS (375 ML)

CONTINUED . . .

QUICK TIP

Like all whole-grain dishes, the jambalaya actually tastes better on day two, and even better on day three.

HEALTH BITE

If you use chorizo sausages, which are typically made from pork, instead of Italian turkey sausages, the nutritional payload changes right across the board, especially in the fat and sodium departments—and not in a good way.

CONTINUED FROM THE PREVIOUS PAGE

INGREDIENTS

- 4 large cloves garlic
- 2 hot Italian turkey or chorizo sausages (about 10 oz/300 g)
- 1 onion, diced
- 3 stalks celery, coarsely chopped
- 1 sweet red pepper, seeded and coarsely chopped
- 1 green pepper, seeded and coarsely chopped
- 1½ cups (375 mL) long-grain brown rice
- 2 tsp (10 mL) ground thyme
- ¼ tsp (1 mL) cayenne
- One 28 oz (796 mL) can diced tomatoes
- 2 cups (500 mL) lower-sodium chicken broth (see page 7)

1 Mince the garlic and set aside.

2 Heat a large saucepan or Dutch oven over medium heat. Wash your hands. Squeeze the sausage meat out of its casings and into the pot. (This is sort of fun and gross all at the same time.) Wash your hands again. Cook the sausage meat until browned, 3 to 5 minutes, breaking it up with the back of a wooden spoon as it cooks.

3 Add the onion, and sauté until the onion starts turning a light golden colour, about 5 minutes. Add the celery, both peppers, and garlic, and sauté for 2 minutes.

4 Add the rice, thyme, and cayenne, and cook, stirring, until the rice is well coated and the spices smell fragrant, 1 to 2 minutes.

5 Stir in the tomatoes and broth, making sure you scrape up all the little browned bits stuck to the bottom of the pot. Aside from adding fabulous flavour, this will prevent the rice from sticking while it's cooking.

6 Bring to a boil. Reduce the heat to a simmer and cook, covered, until the rice is tender, 55 to 60 minutes.

7 Using a rice paddle (a shamoji; see page 11) or a flat spoon, scoop the rice from the bottom of the saucepan to the top to redistribute the moister rice at the bottom. I do 4 scooping turns; this way all the grains will have the same fluffy consistency. Remove the saucepan from the heat. Let sit, covered, for 10 minutes. (Store any leftovers in a resealable container in the fridge for up to 4 days.)

PER SERVING: 318 CALORIES, 6.7 G TOTAL FAT, 2.1 G SATURATED FAT, 0 G TRANS FAT, 512 MG SODIUM, 55.6 G CARBOHYDRATE, 6 G FIBRE, 8.3 G SUGARS, 16 G PROTEIN

DIABETES FOOD CHOICE VALUES PER SERVING: 1½ CARBOHYDRATE, 1½ MEAT AND ALTERNATIVES

Cajun Shrimp Pilau

We say "pilaf," Southerners say "pilau," but they're the same thing. Onions, spices, protein, rice, vegetables, and broth create an all-in-one-bowl dinner. Cajun cooking is usually spicy but I took the heat out of this version, so add some Louisiana hot sauce when serving if you want more punch.

MAKES 6 CUPS (1.5 L) | ONE SERVING = 1½ CUPS (375 ML)

INGREDIENTS

- 6 large cloves garlic
- 1 lb (500 g) frozen, uncooked large shrimp (21 to 25 per lb/500 g), thawed
- 1 tbsp (15 mL) canola oil
- 2 onions, diced
- 2 stalks celery, coarsely chopped
- 1 sweet red pepper, seeded and diced
- 1¼ cups (310 mL) long-grain brown rice
- 1½ tsp (7.5 mL) ground thyme
- 1 tsp (5 mL) dried oregano leaves
- ½ tsp (2.5 mL) cracked black pepper
- One 28 oz (796 mL) can diced tomatoes
- ¼ cup (60 mL) finely chopped parsley

1 Mince the garlic and set aside.

2 Wash your hands. Peel and devein the shrimp. Set aside. Wash your hands again.

3 Heat a large saucepan or Dutch oven over medium heat. Add the oil, then the onions, and sauté until the onions start turning a light golden colour, about 5 minutes.

4 Add the garlic, celery, and sweet pepper, and sauté for 2 minutes.

5 Add the rice, thyme, oregano, and pepper, and cook, stirring, until the rice is well coated and the spices smell fragrant, 1 to 2 minutes.

6 Stir in the tomatoes, making sure you scrape up all the little browned bits stuck to the bottom of the pot. This adds flavour and will also prevent the rice from sticking while it's cooking.

7 Bring to a boil. Add the shrimp and bring back to a boil. Reduce the heat to a simmer and cook, covered, until the rice is tender, 55 to 60 minutes.

8 Using a rice paddle (a shamoji; see page 11) or a flat spoon, scoop the rice from the bottom of the saucepan to the top to redistribute the moister rice at the bottom. I do 4 scooping turns; this way all the grains will have the same fluffy consistency. Remove the saucepan from the heat. Let sit, covered, for 10 minutes. Stir in the parsley. (Store any leftovers in a resealable container in the fridge for up to 2 days.)

PER SERVING: 407 CALORIES, 7.5 G TOTAL FAT, 2 G SATURATED FAT, 0 G TRANS FAT, 529 MG SODIUM, 65.7 G CARBOHYDRATE, 8 G FIBRE, 10.6 G SUGARS, 29 G PROTEIN

DIABETES FOOD CHOICE VALUES PER SERVING: 2 CARBOHYDRATE, 3 MEAT AND ALTERNATIVES

RICE: A SHORT HISTORY

We Canucks can take some of the credit for the way rice has influenced Louisiana cuisine. If the British redcoats didn't like you or your religion, you got the big boot. The Acadians, a French-speaking, rural people, got kicked out of Nova Scotia by the redcoats in the early 1700s. Some of them eventually arrived in Louisiana, via the rice-growing Carolinas, bringing with them rice plants that thrived in the swampland we now call Cajun country.

Brown Rice Pilaf

Healthwise, this sweet-savoury pilaf packs a big punch. The antioxidants in the tart dried cherries are rich in anthocyanins, which reduce inflammation associated with heart disease and arthritis. Pistachios are high in cholesterol-lowering plant sterols and contain the most potassium of all nuts.

MAKES 3 CUPS (750 ML) | ONE SERVING = ½ CUP (125 ML)

INGREDIENTS

- 4 cloves garlic
- 1 tsp (5 mL) dried savory
- ¼ to ½ tsp (1 to 2.5 mL) cracked black pepper
- ¼ tsp (1 mL) ground allspice
- ¼ tsp (1 mL) cinnamon
- 1 tbsp (15 mL) extra virgin olive oil
- 1 onion, diced
- 1 stalk celery, diced
- 1 cup (250 mL) long-grain brown rice
- 2 cups (500 mL) lower-sodium chicken broth (see page 7)
- ¼ cup (60 mL) chopped tart dried cherries
- ¼ cup plus 2 tbsp (90 mL) shelled, unsalted, dry-roasted natural pistachios, coarsely chopped

1 Mince the garlic and set aside.

2 Mix together the savory, pepper, allspice, and cinnamon in a small bowl. Set aside.

3 Heat a large saucepan with a tight-fitting lid over medium heat. Add the oil, then the onion, and sauté until the onion starts turning a light golden colour, about 5 minutes.

4 Add the garlic and celery, and sauté for 1 minute. Add the spice mixture and sauté for 30 seconds.

5 Add the rice and cook, stirring, until the rice is well coated with the spices.

6 Stir in the broth, making sure you scrape up all the little browned bits stuck to the bottom of the saucepan. This ramps up the flavour and will also prevent the rice from sticking while it's cooking.

7 Add the cherries and bring to a boil. Reduce the heat to a simmer and cook, covered, until the rice is tender, 50 to 55 minutes. To see if it's done, quickly lift the lid and check whether or not the pilaf looks very wet. If it is, put the lid back on and cook for a further 5 to 10 minutes. If the rice looks dry, remove the saucepan from the heat.

8 Using a rice paddle (a shamoji; see page 11) or a flat spoon, scoop the rice from the bottom of the saucepan to the top to redistribute the moister rice at the bottom. I do 4 scooping turns; this way all the grains will have the same fluffy consistency. Remove the saucepan from the heat. Let sit, covered, for 10 minutes.

9 Serve each portion of pilaf with 1 tbsp (15 mL) pistachios sprinkled over the top.

PER SERVING: 209 CALORIES, 6.9 G TOTAL FAT, 1 G SATURATED FAT, 0 G TRANS FAT, 68 MG SODIUM, 35 G CARBOHYDRATE, 5 G FIBRE, 4.5 G SUGARS, 5 G PROTEIN

DIABETES FOOD CHOICE VALUES PER SERVING: 1 CARBOHYDRATE, ½ MEAT AND ALTERNATIVES, ½ FAT

WHAT IS . . . ?

Rice comes in three basic types: short-grain, medium-grain, and long-grain.

Short-grain rice is a stickier rice than the other two, and can be used in risottos, puddings, or a dish like sushi where you want the rice grains to stick together. Medium-grain rice has characteristics of both short- and long-grain rice, and is a good all-round rice that works for risottos, desserts, and puddings.

Long-grain rice cooks up into single grains and tends to be fluffier than short-grain rice. It's good for pilafs, side dishes, soups, and fried rice.

Quinoa: Old Is New Again

Quinoa (pronounced *keen*-WAH) is an ancient cereal that's gained popularity in the last few years. There was a time when I would mention this weird little grain and no one would know what I was talking about. Now the odd person can actually pronounce it.

Quinoa Primer

Quinoa is an amazing little grain (actually a seed). Rich in protein, it contains potassium, riboflavin, magnesium, zinc, and copper. It's also a good source of manganese, a trace mineral that plays a role in the metabolism of fats and carbohydrates and the absorption of calcium, and that helps regulate your blood sugar. Manganese is also necessary for normal brain and nerve function.

As if this weren't enough, quinoa has three more pluses:

1 It has a mild flavour.
2 It cooks in about 20 minutes.
3 And, best of all, most kids love it.

Quinoa grains are naturally coated with a bitter resin called saponin. This resin can be rinsed away by washing, but is often removed by mechanical polishing. Unfortunately for us, polishing also removes the germ, making this a less nutritious form of quinoa.

So choose whole-grain quinoa and rinse it well in a fine wire-mesh strainer before cooking. Try whole-grain red quinoa, if you can find it at a bulk store or a health food store; it looks pretty and has a nuttier flavour.

When cooking quinoa, the rule of thumb is 1 cup (250 mL) whole-grain quinoa plus 2 cups (500 mL) liquid yields approximately 3 cups (750 mL) cooked quinoa.

YEAR ROUND
KID FRIENDLY

Side-Dish Quinoa

MAKES 3 CUPS (750 ML) | ONE SERVING = ½ CUP (125 ML)

1 Place the quinoa in a fine wire-mesh strainer and rinse it well. Place the rinsed quinoa in a medium saucepan. Add the broth and bring to a boil. Reduce the heat to medium-low and cook, covered, until the grains are translucent and all the broth has been absorbed, 18 to 20 minutes.

2 Fluff the quinoa with a fork. Remove the saucepan from the heat and let stand, covered, for 5 to 10 minutes.

PER SERVING (MADE WITH CHICKEN BROTH CONTAINING 85 MG SODIUM PER CUP/250 ML): 119 CALORIES, 1.7 G TOTAL FAT, 0 G SATURATED FAT, 0 G TRANS FAT, 18 MG SODIUM, 20 G CARBOHYDRATE, 2 G FIBRE, 0.6 G SUGARS, 6 G PROTEIN

DIABETES FOOD CHOICE VALUES PER SERVING (MADE WITH CHICKEN BROTH CONTAINING 85 MG SODIUM PER CUP/250 ML): 1 CARBOHYDRATE, ½ MEAT AND ALTERNATIVES

INGREDIENTS

1 cup (250 mL) whole-grain quinoa (see page 152)

2 cups (500 mL) lower-sodium chicken or vegetable broth (see page 7), or water

GIVE IT A TWIST

LEMON AND LIME QUINOA:
Follow recipe for Side-Dish Quinoa, adding 1 tsp (5 mL) each of lemon and lime zest in Step 2. Fluff well. This goes well with seafood.

PEANUT QUINOA:
Spoon 2 tbsp (30 mL) peanut sauce (page 93) over each serving of Side-Dish Quinoa.

Quinoa Tabbouleh

Traditional tabbouleh is made with couscous, a tiny, grain-size pasta made from coarsely ground hard durum wheat. My version uses whole-grain quinoa, which makes it nutty-tasting and protein-rich.

Make sure you start this recipe a day ahead of time.

MAKES 4 CUPS (1 L) | ONE SERVING = 1 CUP (250 ML)

1 For the tabbouleh, the night before you want to serve it, place the quinoa in a fine wire-mesh strainer and rinse it well. Place the rinsed quinoa in a medium saucepan. Add 1 cup (250 mL) water and bring to a boil. Reduce the heat to medium-low and cook, covered, until the grains are translucent and all the water has been absorbed, 18 to 20 minutes.

2 Fluff the quinoa with a fork. Remove the saucepan from the heat and let stand, covered, for 5 to 10 minutes. Let the quinoa cool, then refrigerate in an airtight container overnight.

3 The next day, wash and spin-dry the parsley and mint. Make sure the herbs are very dry or the salad will be soggy.

4 Chop the parsley very finely, and chop the mint into slightly bigger pieces.

5 Mix together the quinoa, parsley, mint, tomatoes, and shallot in a salad bowl, and toss well.

6 For the lemon dressing, remove the zest from the lemon using a Microplane grater (see page 8). Set aside.

7 With your palm, roll the lemon on the counter (this makes it yield more juice), then cut it in half and squeeze out ¼ cup (60 mL) juice.

8 Whisk together the lemon juice and oil in a small bowl. Pour the dressing over the salad and toss well. Sprinkle with the lemon zest and toss again.

PER SERVING: 181 CALORIES, 8.5 G TOTAL FAT, 1 G SATURATED FAT, 0 G TRANS FAT, 25 MG SODIUM, 22.8 G CARBOHYDRATE, 4 G FIBRE, 1.7 G SUGARS, 5 G PROTEIN

DIABETES FOOD CHOICE VALUES PER SERVING: 1½ CARBOHYDRATE, ½ MEAT AND ALTERNATIVES, 1½ FAT

QUINOA TABBOULEH

- ½ cup (125 mL) whole-grain quinoa (see page 152)
- 2 cups (500 mL) lightly packed parsley sprigs
- ½ cup (125 mL) lightly packed fresh mint
- 1 cup (250 mL) grape tomatoes, cut in half
- 1 large shallot, diced

LEMON DRESSING

- 1 large lemon, scrubbed well and dried
- 2 tbsp (30 mL) extra virgin olive oil

CAN'T GET ENOUGH QUINOA?

If you like these quinoa recipes, try my Blueberry-Quinoa Salad on page 80, too.

Spinach Lasagna

The only time I make lasagna is when I have some extra homemade tomato sauce in the fridge or freezer. It cuts down on the whole prep part. And lasagna is all about the prep. But in this case you can just assemble the layers and then let the oven do its thing while you drink a glass of red wine. Ahh.

Oh, shoot—I forgot about the dishes. There's always a catch.

MAKES 8 SERVINGS

INGREDIENTS

- Nine 100% whole-grain lasagna noodles
- Two 11 oz (312 g) packages frozen chopped spinach (see below) or 12 cups (3 L) lightly packed fresh spinach
- One 1 lb (454 g) container extra-smooth light ricotta cheese
- ½ cup (125 mL) finely grated, really good Parmesan cheese
- 1 omega-3 egg (see page 13)
- 3 cups (750 mL) Roasted Red Pepper and Tomato Pasta Sauce (see page 156) or your favourite tomato sauce
- ¾ cup (185 mL) shredded light mozzarella cheese

HOW TO

Make sure you press the liquid out of the spinach really, really well, or the lasagna will be very, very wet.

1 Preheat the oven to 350°F (180°C). Line an 11- × 7-inch (2 L) non-metallic baking dish with wet parchment paper (see page 11).

2 Bring a really large pot of water to a boil. Add the noodles and cook for 10 minutes or until al dente.

3 Meanwhile, if using frozen spinach, thaw it according to the package directions. Place the spinach in a colander in the sink and using the back of a fork, press out any excess liquid. Let the spinach drain in the sink.

4 If using fresh spinach, rinse and drain it in a colander. Put the spinach in a large saucepan with just the water clinging to its leaves, and cook, covered, over medium heat until wilted, 3 to 5 minutes. Drain the spinach well and let it sit in the colander in the sink until it is cool enough to handle. Squeeze out any excess water, then chop the spinach coarsely and set aside.

5 Mix together the ricotta, Parmesan, and egg in a medium bowl. Set aside. Get the feeling there's an assembly line happening here?

6 Hopefully you have another colander; if not, place the drained spinach in a separate bowl. When the noodles are done, drain them in the colander and set aside.

7 Lay 3 noodles, slightly overlapping, in the prepared dish to cover the base of the dish. Spread evenly with 1 cup (250 mL) tomato sauce. Evenly dollop one-third of the ricotta mixture over the sauce. Spoon over one-third of the spinach. Evenly sprinkle with one-third of the mozzarella.

8 Repeat these layers twice, ending with mozzarella. Any ingredients left over? I hope not. But if there are, be creative and just sprinkle them on top. Unless it's the noodles ... hmm, better luck next time.

9 Bake, uncovered, until cooked through, 40 to 50 minutes. Check the lasagna after 30 minutes; if the noodles and cheese are browning too much, cover the lasagna loosely with foil and continue baking.

10 Remove the lasagna from the oven and give it a 10-minute time out before serving. This allows all those hot ingredients to mesh together and should prevent the lasagna from turning into a mushy mess when you slice it.

PER SERVING: 318 CALORIES, 9.2 G TOTAL FAT, 4.9 G SATURATED FAT, 0 G TRANS FAT, 392 MG SODIUM, 36.3 G CARBOHYDRATE, 5 G FIBRE, 8.2 G SUGARS, 20 G PROTEIN

DIABETES FOOD CHOICE VALUES PER SERVING: 2 CARBOHYDRATE, 2 MEAT AND ALTERNATIVES, ½ FAT

KICK IT UP A NOTCH WITH WHOLE-GRAIN PASTA

If you are just getting used to cooking and eating whole wheat pasta, crank up the stove, because here comes an even healthier version: whole-grain pasta.

A better choice than whole wheat, whole-grain pasta is the real deal, containing the whole grain and all its benefits.

I like Catelli's Healthy Harvest whole-grain whole wheat pasta and their multigrain pasta, made with five whole-grain flours, including whole wheat semolina, whole rye, whole buckwheat, whole barley, and brown rice. Both varieties are available at most grocery stores across Canada. You could also try whole-grain kamut, spelt, or multigrain pasta, available at most health food stores.

Roasted Red Pepper and Tomato Pasta Sauce

This is my fresh-no-matter-what-time-of-year pasta sauce. It's a gorgeous shade of red and it looks picture-perfect every time you serve it.

Make sure that you have all your ingredients prepped and ready to go, except the basil (chop this just before using). Pretend you're a sous chef working in a world-renowned restaurant. You can even put the prepped ingredients in little bowls.

MAKES ABOUT 4 CUPS (1 L) PURÉED SAUCE | ONE SERVING = ½ CUP (125 ML)

1 Mince the garlic and set aside.

2 Heat a large saucepan over medium heat. Add the oil, then the garlic, and sauté for 30 seconds. Don't let the garlic burn.

3 Add the roasted red peppers and red pepper flakes, and sauté for 2 minutes.

4 Stir in the tomatoes and red wine, and bring to a boil. Reduce the heat to a simmer and cook, uncovered and stirring often, until the sauce thickens, 25 to 30 minutes. This will intensify its flavour.

5 Now you have a choice: you can either serve this as is, or purée it with a hand-held immersion blender (see page 8) or in a regular blender to make a thick sauce. I always purée it; that way no one says, "I don't like those big red things."

6 Chop the basil and stir it into the sauce. For each serving, spoon ½ cup (125 mL) sauce over 1 cup (250 mL) cooked 100% whole-grain pasta. (Store the sauce in an airtight container in the fridge for up to 3 days or freezer for up to 3 months, but don't add the fresh basil until just before serving.)

PER SERVING (WITHOUT PASTA): 80 CALORIES, 2.1 G TOTAL FAT, 0 G SATURATED FAT, 0 G TRANS FAT, 130 MG SODIUM, 10.6 G CARBOHYDRATE, 2 G FIBRE, 5.6 G SUGARS, 2 G PROTEIN

DIABETES FOOD CHOICE VALUES PER SERVING (WITHOUT PASTA): ½ CARBOHYDRATE, ½ FAT

INGREDIENTS

4 large cloves garlic
1 tbsp (15 mL) extra virgin olive oil
1 jar (12 oz/370 mL) flame-roasted red peppers, drained and coarsely chopped, or 5 whole roasted sweet red peppers, seeded and coarsely chopped (see page 25)
¼ to ½ tsp (1 to 2.5 mL) red pepper flakes
One 28 oz (796 mL) can diced tomatoes
1 cup (250 mL) dry red wine
3 tbsp (45 mL) finely chopped fresh basil

BIG-BATCH COOKING ROCKS!

I usually double this recipe and freeze 3 cups (750 mL) for the Spinach Lasagna on page 156.

HOW TO

One of the secrets to this simple pasta sauce is red wine. Whenever you use wine as an ingredient, choose a wine you'd actually drink with your dinner. It doesn't have to be a high-end one but it does need to be something you would buy to drink, not just to cook with.

Greek Barley Salad

Teaming diabetes-friendly barley with a heart-healthy oil and olives, plus antioxidant-rich veggies, creates a colourful summer salad that's a delicious medley of flavours and nutrients.

Start prepping the salad the night before or early on the day you want to serve it.

MAKES 5 CUPS (1.25 L) | ONE SERVING = 1 CUP (250 ML)

GREEK BARLEY SALAD

- ½ cup (125 mL) pot barley
- 3 cups (750 mL) cherry tomatoes, washed and dried
- ½ large unpeeled English cucumber, washed and dried
- 12 kalamata olives, pitted and coarsely chopped (see page 23)
- 1 large shallot, minced
- ½ cup (125 mL) crumbled goat's milk feta cheese (see page 14)

HERB DRESSING

- 2 cloves garlic
- 2 tbsp (30 mL) extra virgin olive oil
- 2 tbsp (30 mL) red wine vinegar
- 1 tbsp (15 mL) fresh basil chiffonade (see page 18)
- 2 tsp (10 mL) chopped fresh oregano

1 For the salad, the night before you want to serve it, place the barley in a wire-mesh colander and rinse it under cold running water. Put the barley in a medium saucepan. Add 1½ cups (375 mL) water and bring to a boil. Reduce the heat to a simmer and cook, covered, until the barley is tender but chewy, 45 to 55 minutes. Stir once or twice to evenly distribute any remaining liquid. Remove the saucepan from the heat, fluff the barley with a fork to separate the grains, and let sit, covered, for 10 minutes. Fluff the barley again, then let it cool for 30 minutes. (Store in an airtight container in the fridge for up to 3 days.)

2 The next day, cut the tomatoes into quarters using a serrated knife. Place the tomatoes in a salad bowl. Add cold barley.

3 Dice the cucumber into pieces about the same size as the tomatoes. Add the cucumber to the tomatoes, along with the olives and shallot.

4 For the herb dressing, mince the garlic and set aside.

5 Whisk together the oil, vinegar, basil, oregano, and garlic in a small bowl.

6 Add the dressing to the barley mixture, along with the cheese, and toss well. Either serve the salad right away or let it sit for 15 minutes to absorb the flavours.

PER SERVING: 238 CALORIES, 13.8 G TOTAL FAT, 5.0 G SATURATED FAT, 0 G TRANS FAT, 457 MG SODIUM, 23 G CARBOHYDRATE, 5 G FIBRE, 3.2 G SUGARS, 9 G PROTEIN

DIABETES FOOD CHOICE VALUES PER SERVING: 1 CARBOHYDRATE, 1 MEAT AND ALTERNATIVES, 2 FAT

Barley: The Unsung Hero of the Whole-Grain World

This supergrain is one of the richest sources of not one, but two types of fibre — soluble and insoluble. These dietary fibres provide your GI (gastrointestinal) tract with friendly bacteria, which helps keep it happy. And trust me, you don't want 26 feet (7.9 metres) of angry GI tract. Make nice with your GI tract and it will make nice with you.

Okay, so you have happy intestines, but barley's true claim to body fame lies in its high levels of beta glucans. This type of fibre helps lower cholesterol, which in turn decreases your chances of developing heart disease. It also promotes healthy blood sugar levels by slowing down the absorption of glucose — a winning combination for people living with diabetes.

Barley Primer

Look for pot barley when grocery shopping. This is the closest you can get to the whole-grain version. You can usually find pot barley with the whole dry beans, which are often by the canned beans. Or try the bulk section. Store barley in a cool dark cupboard or in your fridge for up to one year.

Most people have had barley in a soup, but think outside the soup pot and use barley in salads, as a side dish, or as a substitute for Arborio rice in a risotto, like my Barley Risotto with Porcini Mushrooms (facing page).

Barley How-To

To prep basic pot barley, combine 1 cup (250 mL) pot barley with 3 cups (750 mL) lower-sodium chicken, vegetable, or beef broth, or plain water, and bring to a boil. Reduce the heat to a simmer and cook, covered, until chewy but not rubbery, 45 to 55 minutes. Stir once or twice to evenly distribute any remaining liquid. Remove from the heat and let sit, covered, for 10 minutes. One cup (250 mL) raw pot barley makes about 3 to 4 cups (750 mL to 1 L) cooked barley. Serve right away, or let cool and use instead of rice or beans in a salad.

Barley Risotto with Porcini Mushrooms

This risotto is the equivalent of sending your heart a love letter.

After you've soaked the flavourful dried mushrooms, make sure you keep the soaking liquid *when you drain them. One of my testers didn't and was sunk when she got to Step 6.*

MAKES 5 CUPS (1.25 L) | ONE SERVING = 1 CUP (250 ML)

1 Brush any dirt off the dried mushrooms. Place the mushrooms in a heatproof bowl, pour the boiling water over them, and let sit, covered, for 15 minutes.

2 Mince the garlic and set aside.

3 Place the barley in a wire-mesh colander and rinse it well under cold running water. Set the barley aside to drain.

4 When the 15 minutes are up, drain the mushrooms, reserving the liquid. Chop the mushrooms and set aside.

5 Heat a large saucepan over medium heat. Add the oil, then the onion, and sauté until the onion is just starting to turn golden brown, about 3 minutes. Add the thyme and garlic, and sauté for 1 minute.

6 Add the barley and sauté for 1 minute. Stir in the broth, reserved mushroom soaking liquid, and chopped mushrooms, making sure you scrape up all the little browned bits stuck to the bottom of the saucepan.

7 Bring to a boil, and stir again. Reduce the heat to a simmer and cook, covered and stirring occasionally, until the barley is tender and the risotto is creamy, 50 to 55 minutes. (Stirring occasionally during cooking will make the risotto more creamy — the sign of a good risotto.)

8 Stir in the cheese just before serving.

PER SERVING: 312 CALORIES, 12 G TOTAL FAT, 6.4 G SATURATED FAT, 0 G TRANS FAT, 478 MG SODIUM, 38 G CARBOHYDRATE, 9 G FIBRE, 3 G SUGARS, 15 G PROTEIN

DIABETES FOOD CHOICE VALUES PER SERVING: 2 CARBOHYDRATE, 2 MEAT AND ALTERNATIVES, 1 FAT

INGREDIENTS

- 20 to 24 g (0.7 to 0.85 oz) dried porcini mushrooms (about 1 cup/250 mL; see below)
- 1 cup (250 mL) boiling water
- 6 cloves garlic
- 1 cup (250 mL) pot barley
- 1 tbsp (15 mL) extra virgin olive oil
- 1 onion, diced
- 1 tbsp (15 mL) chopped fresh thyme (see page 25)
- 3 cups (750 mL) lower-sodium chicken broth (see page 7)
- ¾ cup (185 mL) crumbled goat's or sheep's milk feta (see page 14)

WHAT IS . . . ?

Dried porcini mushrooms have an intense flavour that adds a lovely smoky meatiness to any dish. Grocery Store Search: You can find packages of dried porcini mushrooms in the produce department of larger grocery stores. If your grocery store doesn't carry them, check out an Italian grocery store. If that seems like way too much work, or you don't live anywhere close to an Italian grocery store, then buy dried shiitake mushrooms, which are becoming more readily available.

Asian Barley Salad

Cholesterol-lowering barley, combined with two folate stars—peas and peanuts—makes this another heart-healthy dish.

This is one of my all-time favourites for a summer dinner. Plan ahead and cook the barley the night before. Then, in the heat of the day, all you have to do is chop a couple of green onions, throw in some peas and peanuts, and toss it all with a great salad dressing.

MAKES 4 CUPS (1 L) | ONE SERVING = 1 CUP (250 ML)

ASIAN BARLEY SALAD

1 cup (250 mL) pot barley
1 cup (250 mL) cooked fresh or thawed frozen peas (see page 14)
2 large green onions, thinly sliced
1 cup (250 mL) red-skinned peanuts (see sidebar)

PEANUT DRESSING

2 tbsp (30 mL) natural peanut butter (see page 14)
2 tbsp (30 mL) rice vinegar (see page 16)
2 tbsp (30 mL) lower-sodium soy sauce (see page 17)
2 tsp (10 mL) wasabi paste (see page 17)

1 For the salad, the night before you want to serve it, place the barley in a wire-mesh colander and rinse it under cold running water. Put the barley in a medium saucepan. Add 3 cups (750 mL) water and bring to a boil. Reduce the heat to a simmer and cook, covered, until the barley is tender but chewy, 45 to 55 minutes. Stir once or twice to evenly distribute any remaining liquid. Remove the saucepan from the heat, fluff the barley with a fork to separate the grains, and let sit, covered, for 10 minutes. Fluff the barley again, then let cool for 30 minutes. (Store in an airtight container in the fridge for up to 3 days.)

2 The next day, toss together the barley, peas, and green onions in a salad bowl.

3 For the peanut dressing, whisk together the peanut butter, vinegar, soy sauce, and wasabi paste in a small bowl. Pour the dressing over the barley mixture and toss well.

4 Spoon the salad into bowls. Sprinkle each serving with ¼ cup (60 mL) peanuts. Serve right away. (Any leftover salad can be covered and refrigerated overnight, but the barley absorbs the dressing so you may need to add a little more before serving.)

HEALTH BITE

Why red-skinned peanuts? There are loads more antioxidants to be had if you eat the skins, and every little bit helps.

PER SERVING: 483 CALORIES, 24.1 G TOTAL FAT, 3.1 G SATURATED FAT, 0 G TRANS FAT, 354 MG SODIUM, 53.6 G CARBOHYDRATE, 14 G FIBRE, 5.9 G SUGARS, 19 G PROTEIN

DIABETES FOOD CHOICE VALUES PER SERVING: 2½ CARBOHYDRATE, 2½ MEAT AND ALTERNATIVES, 3½ FAT

ME AND MY DIVAS

My claims to fame involve teaching Hockey Hall of Famer Brett Hull home economics when he was in Grade 9, touring and improvising with Mike Myers in The Second City Touring Company, and being given the boot from a book club. Yup, I got kicked out. Okay, that's a bit too dramatic even for me. The truth is I wasn't invited back because I was too opinionated. Who? *Moi*?

I was hurt at first, but after a while I saw the humour in the whole thing. Seriously, who has ever been kicked out of a book club? I'm certainly a trendsetter.

My son had the flu in the summer of 2009, and after a trip to the ER, complete with an isolation booth and a doctor in a hazmat suit, we decided to quarantine ourselves to make sure that if, in fact, he had the dreaded H1N1 virus, we weren't going to be the ones responsible for taking out Toronto.

I live in a one-hundred-year-old home right in Toronto and all the houses have front porches that become gathering points every summer. When I wasn't administering food, drinks, and mommy-ness to my son, I sat on my front porch reading blessed books. I looked at this forced isolation as a gift — I had time to sit and read.

My neighbours Jen, Heather, and Erin would stand at the foot of the steps and we'd chat about life and the weather, and gradually the idea of a book club for the bleak winter months was hatched. The four of us represent four decades of living — thirties, forties, fifties, and sixties — so in January 2010, the Decade Divas was born.

All of us are pretty great home cooks and Jen is a chef so we decided to read only books that had something to do with food; then we'd discuss the book over food taken from its pages.

We started off with very good intentions, but the Decade Divas rapidly turned into an eating, drinking, and frivolity-making group of women who share an evening under the guise of having read a book, which some of us have, and some of us haven't. It doesn't really matter. What does matter is we're spending time together and having way too much fun.

We're an eclectic group. Between us we've had eight husbands, and been to 37 countries, including Liechtenstein, Turkey, and Japan. But our real forte is that together we could design and build you a new house, cater and style any type of occasion, design you a website, manage your career (if you were in a rock band), and administer nursing care. Yes, we're a busy hive of activity. We are women who love life and, apparently, drinking good wine.

On the night we discussed *Under the Tuscan Sun* (my pick), I served this Italian-inspired barley dish to raves, and that was before three bottles of Italian vino and our jam session, which included bass and acoustic guitar, African drum, castanets, tambourines, and piano.

Tuscan Supper

This got a thumbs-up from the Decade Divas the first time I made it and another big thumbs-up from my publisher and his partner the next time I made it. All that praise, and it can lower your cholesterol, too—what a fabulous dish!

MAKES 6 CUPS (1.5 L) | ONE SERVING = 1 CUP (250 ML)

1 Mince the garlic and set aside.

2 Place the barley in a wire-mesh colander and rinse it well under cold running water. Set the barley aside to drain.

3 Heat a large pot over medium heat. Add the oil, then the onion, and sauté until golden brown, about 5 minutes. (This extra bit of time browning the onion pays off in the end as it gives the dish a deeper flavour.)

4 Add the mushrooms and garlic and sauté for 3 minutes. (I know what you're thinking: this pot isn't big enough. Trust me, the principle of shrinkage applies here and in about 3 minutes the mushrooms will have shrunk down.)

5 Add the basil, oregano, and pepper, and sauté for 1 minute. Add the barley and sauté for 1 minute.

6 Stir in the tomatoes and broth, making sure you scrape up all the little browned bits stuck to the bottom of the saucepan.

7 Bring to a boil and stir again. Reduce the heat to a simmer and cook, covered, until the barley is cooked through and soft but not mushy, 45 to 50 minutes. Stir occasionally and adjust the heat so it doesn't burn.

8 Remove the saucepan from the heat, stir once, and let sit, covered, for 10 minutes. Spoon into bowls and top each serving with 2 tbsp (30 mL) grated cheese. (Store any leftovers in the fridge for up to 3 days.)

PER SERVING: 207 CALORIES, 5 G TOTAL FAT, 1 G SATURATED FAT, 0 G TRANS FAT, 309 MG SODIUM, 33 G CARBOHYDRATE, 8 G FIBRE, 5.5 G SUGARS, 9 G PROTEIN

DIABETES FOOD CHOICE VALUES PER SERVING: 2 CARBOHYDRATE, 1 MEAT AND ALTERNATIVES, ½ FAT

INGREDIENTS

4 large cloves garlic
1 cup (250 mL) pot barley
1 tbsp (15 mL) extra virgin olive oil
1 onion, diced
4 cups (1 L) sliced cremini mushrooms (about 24 mushrooms, or one and a half 8 oz/227 g packages)
1 tbsp (15 mL) dried basil leaves (see below)
1 tsp (5 mL) dried oregano leaves (see below)
¼ tsp (1 mL) cracked black pepper
One 19 oz (540 mL) can diced tomatoes
1 cup (250 mL) lower-sodium vegetable or chicken broth (see page 7)
½ cup (125 mL) lightly packed grated Asiago cheese or really good Parmesan or Pecorino cheese

HOW TO

"Can I use fresh herbs?" Yes, you can. Use 3 tbsp (45 mL) chopped fresh basil and 1 tbsp (15 mL) chopped fresh oregano, but add them just before serving so the flavour isn't completely cooked out of the herbs.

Oats: Making Beta Glucan Your Friend

My granny swore that the reason she lived to be 98 was that her father made her eat oatmeal every day until she left home. And you know what? She was on to something.

Good for You

Oats, oat bran, and oatmeal are very high in soluble fibre (the kind that makes your heart healthy). Soluble fibre dissolves in water and becomes a thick viscous gel that travels slowly through the intestine. This thick goo slows down the absorption of glucose, in turn helping to stabilize blood sugars, a definite bonus for people living with diabetes.

The soluble fibre in oat bran is considered very helpful for those with diabetes. Foods containing soluble fibre may help control blood sugar by delaying stomach-emptying, slowing down the entry of glucose into the bloodstream, and lessening the rise in blood sugar after a meal that included soluble fibre.

Beta glucans — soluble-fibre compounds — are responsible for all the pluses in oats. Your liver is on a mission to find cholesterol. It's believed that beta glucans prevent the reabsorption of bile, which forces your liver to get its cholesterol from your blood. The beta glucans in your blood in turn sop up the bad LDL cholesterol. I like to envision beta glucans working like those little smiley-faced mini scrub brushes in a popular TV ad, the foamy, soluble-fibre cleaners unplugging your arteries as they go through your system. The oat fibre may also bind to any cholesterol in your intestines, soaking it up and escorting it out of your body.

How much soluble fibre do you need in your diet to lower your cholesterol? You need to eat at least 3 grams of soluble fibre from oat products every day to achieve a notable decrease in cholesterol levels. The nutrient breakdowns of the oat recipes that follow include the amount of soluble fibre, so you can see just how much you're getting in each serving.

So, eat your oats. Your heart will thank you and my grandmother will smile down on you from heaven, and that's a blessing on its own.

Attention Menopausal Women!

As our estrogen leaves the building, so do its protective powers over our cholesterol levels. Perimenopausal and menopausal women all need to be eating more soluble fibre. Enter the power of oats. Eating whole-grain oats and oat bran can help reduce your cholesterol levels.

large-flake oats, oat bran, and steel-cut oats (top to bottom)

Oat Primer

There's a dizzying array of different varieties of oats available, all called different things. So, what's in a name?

Steel-cut oats are whole-grain oats that have been cut with — wait for it — steel cutters, hence the name. But just to keep you on your toes, they're sometimes called Scottish or Irish oats. Used mostly for hot cereal, these oats are chewy when cooked, with a nuttier flavour than rolled oats. (They're the kind my granny ate for breakfast.) Once you've tried steel-cut oats, you probably won't even think about eating the large-flake type again. I use steel-cut oats for my hot breakfast cereal, and in cookie recipes.

Another winner in the "Obvious Name" game, *rolled oats* are whole-grain oats that have been steamed and then rolled (now, there's a surprise). Rolled oats come in different sizes: instant, quick-cooking, and large-flake (sometimes called old-fashioned rolled oats). These oats can usually be used interchangeably in hot cereal and cookie recipes, or as a topping for fruit crisp.

Oat bran is the outer husk of the whole-oat grain and contains most of the fibre and some of the fat. In Canada, Rogers and Quaker both sell plain oat bran. Can't find these brands? Read the label to be sure that the list of ingredients only says oat bran. Store oat bran in a cool, dry place; I keep mine in the fridge or freezer.

Scott's Muesli for One

The Swiss aren't famous just for chocolate. A lesser-known but just as delicious invention of theirs is a truly wonderful breakfast concoction called muesli.

This revolutionary food—a combination of raw oat flakes, dried fruit, and nuts and/or seeds—was created by Swiss physician Maximilian Oskar Bircher-Benner in the early 1900s. If there were a father of the raw food movement, Dr. Bircher-Benner would be your man. Bircher-Benner believed in the power of raw foods to heal the body.

Muesli is a rib-sticking breakfast, and when eaten with milk, basically has all the food groups present and accounted for.

This is my partner Scott's breakfast all year long.

MAKES 1 SERVING

INGREDIENTS

½ cup (125 mL) large-flake rolled oats
¼ cup (60 mL) dried berries or ½ cup (125 mL) fresh seasonal berries
2 tbsp (30 mL) walnuts
1 tbsp (15 mL) ground flaxseed (see page 13)
1 tbsp (15 mL) cocoa nibs (see page 12)
Generous sprinkle of cinnamon
1 cup (250 mL) skim milk or fortified organic soy beverage

1 In a cereal bowl, mix together the oats, berries, walnuts, flaxseed, cocoa nibs, and cinnamon. Pour the milk into the bowl, stir, and eat.

PER SERVING: 485 CALORIES, 19.4 G TOTAL FAT, 4.3 G SATURATED FAT, 0 G TRANS FAT, 129 MG SODIUM, 58.4 G CARBOHYDRATE, 11 G FIBRE, 1.3 G SOLUBLE FIBRE, 16.9 G SUGARS, 20 G PROTEIN

DIABETES FOOD CHOICE VALUES PER SERVING: 3 CARBOHYDRATE, 1 MEAT AND ALTERNATIVES, 3½ FAT

HEALTH BITE

The fat grams in Scott's muesli come from the heart-healthy walnuts, flaxseed, and cocoa nibs—and the flaxseed also helps lower bad cholesterol. Don't skip these all-important ingredients just to save yourself some calories. This is a power breakfast that will stay with you all morning, helping you to think better and preventing the 10:00 a.m. let's-grab-a-sugary-doughnut-and-a-coffee attack.

MAKE IT EASY, FOR THE TIME PRESSED

You can also buy ready-made muesli. I like Dorset Cereals's line made with whole grains, dried fruits, nuts, and seeds.

Overnight Blueberry Irish Oatmeal for Two

If you don't think you have time to make oatmeal from scratch every morning, this recipe will prove you wrong. The nutty, chewy goodness of cooked steel-cut oats can be in your bowl in about 10 minutes.

You can double, triple, or quadruple this recipe; just use a bigger saucepan.

MAKES ABOUT 1½ CUPS (375 ML) | ONE SERVING = ¾ CUP (185 ML)

INGREDIENTS

¼ cup (60 mL) Irish, Scottish, or steel-cut oats
¼ cup (60 mL) oat bran
¼ cup (60 mL) dried blueberries
½ cup (125 mL) skim milk or fortified organic soy beverage, heated
Generous sprinkle of cinnamon
Honey or your choice of sweetener to taste (optional)

1 The night before, a couple of hours before you get ready for bed, bring 1¼ cups (310 mL) water to a boil in a medium microwaveable bowl. When the water boils, stir in the oats, cover, and let sit for 30 minutes. (If you don't have a microwave, just boil the water, then stir the oats and boiling water together in a medium bowl.)

2 After 30 minutes, put the bowl in the fridge. (I wrote to Health Canada to ask if it was safe to leave the bowl out all night on the counter. The short answer to that question was "ARE YOU OUT OF YOUR MIND? *No!*")

3 The next morning, scrape the contents of the bowl into a small saucepan and stir well. If the oatmeal looks really thick, add a little more water.

4 Bring to a boil over medium heat. Stir in the oat bran and blueberries, and simmer for 5 minutes, stirring occasionally.

5 Remove the saucepan from the heat and stir the oatmeal. Spoon the oatmeal into 2 bowls and add the milk, dividing evenly. Sprinkle with the cinnamon, and sweeten to taste with honey or a sweetener of your choice (if using).

THUMBS UP

When Catherine, my I-never-cook-from-scratch friend, had a bowl of this oatmeal with me one morning while we waited for our cars to be repaired (we have the same mechanic down the street), she said, "Hey, this tastes okay." This may sound like faint praise, but if you knew Catherine, trust me, you'd know it's a ringing endorsement.

PER SERVING (WITHOUT HONEY): 188 CALORIES, 2.4 G TOTAL FAT, 0.4 G SATURATED FAT, 0 G TRANS FAT, 36 MG SODIUM, 37.8 G CARBOHYDRATE, 5 G FIBRE, 1.75 G SOLUBLE FIBRE, 13.9 G SUGARS, 8 G PROTEIN

DIABETES FOOD CHOICE VALUES PER SERVING (WITHOUT HONEY): 2 CARBOHYDRATE, ½ MEAT AND ALTERNATIVES, ½ FAT

YEAR ROUND
KID FRIENDLY

Blueberry-Oatmeal Muffins

Here's an all-season muffin that, unlike all-season tires, actually works all year round in Canada. When your local blueberries are ripe and ready, use fresh berries; in the dead of winter, switch to frozen. Frozen berries will taste better and be more nutrient-dense than the little blueberry that's travelled up to Canada on the Big Blueberry Bus from the sunny warm climates I start fantasizing about in mid-February.

MAKES 12 MUFFINS | ONE SERVING = 1 MUFFIN

INGREDIENTS

3/4 cup (185 mL) 1% plain yogurt
1/2 cup (125 mL) packed dark brown sugar
1/2 cup (125 mL) mashed ripe banana (about 1 large really ripe banana)
1 omega-3 egg (see page 13)
1 cup (250 mL) large-flake rolled oats
1 cup (250 mL) whole wheat flour
3/4 cup (185 mL) ground flaxseed (see page 13)
2 tbsp (30 mL) wheat germ
1 tsp (5 mL) baking powder
1 tsp (5 mL) baking soda
2 tsp (10 mL) cinnamon
1 cup (250 mL) fresh or frozen blueberries (no need to thaw)

1 Preheat the oven to 375°F (190°C). Line a 12-cup muffin pan with paper liners.

2 Whisk together the yogurt, brown sugar, banana, and egg in a large bowl. Stir in the oats and let sit for 10 minutes.

3 Whisk together the flour, flaxseed, wheat germ, baking powder, baking soda, and cinnamon in a small bowl.

4 Add the flour mixture to the yogurt mixture, and stir just until combined. Fold in the blueberries.

5 Divide the batter evenly among the muffin cups (I use a 1/4-cup / 60 mL ice-cream scoop with a release lever). Bake until a toothpick inserted in the centre of a muffin comes out clean, 20 to 25 minutes. Let the muffins cool in the pan on a wire rack for 5 minutes. Remove the muffins and let them cool completely on the wire rack. (Store the muffins in an airtight container for up to 2 days, or freeze for up to 2 months.)

PER MUFFIN: 173 CALORIES, 4.5 G TOTAL FAT, 0.7 G SATURATED FAT, 0 G TRANS FAT, 153 MG SODIUM, 29 G CARBOHYDRATE, 4 G FIBRE, TRACE SOLUBLE FIBRE, 11.7 G SUGARS, 5 G PROTEIN

DIABETES FOOD CHOICE VALUES PER MUFFIN: 2 CARBOHYDRATE, 1 FAT

BANANA BONANZA

You need to use thawed frozen bananas for this recipe because freezing really ripe bananas helps break down their cell walls, making them extremely mushy.

Toss unpeeled ripe bananas into the freezer so you'll have them on hand for these muffins. When ready to bake, just thaw the bananas, cut off one end, and squeeze the mushy fruit into a measuring cup.

YEAR ROUND
KID FRIENDLY

Breakfast Grab-and-Gos

I am a fan of the sit-down breakfast. I like to give myself enough time in the morning to eat a bowl of cereal before I dash off for the day. But I realize that many of us need a grab-and-go type of petit déjeuner *that's equivalent to a bowl of cereal.*

This whole-grain power recipe is the perfect solution. Each Grab-and-Go is loaded with great ingredients that supply your morning body with complex carbohydrates and three forms of cholesterol-lowering oats, plus flaxseed, dried fruit, and a tiny bit of chocolate for your soul.

Please note that these aren't very sweet, so if you're expecting a great big sweet cookie, you're barking up the wrong tree. You can sweeten them up a little by adding an extra ½ cup (125 mL) dried cranberries or blueberries.

MAKES 18 GRAB-AND-GOS | ONE SERVING = 1 GRAB-AND-GO

INGREDIENTS

1½ cups (375 mL) oat bran
1½ cups (375 mL) large-flake rolled oats
1 cup (250 mL) whole wheat flour
¾ cup (185 mL) ground flaxseed (see page 13)
½ cup (125 mL) Scottish, Irish, or steel-cut oats
2 tbsp (30 mL) wheat germ
2 tbsp (30 mL) cinnamon
1 tsp (5 mL) baking soda
1 cup (250 mL) dried cranberries or blueberries
¼ cup (60 mL) chocolate chips with at least 60% cocoa mass
½ cup (125 mL) coarsely chopped walnuts
¾ cup (185 mL) packed dark brown sugar
2 omega-3 eggs (see page 13)
One 4.5 oz (128 mL) jar strained prunes baby food
¼ cup (60 mL) canola oil (be sure to measure accurately; see page 21)
1 tbsp (15 mL) pure vanilla extract

1 Position a rack in the middle of the oven. Preheat the oven to 375°F (190°C). Line 2 large baking sheets with parchment paper.

2 Mix together the oat bran, large-flake oats, flour, flaxseed, steel-cut oats, wheat germ, cinnamon, and baking soda in a large bowl.

3 Stir in the cranberries or blueberries, chocolate chips, and walnuts.

4 Whisk together the brown sugar, eggs, prunes, oil, and vanilla in a medium bowl, until well blended.

5 Add the sugar mixture to the oat bran mixture, and stir until really well combined. I like to mix this with my hands but the dough is sticky, so you may want to use a large spoon or mix it in a stand mixer.

HEALTH BITE

Eat one Grab-and-Go with a glass of skim milk and an apple, and up your soluble-fibre intake to 23 grams. The extra gram comes from the whole unpeeled apple.

6 You want to make 18 Grab-and-Gos, so eyeball an amount that's bigger than a golf ball but smaller than a tennis ball. Scoop out the batter (a ¼-cup / 60 mL ice-cream scoop with a release button is perfect for this) onto the prepared baking sheets, spacing the balls of dough about 2 inches (5 cm) apart. Press each ball of batter down to make a 3½-inch (9 cm) cookie that's ¾ inch (2 cm) thick. The batter will be sticky, so lightly press down with either the back of a metal spoon or use your dampened hands (I use my hands). Bake until medium brown, 13 to 15 minutes.

7 Let the cookies cool slightly on the baking sheets before removing them and letting them cool completely on wire racks. (Store in an airtight container for up to 2 weeks or freeze for up to 3 months. I freeze them in individual bags and pop one in my purse the night before I know I'm going to have a grab-and-go kind of morning.)

PER GRAB-AND-GO: 256 CALORIES, 10.4 G TOTAL FAT, 1.7 G SATURATED FAT, 0 G TRANS FAT, 81 MG SODIUM, 37.8 G CARBOHYDRATE, 5 G FIBRE, 1.3 G SOLUBLE FIBRE, 14.7 G SUGARS, 7 G PROTEIN

DIABETES FOOD CHOICE VALUES PER GRAB-AND-GO: 2 CARBOHYDRATE, 2 FAT

HOW TO

I use Ghirardelli 60% cocoa mass chocolate chips in this recipe because they taste great and are really big. There aren't many chocolate chips in the recipe so the bigger the chip the bigger the chocolate hit. And remember, the chocolate is for your soul. Feel free to use 70% cocoa mass chocolate chunks instead.

NUT-FREE AND STILL NICE

When you bake, in addition to adding flavour, every ingredient has a function. One of the functions of the walnuts in a Grab-and-Go is to keep it from drying out as it sits patiently waiting for you to eat it. If you want to omit the walnuts, add an extra 2 tbsp (30 mL) canola oil to the batter. You need that extra bit of fat to keep the Grab-and-Gos from turning into hockey pucks.

PICTURED ON PAGE 259
YEAR ROUND
KID FRIENDLY

Triple-Oat Cookies

A trio of oats—large-flake oats, steel-cut oats, and oat bran—makes these cookies just about as oaty as you can get.

Dates not only add sweetness to these cookies but are a good source of fibre and potassium, that all-important mineral that helps to regulate blood pressure.

MAKES 30 COOKIES | ONE SERVING = 1 COOKIE

INGREDIENTS

- 1/2 cup (125 mL) packed dark brown sugar
- 1/2 cup (125 mL) canola oil (be sure to measure accurately; see page 21)
- 1/4 cup (60 mL) granulated sugar
- 1 omega-3 egg (see page 13)
- 1 tsp (5 mL) pure vanilla extract
- 1 1/4 cups (310 mL) large-flake rolled oats
- 1 cup (250 mL) whole wheat flour
- 1/2 cup (125 mL) Scottish, Irish, or steel-cut oats
- 1/4 cup (60 mL) oat bran
- 2 tbsp (30 mL) wheat germ
- 2 tsp (10 mL) cinnamon
- 1/2 tsp (2.5 mL) baking powder
- 1/4 cup (60 mL) finely chopped dates (see page 13)

1 Position a rack in the middle of the oven. Preheat the oven to 375°F (190°C). Line 2 large baking sheets with parchment paper.

2 Beat together the brown sugar, oil, and granulated sugar in a large bowl. The mixture will look like wet sand; don't worry, it's supposed to.

3 Beat in the egg and vanilla until the mixture thickens slightly and is sort of smooth.

4 Stir together the large-flake oats, flour, steel-cut oats, oat bran, wheat germ, cinnamon, and baking powder in a medium bowl. Add the dates and toss until they are coated with the oat mixture.

5 Add the oat mixture to the sugar mixture, and stir with a large spoon until the dough comes together.

6 Wash your hands and roll up your sleeves. You have to use your hands to finish mixing this; the heat from your hands helps meld all the ingredients together. The dough will be very stiff so some elbow grease is required. This is a great recipe to make when you're crabby—all that mixing gets rid of a ton of tension.

GIVE IT A TWIST

If you want really crispy cookies, flatten them out to 1/4-inch (5 mm) thickness.

7 When the dough is mixed, scoop out 1 tbsp (15 mL) dough, roll it between your palms, and place the ball on one of the prepared baking sheets. Repeat with the remaining dough, spacing the balls about 1 inch (2.5 cm) apart. (You should get 30 balls of dough in total, 15 per baking sheet.) When you have finished scooping out the balls of dough, lightly press down on them with your palm to flatten them. If the dough sticks to your hands, wash your hands, then lightly press down with slightly damp palms.

8 Bake until lightly browned, 12 to 14 minutes. Let the cookies cool on the baking sheets for 5 minutes, then remove the cookies and let them cool completely on wire racks. (Store the cookies in an airtight container for up to 2 weeks, or freeze for up to 3 months.)

PER COOKIE: 105 CALORIES, 4.6 G TOTAL FAT, 0.4 G SATURATED FAT, 0 G TRANS FAT, 8 MG SODIUM, 14.2 G CARBOHYDRATE, 1 G FIBRE, 0.3 G SOLUBLE FIBRE, 5.1 G SUGARS, 2 G PROTEIN

DIABETES FOOD CHOICE VALUES PER COOKIE: 1 CARBOHYDRATE, 1 FAT

The Venerable Oatcake

If your ancestors came from Scotland, you may be familiar with the oatcake. Oatcakes are a round cookie-type treat made from Scottish oats and not much else.

They aren't sweet. I repeat, they are not sweet. They get their natural sweetness from heart-healthy oats. If you want an oat *cookie*, then check out my Triple-Oat Cookies on page 174. I absolutely love oatcakes as a snack with a cup of tea, maybe with a touch of pure raspberry jam.

Traditionally, the Scots never threw anything out, and made do with what they had. In the middle of a bitter winter when the sugar was almost gone, the chickens had stopped laying eggs, and there wasn't much left in the pantry but oats, these passed as a treat. Oh, those stoic Scots!

Glam It Up

For a treat, try my ginger-spiked oatcakes (see sidebar) with a tiny bit of melted chocolate on top. Place one large chocolate chip (I use Ghirardelli 60% cocoa mass chocolate chips) on top of each oatcake as soon as they come out of the oven. When the chocolate chips have melted, spread the chocolate evenly over the top of each oatcake. Remove the oatcakes from the baking sheet and let them cool on a wire rack.

Traditional Oatcakes

Okay, okay, traditional oatcakes are made with either lard or butter, but you know I can't do that. Here is the Mairlyn-ized version of a traditional oatcake.

MAKES (IN A PERFECT WORLD) 18 OATCAKES | ONE SERVING = 1 OATCAKE

1 Position a rack in the middle of the oven. Preheat the oven to 400°F (200°C). Line a large baking sheet with parchment paper.

2 Using a fork, mix together the flour, steel-cut oats, large-flake oats, brown sugar, baking soda, and salt in a large bowl.

3 Still using the fork, stir in the oil until the dry ingredients are well coated.

4 Now, wash your hands. Pour the hot water over the flour mixture and mix with your hands, squeezing the dough until it starts to stick together. Keep squeezing and kneading until the dough forms a ball. Any dry bits in the bottom of the bowl? Keep squeezing and mixing until it all sticks together. Squeezing the ball of dough gets rid of tension and develops grip strength, just like those stress balls. Who says baking can't be good for you?

5 Pinch off golf-ball–size balls of dough (think giant meatballs or really decadent truffles) and place them about 1 inch (2.5 cm) apart on the prepared baking sheet. If you've got a good eye for size, you'll get 18 balls. If you get more or fewer, who cares? Don't worry, it's no big deal. Press down on the balls until they're about ½ inch (1 cm) thick.

6 Bake until the oatcakes are golden brown, about 12 minutes. (If you made more than 18, bake them for about 10 minutes or until golden brown. If you made fewer than 18, bake them for about 15 minutes or until golden brown.) Let the oatcakes cool on the baking sheet for 5 minutes, then remove the oatcakes from the baking sheet and let them cool completely on a wire rack.

PER OATCAKE: 157 CALORIES, 7.6 G TOTAL FAT, 0.7 G SATURATED FAT, 0 G TRANS FAT, 52 MG SODIUM, 18.5 G CARBOHYDRATE, 2 G FIBRE, 0.6 G SOLUBLE FIBRE, 1.7 G SUGARS, 4 G PROTEIN

DIABETES FOOD CHOICE VALUES PER OATCAKE: 1 CARBOHYDRATE, 1½ FAT

INGREDIENTS

1½ cups (375 mL) whole wheat flour
1 cup (250 mL) Scottish, Irish, or steel-cut oats
1 cup (250 mL) large-flake rolled oats
2 tbsp (30 mL) packed dark brown sugar
½ tsp (2.5 mL) baking soda
Pinch of salt
½ cup (125 mL) canola oil (be sure to measure accurately; see page 21)
6 tbsp (90 mL) hot water

GIVE IT A TWIST

For oatcakes with a hint of ginger, replace the sugar in my traditional oatcake recipe with ¼ cup (60 mL) finely chopped crystallized ginger (see page 29).

Per oatcake: 163 calories, 7.7 g total fat, 0.7 g saturated fat, 0 g trans fat, 52 mg sodium, 19.9 g carbohydrate, 2 g fibre, 0.6 g soluble fibre, 2.6 g sugars, 4 g protein

Diabetes Food Choice Values per oatcake: 1 Carbohydrate, 1½ Fat

Whole-Grain Cornmeal: The Elusive Grain

You know cornmeal, right? It's yellow, comes in a bag, and in your local grocery store, is usually in the same aisle as the wheat germ. Sorry, guys, that's probably not whole-grain cornmeal.

Whole-grain cornmeal starts off as a whole kernel of corn, but in most commercial brands of cornmeal, the thick outer skin and the germ are removed before it is ground.

Look for stone-ground whole-grain cornmeal to get the grain's full nutritional benefits. In Canada, look for Bob's Red Mill stone-ground whole-grain cornmeal in a medium grind in larger grocery stores and health food stores. It's perfect for my Pumpkin-Cornmeal Griddle Cakes.

Pumpkin-Cornmeal Griddle Cakes

Pancakes on the weekend have been a tradition in our house since my son was a little guy. These are great in the fall. They smell amazing while you're cooking them, and taste even better, especially when drizzled with pure maple syrup.

These are grown-up pancakes. If you have kids, either make the Chocolate Pancakes with Strawberry Sauce on page 72, or do what my son suggested and add chocolate chips to the batter. "Kids will eat anything with chocolate chips," says he.

Feel free to substitute Splenda for the sugar.

MAKES TWENTY 4-INCH (10 CM) PANCAKES | ONE SERVING = 4 PANCAKES

INGREDIENTS

1¼ cups (310 mL) non-fat plain yogurt
¾ cup (185 mL) pure pumpkin purée (not pumpkin-pie filling; see page 16)
½ cup (125 mL) skim milk or fortified organic soy beverage
1 omega-3 egg (see page 13)
2 tbsp (30 mL) packed dark brown sugar, or your choice of sweetener
1 tbsp (15 mL) canola oil
¾ cup (185 mL) whole wheat flour
¾ cup (185 mL) whole-grain medium-grind cornmeal
2 tbsp (30 mL) wheat germ
1 tbsp (15 mL) cinnamon
½ tsp (2.5 mL) baking soda
½ tsp (2.5 mL) ground ginger
¼ tsp (1 mL) ground cloves
Canola oil or non-stick baking spray
Pure maple syrup (see page 14) to serve

1 Preheat the oven to 200°F (95°C).

2 Whisk together the yogurt, pumpkin, milk, egg, brown sugar, and oil in a medium bowl.

3 Whisk in the flour, cornmeal, wheat germ, cinnamon, baking soda, ginger, and cloves. Let the batter sit while the skillet is heating (it will get a little thicker).

4 Heat a large non-stick skillet over medium heat. Grease the skillet lightly with canola oil or spray lightly with baking spray.

5 Stir the batter well. Spoon 2 tbsp (30 mL) batter into the skillet, swirling the batter with the back of a spoon to make a 4-inch (10 cm) pancake. Repeat to form 2 or 3 more pancakes in the skillet.

CONTINUED . . .

CONTINUED FROM THE PREVIOUS PAGE

6 Cook until bubbles form on the top of the pancakes and the undersides are dark golden brown. Flip the pancakes and cook on the other side until the undersides are dark golden brown. Remove the pancakes from the skillet and keep them warm in the oven on an ovenproof plate until all the pancakes are cooked.

7 Serve with pure maple syrup or a topping of your choice.

PER SERVING (WITHOUT PURE MAPLE SYRUP OR TOPPING): 261 CALORIES, 5.2 G TOTAL FAT, 0.6 G SATURATED FAT, 0 G TRANS FAT, 197 MG SODIUM, 43.8 G CARBOHYDRATE, 6 G FIBRE, 10.2 G SUGARS, 10 G PROTEIN

DIABETES FOOD CHOICE VALUES PER SERVING (WITHOUT PURE MAPLE SYRUP OR TOPPING): 1½ CARBOHYDRATE, 1½ MEAT AND ALTERNATIVES

HEALTH BITE

Those other corn products, corn tortilla chips and yes, even popcorn, are also considered whole grains, but be smart. Buy either lightly salted or unsalted chips, and remember portion size matters. Don't eat an entire bag and then congratulate yourself for eating six servings of whole grains in a day. You're just kidding yourself. I use tortilla chips in Black Bean Tortilla Chip Soup (page 48) and Nachos for One (page 59).

When it comes to popcorn, watch the butter, additives, and salt that most packaged popcorn contains. Your best bet is to air-pop your own popcorn, then add toppings in moderation.

YEAR ROUND
KID FRIENDLY

Sunday Morning Pancakes with Blueberry-Honey Sauce

Blueberry-honey sauce makes these weekend pancakes extra special. Make the sauce (recipe follows) before you make the pancakes. Or if you prefer, serve them simply with pure maple syrup.

MAKES SIXTEEN 4-INCH (10 CM) PANCAKES | ONE SERVING = 4 PANCAKES

1 Preheat the oven to 200°F (95°C).

2 Whisk together the milk, egg, and oil in a medium bowl.

3 Whisk in the flour, oat flakes, wheat germ, flaxseed, oat bran, cinnamon, and baking powder. Let the batter sit while the skillet is heating (the batter will get a little thicker).

4 Heat a large non-stick skillet over medium heat. Grease the skillet lightly with canola oil or spray lightly with baking spray.

5 Stir the batter well. Spoon 2 tbsp (30 mL) batter into the skillet, swirling the batter with the back of a spoon to make a 4-inch (10 cm) pancake. Repeat to form 2 or 3 more pancakes in the skillet.

6 Cook until bubbles form on the top of the pancakes and the undersides are dark golden brown. Flip the pancakes and cook on the other side until the undersides are dark golden brown. Remove the pancakes from the skillet and keep warm in the oven on an ovenproof plate until all the pancakes are cooked.

7 Serve the pancakes with the Blueberry-Honey Sauce or pure maple syrup.

PER SERVING (WITHOUT SAUCE): 227 CALORIES, 7.8 G TOTAL FAT, 1 G SATURATED FAT, 0 G TRANS FAT, 235 MG SODIUM, 30 G CARBOHYDRATE, 5 G FIBRE, 4.9 G SUGARS, 10 G PROTEIN

DIABETES FOOD CHOICE VALUES PER SERVING (WITHOUT SAUCE): 1½ CARBOHYDRATE, 1 MEAT AND ALTERNATIVES, 1 FAT

INGREDIENTS

1¼ cups (310 mL) skim milk or fortified organic soy beverage
1 omega-3 egg (see page 13)
1 tbsp (15 mL) canola oil
¾ cup (185 mL) whole wheat flour
¼ cup (60 mL) large oat flakes
2 tbsp (30 mL) wheat germ
2 tbsp (30 mL) ground flaxseed (see page 13)
2 tbsp (30 mL) oat bran
2 tsp (10 mL) cinnamon
2 tsp (10 mL) baking powder
Canola oil or non-stick baking spray
Blueberry-Honey Sauce (recipe follows), or pure maple syrup (see page 14)

KID ZONE

When my son did the recipe testing for these pancakes, instead of making 16 pancakes, he made 4 extra-large ones. He's a university student and said it was quicker that way.

Blueberry-Honey Sauce

This sauce tastes great drizzled over plain yogurt, too. Feel free to use Splenda instead of honey, if you prefer.

MAKES ABOUT 1¼ CUPS (310 ML) | ONE SERVING = ¼ CUP (60 ML)

INGREDIENTS

1½ cups (375 mL) fresh or frozen blueberries

½ cup (125 mL) cup honey, or your choice of sweetener to taste

1 tbsp (15 mL) orange zest

2 tbsp (30 mL) fresh orange juice

1 If using fresh blueberries, rinse them well and pick out any stems.

2 Mix together the blueberries and honey in a small saucepan, and bring to a boil. Boil gently until slightly thickened and berries start to pop, about 5 minutes. Remove the saucepan from the heat and add the orange zest and juice.

3 Let the sauce cool slightly before drizzling over the pancakes. (Refrigerate the sauce in a sealed glass jar for up to 3 days.)

PER SERVING: 133 CALORIES, 0.3 G TOTAL FAT, 0 G SATURATED FAT, 0 G TRANS FAT, 2 MG SODIUM, 35.3 G CARBOHYDRATE, 2 G FIBRE, 32.6 G SUGARS, 0 G PROTEIN

DIABETES FOOD CHOICE VALUES PER SERVING: 2 CARBOHYDRATE

Flour: Whole Grain v. Whole Wheat

You would assume that whole wheat flour was the real deal. That it contained the bran, the germ, and the endosperm. Well, you'd be wrong, my friend. I was.

Here's the scoop: in Canada, whole wheat flour is refined white flour with the bran added back in, but not the wheat germ, which is the bigger health contributor. So, when you're buying whole wheat bread, look for "whole-grain whole wheat flour" on the ingredients list or you'll be missing out on wheat germ's health benefits.

The wheat *germ* is a concentrated source of nutrients, including thiamine, folate, magnesium, phosphorus, zinc, and vitamin E. The germ also contains protein, fibre, and some fat. It's because of the fat that I like to store my wheat germ in the fridge or freezer to prolong its shelf life.

In all the recipes using whole wheat flour in this book, except Don't-Forget-to-Leave-Room-for-Chocolate Cake! (page 329), I've added wheat germ to the batter, making all the baked goods in this book whole-grain whole wheat, and good for you. (If you use stone-ground whole wheat flour, there's no need to add wheat germ, as it remains in whole wheat flour processed this way.)

Whole-Grain Irish Soda Bread

Bake up a batch of this quick bread while you're fixing a bean dish or a pot of soup, and you have the perfect cold-weather supper.

MAKES 16 WEDGES | ONE SERVING = 1 WEDGE

INGREDIENTS

2 cups (500 mL) whole wheat flour
2 tbsp (30 mL) wheat germ
2 tbsp (30 mL) ground flaxseed (see page 13)
1 tbsp (15 mL) packed dark brown sugar
1½ tsp (7.5 mL) baking powder
½ tsp (2.5 mL) baking soda
¾ cup (185 mL) 1% plain yogurt
1 omega-3 egg
2 tbsp (30 mL) canola oil
Whole wheat flour for dusting

1 Preheat the oven to 375°F (190°C). Line a baking sheet with parchment paper, or lightly grease the baking sheet.

2 Whisk together the flour, wheat germ, flaxseed, brown sugar, baking powder, and baking soda in a large bowl. Set aside.

3 Whisk together the yogurt, egg, and oil in a small bowl.

4 Add the yogurt mixture to the flour mixture and stir until combined. If the dough is sticky, add a bit more flour. Now, roll up your sleeves: you're going to knead the bread.

5 Lightly flour a board or your counter with whole wheat flour. Place the dough in the centre of floured area. Push the dough down and away from you with the heels of your hands, then turn it one-quarter of a turn and bring the top flap of dough over to fold it in half. Repeat this process 19 more times.

6 Shape the dough, with its smooth side facing up, into a round loaf, 1½ inches (4 cm) thick and 6 inches (15 cm) in diameter.

7 Place the dough on the prepared baking sheet. Using a sharp knife, make a shallow X in the top.

8 Bake until golden brown on top and darker brown on the bottom, 35 to 40 minutes. The loaf should look like a giant biscuit. To tell whether the loaf is ready or not, knock gently on the top of it. It should sound hollow.

9 Remove the loaf from the baking sheet and let it cool on a wire rack for 10 minutes. Serve the loaf cut into 16 wedges.

PER SERVING: 91 CALORIES, 3 G TOTAL FAT, 0.4 G SATURATED FAT, 0 G TRANS FAT, 85 MG SODIUM, 12.7 G CARBOHYDRATE, 1 G FIBRE, 1.6 G SUGARS, 3 G PROTEIN

DIABETES FOOD CHOICE VALUES PER SERVING: 1 CARBOHYDRATE, ½ FAT

PICTURED ON PAGE 121
YEAR ROUND
ADULTS ONLY

Really, Really High-Fibre Banana Chocolate Chip Muffins

I created this recipe for a neighbour of mine who was constipated as a result of taking pain meds while she was in the hospital. These are serious muffins; no fooling around with these babies. Make sure that you drink an extra glass or two of water on days when you eat them, as an overabundance of fibre and not enough liquid can actually constipate you.

Each of these muffins contains 10 grams of fibre. They're perfect for an adult but may be a little too powerful for a child. So adults only, please.

MAKES 12 MUFFINS | ONE SERVING = 1 MUFFIN

INGREDIENTS

- 1½ cups (375 mL) frozen and thawed mashed banana (about 4 really ripe bananas; see sidebar on page 171)
- ¾ cup (185 mL) packed dark brown sugar
- ¾ cup (185 mL) whole psyllium husks (see page 16)
- ¾ cup (185 mL) buttermilk
- 1 omega-3 egg (see page 13)
- 1 cup (250 mL) whole wheat flour
- ¾ cup (185 mL) ground flaxseed (see page 13)
- 2 tbsp (30 mL) wheat germ
- 2 tbsp (30 mL) cinnamon
- 1½ tsp (7.5 mL) baking powder
- 1 tsp (5 mL) baking soda
- ¼ cup (60 mL) finely chopped walnuts
- ¼ cup (60 mL) chocolate chips with at least 60% cocoa mass or chocolate chunks with at least 70% cocoa mass

1 Preheat the oven to 400°F (200°C). Line a 12-cup muffin pan with paper liners.

2 Mix together the bananas, brown sugar, psyllium husks, buttermilk, and egg in a large bowl. Let the mixture sit for 10 minutes, then stir well.

3 Whisk together the flour, flaxseed, wheat germ, cinnamon, baking powder, and baking soda in a medium bowl. Stir in the walnuts and chocolate chips.

4 Stir the flour mixture into the banana mixture until well combined. The batter will be very thick.

5 Divide the batter evenly among the muffin cups (I use a ¼-cup / 60 mL ice-cream scoop with a release lever). Bake until a toothpick comes out clean, 20 to 25 minutes. Let the muffins cool in the pan on a wire rack for 5 minutes. Remove the muffins and let them cool completely on the wire rack. (Store the muffins in an airtight container for up to 2 days, or freeze for up to 2 months.)

PER MUFFIN: 208 CALORIES, 7 G TOTAL FAT, 1.6 G SATURATED FAT, 0 G TRANS FAT, 182 MG SODIUM, 40 G CARBOHYDRATE, 10 G FIBRE, 19.1 G SUGARS, 5 G PROTEIN

DIABETES FOOD CHOICE VALUES PER MUFFIN: 2 CARBOHYDRATE, 1½ FAT

MY FAVOURITE BIG F-WORD

There are so many things we just don't get enough of — fun, fitness, flamboyance — and my favourite F-word of them all, *fibre*.

Most of us aren't even coming close to consuming the recommended daily amount of fibre — 25 g for women and 38 g for men. No wonder we're all so tense.

Fibre comes in two forms: insoluble and soluble. Both play important roles in making happy campers out of your GI (gastrointestinal) tract and heart. And trust me, an unhappy GI tract will make your life miserable, and an unhappy heart can kill you. Yup, good old reliable fibre helps our bodies out with two for the price of one. What a nutritional bargain.

Insoluble fibre, which is the type found in whole-grain whole wheat and wheat bran, doesn't easily dissolve in water. It actually holds water, keeping all that digested food moving through your GI tract, gently cleaning your colon along the way.

Soluble fibre, on the other hand, dissolves in water. Your body turns it into a thick, gooey gel that moves very slowly through your body. One of the big pluses of eating something rich in soluble fibre is that your stomach stays fuller longer, making you *feel* fuller longer. Ever had a sugar high followed by the crash and burn? Soluble fibre helps prevent this by slowing the absorption of glucose into the body.

The big prize is that soluble fibre forces your liver to get its cholesterol from your blood, which in turn helps lower your bad LDL cholesterol. It's the reason that oatmeal is getting all that good press these days. Whole oats contain soluble fibre, and so do oat bran, barley, apples, eggplant, and — Mother Nature's answer to dynamite — psyllium.

Most of us know that a diet low in fibre makes you constipated. But having too much fibre without enough liquid can make you constipated, too. What we're aiming for is a balance of fibre plus enough liquid to keep everything moving. Throw in some exercise and you have the recipe for ARGBM (A Really Great Bowel Movement).

The Glycemic Index for Beginners

The less a whole grain is refined, the better it is for your body. When you remove the fibre-rich bran and the nutrient-dense germ, leaving just the starch-rich endosperm, your body will convert that starch into blood sugar very quickly.

A system called the glycemic index ranks how quickly and how high a carbohydrate can boost your blood sugar compared to pure glucose. The ranking is given a score: foods with a score of 70 or higher are labelled as having a high glycemic index (GI); those with a score of 55 or below have a low GI.

Foods with a high GI, like white bread, will produce rapid spikes in your blood sugar. Foods with a low glycemic index, such as whole-grain oats, cause a "slow, easy" change in your blood sugar. In general, fruits, vegetables, beans and lentils, nuts, and barley all have a low GI.

The way a grain is processed, the type of starch and sugars present, and how much protein a meal contains all affect the glycemic index.

People who consume high-GI foods on a regular basis have a much greater chance of developing type 2 diabetes. According to the Canadian Diabetes Association, people with type 2 diabetes who eat a low-GI diet may help improve their glycemic control, especially if the diet they are following also helps them maintain a healthy weight.

Super Snack Bars (Spin #21)

I've been making a variation of Rice Krispies squares—my favourite childhood treat—for years. This, the 21st version, is my latest twist on the old classic. It's a great recipe to get younger kids to help you with. Remember, if they made it, they will usually eat it.

The dilemma was in which chapter did this recipe belong—the berry chapter, the chocolate chapter, or what? I finally settled on this chapter because, with 5 cups (1.25 L) of grains in the mixture, grains are really the stars.

These pack a great punch of fibre—5 grams in each bar, higher than most commercial bars.

MAKES 16 BARS | ONE SERVING = 1 BAR

INGREDIENTS

4 cups (1 L) whole-grain cereal flakes (try Nature's Path)
1 cup (250 mL) Kellogg's All-Bran Buds
½ cup (125 mL) dried cranberries or blueberries
½ cup (125 mL) chocolate chips with at least 60% cocoa mass
¼ cup (60 mL) raw, unsalted sunflower seeds
½ cup (125 mL) brown rice syrup (see below)
2 tbsp (30 mL) smooth natural peanut butter (see page 14)
Non-stick baking spray (optional)

1 Line an 8-inch (20 cm) square baking pan with parchment paper or lightly spray the pan with baking spray. Set aside.

2 Mix together the cereal flakes, All-Bran Buds, cranberries, chocolate chips, and sunflower seeds in a large bowl. Set aside.

3 Mix together the brown rice syrup and peanut butter in a small saucepan. Heat over medium heat, stirring often, until the peanut butter has melted. Quickly pour the syrup mixture over the cereal mixture and stir until the dry ingredients are well coated with the syrup mixture.

4 Spoon the mixture into the prepared pan. Dampen your hands and press down firmly on the mixture to fit it into the pan (*firmly* is the operative word here). Pop the pan in the fridge until firm, about 2 hours, then cut into 16 bars. No room in the fridge? Leave it on the counter to firm up. This will take about 4 hours, unless it's a damp, humid day, in which case you'll have to make some space in your fridge. (Store the bars in an airtight container at room temperature for up to 4 days.)

PER BAR: 147 CALORIES, 5.2 G TOTAL FAT, 1.7 G SATURATED FAT, 0 G TRANS FAT, 70 MG SODIUM, 24.7 G CARBOHYDRATE, 5 G FIBRE, 13.9 G SUGARS, 2 G PROTEIN

DIABETES FOOD CHOICE VALUES PER BAR: 1½ CARBOHYDRATE, 1 FAT

WHAT IS . . . ?

Brown rice syrup is made by steeping brown rice in a special enzyme preparation. The starches in the rice are broken down and converted into a smooth, sweet liquid. Once opened, store in the fridge for up to 10 months. Place the refrigerated jar in a pot of warm water to make it runnier and easier to measure. Grocery Store Search: I use Lundberg Organic Brown Rice Syrup. Larger grocery stores that have a health food department should have it.

PICTURED ON PAGE 259
FALL / WINTER
KID FRIENDLY

Pumpkin-Date Spice Cookies

Whenever I go home to Vancouver to visit my parents, I look through my mom's recipe file. Some of her recipes are written on index cards, others are clippings cut out of the Vancouver Sun, *and all are splashed with ingredients. Reading them is like going on a culinary archaeological dig.*

You can tell a lot about our family by reading those recipes. The most-used ones have the most splatters. You can tell we all loved chocolate, cookies, and, apparently, French pancakes, which I have no recollection of. Darn menopause!

I adapted this soft, cake-like cookie recipe, which was popular in the 1950s, from one of my mom's splattered newspaper clippings.

Since all my treats have to have something healthy about them, these cookies get their flavour from dates, spices, and some beta-carotene-rich pumpkin.

MAKES 42 COOKIES (USING A 2 TSP / 10 ML MINI-SCOOP, SEE PAGE 11)
ONE SERVING = 2 COOKIES

INGREDIENTS

1¼ cups (310 mL) whole wheat flour
2 tbsp (30 mL) wheat germ
1 tbsp (15 mL) cinnamon
1 tsp (5 mL) baking powder
½ tsp (2.5 mL) grated nutmeg
½ tsp (2.5 mL) ground ginger
2 tbsp (30 mL) finely chopped crystallized ginger (see page 29)
1 cup (250 mL) pitted baking dates (see page 13)
¼ cup plus 2 tbsp (90 mL) unsalted non-hydrogenated margarine
1 cup (250 mL) packed dark brown sugar
1 omega-3 egg (see page 13)
½ cup (125 mL) pure pumpkin purée (not pumpkin-pie filling; see page 16)

1 Position a rack in the middle of the oven. Preheat the oven to 350°F (180°C). Line a large baking sheet with parchment paper.

2 Whisk together the flour, wheat germ, cinnamon, baking powder, nutmeg, and ground ginger in a medium bowl. Stir in the crystallized ginger.

3 Break up the dates into small pieces with your fingers, dropping them into the bowl as you go. Toss well until the dates are coated in the flour mixture. Set aside.

4 Cream the margarine in another medium bowl. Beat in the brown sugar until fluffy.

5 Add the egg and beat until fluffy. Add the pumpkin and beat just until mixed. Add the flour mixture and stir until well combined.

6 Drop the batter by rounded teaspoonfuls (10 mL) onto the prepared baking sheet, or use a 2 tsp (10 mL) mini-scoop (see page 11), spacing the cookies about 1 inch (2.5 cm) apart. Bake until cookies look firm and are lightly browned, 13 to 15 minutes.

7 Let the cookies cool slightly on the baking sheet before removing them and letting them cool completely on a wire rack. (Store the cookies in an airtight container for up to 1 week, or freeze for up to 2 months.)

HOW TO

I use electric beaters when I make cookies, but feel free to mix the batter using a wooden spoon.

PER SERVING: 126 CALORIES, 4 G TOTAL FAT, 0.6 G SATURATED FAT, 0 G TRANS FAT, 65 MG SODIUM, 21 G CARBOHYDRATE, 2 G FIBRE, 11 G SUGARS, 2 G PROTEIN

DIABETES FOOD CHOICE VALUES PER SERVING: 1½ CARBOHYDRATE, 1 FAT

9

Greens:
Nature's Perfect Colour

The virtues of eating your greens reads like Olympian Clara Hughes's list of medals (you may remember she's the only Canadian to have won medals in both the Summer and Winter Olympics). Ms. Hughes and leafy greens are both champions. So much so that Health Canada lists leafy greens (though not Ms. Hughes) as one of the must-haves in Canada's Food Guide.

The guide says, and I quote, "Eat one dark green and one orange vegetable each day." Okay, if you want to be really picky, it says "dark green" not "leafy green," but it *is* pretty close.

Canada's Food Guide does single out three vegetables—romaine lettuce, spinach, and broccoli—two of which *are* leafy greens, the third not so much, but still dark green.

Broccoli is such a powerful food it has its own chapter in this book, along with fellow members of the cruciferous team (Broccoli, Brussels Sprouts, Cabbage, and Cauliflower: The Cruciferous Family of Superheroes, page 90).

The guide also talks up carrots, sweet potatoes, and winter squash, and I've given them their own chapter, too (Carrots, Sweet Potatoes, Winter Squash, and Pumpkin: Golden and Good for You, page 106).

If Canada's Food Guide is naming names, I think we need to listen. And leafy greens are so extraordinary, I believe they deserve their very own chapter, too.

GOOD FOR YOU

"Eat your greens" might be something your mom said, but I'm betting it will be the catchphrase of the 21st century. That's because leafy greens are powerhouses of folate, the amazing B vitamin that prevents damage to your valuable and unique DNA.

Leafy greens also contain vitamin K, which plays an integral role in bone development and heart health. Add immune-enhancing vitamin C and beta-carotene, potassium, magnesium, calcium, and iron, and greens become the rock 'n' roll stars of the veggie world.

PARSLEY

Leafy greens offer yet more proof that Mother Nature knows best. There are two forms of dietary iron: heme and nonheme. Heme iron is found in animal sources and is easily absorbed by the body. Nonheme iron is found in some plants, beans, and grains and is not readily absorbed. Vitamin C helps in the absorption of iron. All leafy greens contain both nonheme iron and vitamin C: Mother Nature at her best.

Kale, mustard greens, bok choy, arugula, watercress, and collards are considered leafy greens but are also certified members of the disease-reducing cruciferous family (see page 91). Not only do you get the benefits of the antioxidants responsible for reducing your chances of developing cancer, but every time you eat a folate-rich leafy green, you also reduce your chances of developing heart disease.

IT'S QUIZ TIME!

Take this test to see how much you know about leafy greens:

1 In ten seconds, name as many edible leafy greens as you can.

2 In ten seconds, name as many types of potato chips as you can.

Give yourself a point for every one of these leafy greens you named: kale, mustard greens, dandelions, arugula, watercress, spinach, collards, Swiss chard, Chinese greens (including bok choy), romaine, and beet tops.

How did you do? If you could name all the leafy greens listed you're either a dietitian or a food-and-nutrition junkie. But if you're like most Canadians, you could probably name more types of chips.

I've tried to figure out why health doesn't sell. In this world of glitz, hype, and scandals, eating your greens just doesn't seem to cut it.

Here's my idea. We all love firefighters, so why don't we get some really hot-looking firemen to pose for a calendar wearing only leafy greens.

Just picture Mr. April lying in a bed of dandelions, Mr. July wearing nothing but a smile and some strategically placed arugula, or Mr. September waist-deep in a field of really tall kale. Women would be all over that calendar. And for men, there could be a female version. That's the campaign the eat-more-fruits-and-vegetables people need. I'm sure that leafy greens sales would go through the roof.

Let's get to know these fabulous veggies better.

Arugula 101

Arugula (pronounced a-roo-gull-la), or rocket, as it's called in the UK, adds a peppery-tasting kick to any salad.

Arugula contains fibre, vitamins A, C, and K, folate, calcium, iron, magnesium, phosphorus, potassium, and manganese — all those nutrients and only 4 calories per cup (250 mL)!

I have been growing this incredible green in my backyard for years. I start my first crop at the end of April and continue to plant seeds all the way through September.

Buy It, Store It

Arugula looks a bit like an oak leaf, and the bigger and older the leaves, the spicier they become. Think of mature arugula as the Lauren Bacall of leafy greens.

Baby or young arugula can be eaten stalk and all, but older bunches need to have their stalks removed. Wash arugula really well to get rid of the dirt and grit, then eat it right away; like other delicate leafy greens, arugula doesn't like to hang out in your fridge.

Mairlyn's Summer Main Course Salad for One

This salad is huge. In fact, it's enormous, and it's loaded with heart-healthy ingredients, so you can feel virtuous while eating it. You can double, triple, or quadruple the salad, and—what the heck—serve some red wine with it and have a salad party.

MAKES 1 HUGE SERVING

INGREDIENTS

- 3 cups (750 mL) lightly packed baby arugula
- ½ cup (125 mL) uncooked fresh or thawed frozen peas (see page 14)
- 1 can of artichoke hearts, drained and thinly sliced (see recipe intro on page 51)
- 3 kalamata olives, pitted and chopped (see page 23)
- 1 tsp (5 mL) capers, drained and rinsed (see page 12)
- One 3 oz (80 to 90 g) can skipjack tuna packed in oil, well drained (see below for other options)
- 2 tbsp (30 mL) finely chopped parsley
- 2 tbsp (30 mL) finely chopped fresh basil
- 1 tbsp (15 mL) finely chopped fresh oregano
- 1 green onion, thinly sliced
- 2 tsp (10 mL) extra virgin olive oil or canola oil
- 2 tbsp (30 mL) good-quality balsamic or white wine vinegar
- Cracked black pepper to taste

1 Swish the arugula in a clean sink of cold water to make sure there isn't any sand or dirt clinging to it. Place in a salad spinner and spin-dry (or pat dry on paper towels). Tear the arugula into bite-sized pieces (or leave as is). Place arugula on a really large plate.

2 Working your way down the list of ingredients, top the arugula with the peas, artichokes, olives, and capers.

3 Break the tuna (if using) into bite-sized pieces and sprinkle it over the salad. Scatter the parsley, basil, oregano, and green onion.

4 Drizzle the salad with the oil, then with the vinegar. Sprinkle with the black pepper and dinner is ready.

PER SERVING: 233 CALORIES, 12.3 G TOTAL FAT, 1.1 G SATURATED FAT, 0 G TRANS FAT, 373 MG SODIUM, 20.6 G CARBOHYDRATE, 9 G FIBRE, 6.5 G SUGARS, 8 G PROTEIN

DIABETES FOOD CHOICE VALUES PER SERVING: 1 CARBOHYDRATE, 1 MEAT AND ALTERNATIVES, 2 FAT

GIVE IT A TWIST

If you're not a tuna fan, add 2½ oz (75 g) cooked chicken or salmon, or ¾ cup (185 mL) drained and rinsed canned chickpeas to ensure protein in this meal.

January Salad

Thank goodness for January citrus. Just when the produce department is starting to look a tad bleak, the sunny-looking US citrus fruit rolls in.

This salad is a fabulous combination of peppery arugula and sweet and tangy citrus, with a semi-sweet salad dressing. It will brighten up your January with zesty flavours that come with a great hit of vitamin C and folate, too.

MAKES 4 SERVINGS | ONE SERVING = ONE PLATEFUL

SALAD

4 cups (1 L) lightly packed baby arugula
2 red grapefruit
2 large oranges
1 small shallot

HONEY-MUSTARD DRESSING

1 tbsp (15 mL) frozen orange juice concentrate, thawed (see page 13)
1 tbsp (15 mL) canola oil
1 tbsp (15 mL) apple cider vinegar (see page 12)
1 tbsp (15 mL) honey
1 tsp (5 mL) Dijon mustard

1 For the salad, swish the arugula in a clean sink of cold water to make sure there isn't any sand or dirt clinging to it. Place in a salad spinner and spin-dry (or pat dry on paper towels). Place arugula in a large bowl and set aside.

2 Scrub the grapefruit and oranges. Peel the fruit and cut into segments (see page 24). Set aside.

3 Mince the shallot and set aside.

4 For the salad dressing, whisk together the orange juice concentrate, oil, vinegar, honey, and mustard in a small bowl.

5 Pour the dressing over the arugula and toss well.

6 Divide the arugula evenly among 4 large plates. Top each portion of arugula with one-quarter of the grapefruit and one-quarter of the orange segments. Sprinkle each salad with one-quarter of the minced shallot.

PER SERVING: 163 CALORIES, 4 G TOTAL FAT, 0.3 G SATURATED FAT, 0 G TRANS FAT, 36 MG SODIUM, 29 G CARBOHYDRATE, 4 G FIBRE, 23.6 G SUGARS, 3 G PROTEIN

DIABETES FOOD CHOICE VALUES PER SERVING: 1½ CARBOHYDRATE, 1 FAT

HEALTH BITE

Grapefruit contains compounds that may interfere with certain prescription drugs. Check with your doctor.

A PERFECT TEN

Check out these unsolicited comments from reality tester Vivien, of Vancouver: "Wow! What a mixture of tastes and textures! I loved the combo of citrus and peppery arugula, which surprisingly complemented each other very well. Marks out of ten? Why, ten!"

Arugula with Roasted Beets and Goat Cheese

This upscale, trendy salad is a winner in both the taste and nutrition categories. Beets are rich in antioxidants that reduce levels of homocysteine, an amino acid that may cause damage to your blood vessels.

Beets aren't considered a spring vegetable but local beets are stored through the winter and are still available in most grocery stores until the end of March.

Roasting the beets gives them a sweeter, richer flavour than boiling them.

Even my brother John, who isn't a beet fan, gives this salad top marks.

MAKES 4 SERVINGS | ONE SERVING = ONE PLATEFUL

SALAD

8 cups (2 L) lightly packed baby arugula (or one 5 oz/142 g container)
4 beets, tops trimmed
2 oz (60 g) soft goat cheese, at room temperature

BALSAMIC DRESSING

2 tbsp (30 mL) balsamic vinegar
4 tsp (20 mL) extra virgin olive oil
2 tsp (10 mL) grainy Dijon mustard
2 tsp (10 mL) honey
1 large shallot, minced

1 For the salad, the night before you plan to serve it, preheat the oven to 350°F (180°C). Line an 8-inch (20 cm) square metal baking pan with foil or parchment paper.

2 Wash the beets and place them in the prepared pan. Roast until tender, 1 to 2 hours, depending on the size of the beets and how tender you like them. (I like my beets on the firmer side.) When the beets are cooked, cool them, then cover and refrigerate overnight.

3 The next day, swish the arugula in a clean sink of cold water to make sure there isn't any sand or dirt clinging to it. Place in a salad spinner and spin-dry (or pat dry on paper towels). Place the arugula in a large bowl and set aside.

4 Peel the beets and slice them thinly. (Unless you want to have purple fingers, wear rubber gloves for this little dye-your-hands exercise.) Set aside.

5 For the dressing, whisk together the vinegar, oil, mustard, and honey in a small bowl. Add the shallot and mix well. Reserving 2 tsp (10 mL) dressing, pour the remainder over the arugula and toss well.

6 Divide the arugula evenly among 4 plates. Top each with one-quarter of the sliced beets. Using your fingers, pinch off equal amounts of goat cheese and sprinkle it over the beets. Drizzle each salad with the reserved dressing.

PER SERVING: 162 CALORIES, 8.5 G TOTAL FAT, 3.1 G SATURATED FAT, 0 G TRANS FAT, 354 MG SODIUM, 15.7 G CARBOHYDRATE, 2 G FIBRE, 11.0 G SUGARS, 6 G PROTEIN

DIABETES FOOD CHOICE VALUES PER SERVING: 1 CARBOHYDRATE, ½ MEAT AND ALTERNATIVES, ½ FAT

WORDS FROM THE WISE

Whenever I prep beets, I roast them while I'm cooking something else in the oven. I was raised by parents who lived through the Depression, and conserving energy is second nature to me. The roasted beets will keep in the fridge for up to three days.

Bok Choy 101

Bok choy is an Asian leafy green that's an excellent source of vitamins A and C. It also contains folate, fibre, potassium, calcium, and magnesium.

A member of the cancer-fighting cruciferous family, bok choy should really be in that chapter (Broccoli, Brussels Sprouts, Cabbage, and Cauliflower: The Cruciferous Family of Superheroes, page 90), but it's leafy, it's green, and it's staying put.

Buy It, Store It

Choose perky-looking bok choy with bright green leaves and no bruises on the white stalks. Bok choy doesn't like sitting in your fridge so plan to eat it as soon as possible after you buy it.

Stir-Fried Bok Choy

This easy side dish goes well with poultry or fish, especially if they have an Asian flair. Serve with a side dish of brown rice and you're good to go.

Baby bok choy is an amazing, nutrient-dense Asian green that looks really beautiful on a plate. It resembles a miniature version of regular bok choy, but cooks up faster.

MAKES 3 CUPS (750 ML) | ONE SERVING = ½ CUP (125 ML)

INGREDIENTS

- 2 large cloves garlic
- ¼ cup (60 mL) lower-sodium vegetable or chicken broth (see below)
- 1 tbsp (15 mL) lower-sodium soy sauce (see page 17)
- ¼ tsp (1 mL) red pepper flakes
- 1 tsp (5 mL) cornstarch
- 1 lb (500 g) baby bok choy
- 1 tbsp (15 mL) canola oil

1 Mince the garlic and set aside.

2 Whisk together the broth, soy sauce, red pepper flakes, and cornstarch in a small bowl. Stir in the garlic and set aside.

3 Wash the bok choy under cold running water and drain well. Cut off about ½ inch (1 cm) from the base of each stalk.

4 Heat a large non-stick skillet over medium heat. Add the oil, then the bok choy. Stir-fry until the green part of the bok choy starts to wilt, 1 to 2 minutes.

5 Stir the broth mixture again and pour it over the bok choy. Cook, stirring, until the sauce comes to a boil and is clear and shiny.

HOW TO

Freeze any leftover broth in ¼- or ½-cup (60 mL or 125 mL) portions.

PER SERVING: 38 CALORIES, 2.6 G TOTAL FAT, 0 G SATURATED FAT, 0 G TRANS FAT, 159 MG SODIUM, 2.8 G CARBOHYDRATE, 1 G FIBRE, 1.1 G SUGARS, 2 G PROTEIN

DIABETES FOOD CHOICE VALUES PER SERVING: ½ MEAT AND ALTERNATIVES, 1 EXTRA

Crispy Kale

My friend Joanne called me one day to ask if I had tried roasting kale in the oven. No, I hadn't. Apparently, the leafy green kale turns crispy. A leafy green turning crispy? I don't think so.

I was a skeptic until I visited the farmers market at Artscape Wychwood Barns in Toronto. The market is housed in an old TTC *(Toronto Transit Commission) barn, and is awash with natural light and a community spirit I'd never experienced at any other farmers market. It made me feel as if I had stepped back in time to a more hands-on era when people knew who grew their food and where it came from.*

Vendors at Wychwood Barns sell freshly caught lake fish, baby greens, natural wool, artisanal goat cheeses, mushrooms, seasonal fruits and vegetables, honey, bread, organic handmade crackers, organic seeds, coffee, chocolate, and ... crispy kale.

One bite from a package of Krispy Kale (spelled with two ks*) and I flew home to try to re-create the taste experience. Sorry, Joanne, for not believing you!*

Here's my version of this fabulous snack.

MAKES ABOUT 4 CUPS (1 L), DEPENDING ON THE SIZE OF THE KALE LEAVES | ONE SERVING = BIG DILEMMA (I HAVE BEEN KNOWN TO EAT THE WHOLE LOT, BUT LET'S GO WITH ½ CUP/125 ML PER SERVING FOR THE AVERAGE PERSON)

INGREDIENTS

1 lb (500 g) kale

1 tbsp (15 mL) extra virgin olive oil

2 tbsp (30 mL) very finely grated, really good Parmesan cheese (optional, but so worth adding)

1 Position a rack in the middle of the oven. Preheat the oven to 325°F (160°C). Line a 15- × 11-inch (38 × 28 cm) rimmed baking sheet with parchment paper.

2 Wash the kale really well. Tear the leaves from the stems, discarding the stems. Tear the leaves into bite-sized pieces.

3 Place the leaves in a salad spinner and spin them dry. Pat the leaves dry on paper towels or a clean tea towel. The leaves need to be totally dry.

CONTINUED ...

CONTINUED FROM THE PREVIOUS PAGE

4 Place the dry kale on the prepared baking sheet. Drizzle the kale with the oil. Now, here comes the fun part: use your hands and gently massage the oil into the kale leaves. You are trying to coat every leaf. It sounds tedious, but as soon as they're all shiny, they're ready.

5 Roast the kale in the oven until the leaves are dark and crunchy, 15 to 20 minutes. If necessary, pop them back in the oven for another 5 to 15 minutes. The timing depends on how dry the leaves were. Whatever you do, don't burn them; they go from great to yuck fairly quickly.

6 Remove the kale from the oven and let it sit for 5 minutes. Place the crispy leaves on a large plate and sprinkle with cheese (if using).

PER SERVING: 88 CALORIES, 2.8 G TOTAL FAT, 0.4 G SATURATED FAT, 0 G TRANS FAT, 62 MG SODIUM, 14.8 G CARBOHYDRATE, 4 G FIBRE, 0 G SUGARS, 5 G PROTEIN

DIABETES FOOD CHOICE VALUES PER SERVING: 1½ CARBOHYDRATE, ½ MEAT AND ALTERNATIVES, ½ FAT

HOW TO

To prep collards, mustard greens, or Swiss chard, wash the greens well. Remove each leaf from its central stem, which tends to be bitter, and discard the stems. Stack the leaves on top of each other and slice into strips. There's no need to blanch collards, mustard greens, or Swiss chard. Sauté the greens in oil with garlic until they start to wilt. Cover and cook until the greens are tender, 5 to 10 minutes.

Kale 101

Don't be intimidated by kale. It looks big and scary but it has a very mild flavour. There are many varieties of this super green. Check out your farmers market for purple kale.

Kale contains vitamins A, C, and K. Vitamin K plays an important role in bone metabolism.

Buy It, Store It

Choose dark green leaves that aren't wilted. Store kale for up to three days in your crisper in an open plastic bag. The longer it sits around in your fridge, the stronger its flavour will be.

Wash kale well before using, and remove each leaf from its central stem, which tends to be bitter. Stack the leaves on top of each other and slice them into strips. There's no need to blanch kale before using it in a recipe.

Kale is great sautéed with olive oil and garlic (it takes 5 to 7 minutes), or added to soups and stews.

Peas Are Important

Why are peas in the leafy green chapter? They're green, they're good for you, and they just didn't fit anywhere else.

Peas are full of fibre (including the soluble kind), vitamins C and K, and DNA-protecting folate.

Winter Pea Salad

Okay, you are dying for a fresh green salad and all the lettuce in your crisper has turned to slime. What's a cook to do?

My secret weapon is frozen peas. You can add them to soups and stir-fries, or even create a salad out of them.

This is my winter house salad when there isn't a lettuce leaf to be found.

MAKES 4 CUPS (1 L) | ONE SERVING = ½ CUP (125 ML), BUT I USUALLY EAT A WHOLE CUP, WHICH IS GREAT WAY TO REACH MY FOLATE QUOTA

PEA SALAD

2½ cups (625 mL) frozen peas
1 cup (250 mL) thinly sliced celery (2 or 3 large stalks)
½ cup (125 mL) finely chopped parsley
1 shallot, minced

CREAMY LIME DRESSING

¼ cup (60 mL) low-fat mayonnaise
1 tbsp (15 mL) fresh lime juice
1 tbsp (15 mL) apple cider vinegar (see page 12)

1 For the salad, rinse the frozen peas in a colander under cold running water until they feel like fresh peas. (Don't over-rinse; they actually taste really great when they are still cold.) Drain well and place in a medium bowl.

2 Add the celery, parsley, and shallot and toss well.

3 For the dressing, whisk together the mayonnaise, lime juice, and vinegar in a small bowl.

4 Pour the dressing over the salad and toss well.

PER SERVING: 69 CALORIES, 2.2 G TOTAL FAT, 0 G SATURATED FAT, 0 G TRANS FAT, 76 MG SODIUM, 10 G CARBOHYDRATE, 3 G FIBRE, 3.1 G SUGARS, 3 G PROTEIN

DIABETES FOOD CHOICE VALUES PER SERVING: ½ CARBOHYDRATE, ½ MEAT AND ALTERNATIVES

Summer Pea and Mint Salad

New summer peas right out of the shell can't be beat. When they hit the farmers market, I have been known to eat a one-quart basket all by myself.

If you do manage to get those fresh peas home from the store or market, this salad is a winner.

MAKES 2½ CUPS (625 ML) | ONE SERVING = ½ CUP (125 ML)

SALAD

1½ cups (375 mL) cooked, chilled fresh peas or thawed frozen baby peas

2 stalks celery, thinly sliced

¾ cup (185 mL) finely chopped parsley

¼ cup (60 mL) finely chopped fresh mint (see below)

¼ cup (60 mL) snipped fresh chives (see below)

ORANGE-DIJON DRESSING

1 tbsp (15 mL) canola oil

1 tbsp (15 mL) frozen orange juice concentrate, thawed (see page 13)

1 tbsp (15 mL) apple cider vinegar (see page 12)

1 tsp (5 mL) Dijon mustard

1 For the salad, toss together the peas, celery, parsley, mint, and chives in a large salad bowl.

2 For the dressing, whisk together the oil, orange juice concentrate, vinegar, and Dijon in a small bowl.

3 Pour the dressing over the salad, and toss well. Serve right away. (It still tastes great the next day but the vinegar turns the peas a terrible-looking grey-green. Just warning you.)

PER SERVING: 79 CALORIES, 3.2 G TOTAL FAT, 0 G SATURATED FAT, 0 G TRANS FAT, 45 MG SODIUM, 9.9 G CARBOHYDRATE, 3 G FIBRE, 4.4 G SUGARS, 3 G PROTEIN

DIABETES FOOD CHOICE VALUES PER SERVING: ½ CARBOHYDRATE, ½ MEAT AND ALTERNATIVES, ½ FAT

BACKYARD HERBS

Chives and mint may be growing in your garden from late spring through the summer, but if they aren't or if you don't have access to any fresh herbs, most large grocery stores carry them year round.

Spinach 101

Mighty spinach made it onto Liz Pearson's Disease-Fighting Superstar list in our book *Ultimate Foods for Ultimate Health … and don't forget the chocolate!* So, it has to be amazing.

The antioxidants found in spinach — beta-carotene, lutein, and zeaxanthin — reduce your chances of developing age-related vision diseases, such as macular degeneration and night blindness.

Spinach is full of folate, which can reduce your chances of developing heart disease and certain cancers, plus vitamin K, a super vitamin that may prevent hardening of the arteries. Spinach is also rich in magnesium, which has been shown to fight high blood pressure, heart disease, diabetes, migraines, and osteoporosis.

Buy It, Store It

I prefer baby spinach to bunch leaf spinach because I find the baby variety is more tender. I also love the convenience of buying baby spinach in containers because it's so much easier than having to super-wash the leafy bunches in a clean sink to make sure any dirt or sand is rinsed off. (And yes, I know that sounds lazy.)

I buy the containers of prewashed baby spinach … but I rinse it anyway. (So, Mairlyn, what are we talking here, about one minute of work? You rinse the prewashed spinach anyway. You're going to pay more for those containers for a one-minute time saver?)

Okay, so after much soul searching, I realize that I am shallow and lazy. I've nearly talked myself back into buying bunches of spinach again. Unless they have tough-looking leaves; then I am all over those containers. (I am so fibbing; I'm always all over those containers, even if it does mean I'm shallow and lazy.)

If you do choose bunched leaf spinach, swish it well in a clean sink of cold water to make sure there isn't any sand or dirt clinging to the leaves. You may have to do this two or three times, especially if you buy unwashed spinach at a farmers market. Once all the grit is gone, spin-dry the spinach in a salad spinner or pat it dry on paper towels.

Spinach Salad with Pears and Walnuts

When I was growing up, aside from peanuts, walnuts were the only other edible nut in the house.

I'm always surprised when someone tells me they don't like walnuts. It usually boils down to a bitter-walnut experience. Be sure to buy a variety with the best possible flavour.

If you're lucky enough to have a walnut tree in your yard that produces sweet walnuts, I'm extremely jealous and want you to send me some for Christmas. But until that happens, the only walnuts I eat are California walnuts, because they are never bitter. Costco sells them, as do many larger grocery store chains. I keep a jar on my counter for my morning cereal but store most of my stash in the freezer. Walnuts love the cold and will be happy in your freezer for up to six months.

MAKES 4 SERVINGS | ONE SERVING = ONE PLATEFUL

MAPLE-MUSTARD DRESSING

2 tbsp (30 mL) white wine vinegar
1 tbsp (15 mL) extra virgin olive oil
1 tbsp (15 mL) pure maple syrup (see page 14)
2 tsp (10 mL) Dijon mustard

SPINACH SALAD

8 cups (2 L) lightly packed baby spinach
2 pears (I prefer Bartlett), washed and patted dry
¼ cup (60 mL) coarsely chopped walnuts
2 oz (60 g) really good blue cheese of your choice, crumbled

1 For the dressing, whisk together the vinegar, oil, maple syrup, and Dijon in a small bowl. Set aside.

2 For the salad, rinse the spinach under cold running water. Place in a salad spinner and spin-dry, or pat dry on paper towels. Place in a large bowl.

3 Cut the pears into quarters and remove the cores. Cut each quarter into 4 slices. Set aside. (The pear slices won't turn brown by the time you need them, unless you are going out somewhere right now.)

4 Pour the dressing over the spinach and toss well.

5 Divide the spinach evenly among 4 plates. Top each portion with 4 slices of pear. Sprinkle each salad with 1 tbsp (15 mL) chopped walnuts and one-quarter of the blue cheese.

PER SERVING: 212 CALORIES, 12 G TOTAL FAT, 3.4 G SATURATED FAT, 0 G TRANS FAT, 333 MG SODIUM, 21.2 G CARBOHYDRATE, 6 G FIBRE, 11.1 G SUGARS, 7 G PROTEIN

DIABETES FOOD CHOICE VALUES PER SERVING: 1 CARBOHYDRATE, 1 MEAT AND ALTERNATIVES, 2 FAT

THE GREAT WALNUT HUNT

Can't find California walnuts? According to my publisher, Robert McCullough, there are three Persian markets on Lonsdale Avenue in North Vancouver, and their walnuts are never bitter either. But it's kind of a long way to go if you live in Halifax, so do your best to scout out great local nuts.

HEALTH BITE

Walnuts provide us with more heart-healthy omega-3 fatty acids than any other nut.

Spinach Salad with Blackberries

This gorgeous-looking salad is a summer treat. Big, juicy, ripe blackberries combine with spinach to make this a sweet-tart salad with just the right amount of dressing. Remember: it's a dressing, not a drowning. We want the flavours of the foods to be complemented by the salad dressing, not annihilated.

In the health department, your body will be absolutely jumping for joy after each forkful of folate-rich, antioxidant-dense spinach and blackberries.

MAKES 4 SERVINGS | ONE SERVING = ONE PLATEFUL

BLACKCURRANT DRESSING

4 tsp (20 mL) canola oil

4 tsp (20 mL) apple cider vinegar (see page 12)

2 tbsp (30 mL) Ribena (see page 16)

1 tsp (5 mL) Dijon mustard

SPINACH SALAD

8 cups (2 L) lightly packed baby spinach

2 cups (500 mL) ripe, juicy blackberries

4 tsp (20 mL) minced shallot

1 For the dressing, whisk together the oil, vinegar, Ribena, and Dijon in a small bowl.

2 For the salad, rinse the spinach under cold running water. Place in a salad spinner and spin-dry, or pat dry on paper towels. Place in a large bowl.

3 Just before serving, rinse the blackberries gently under cold running water. Place on paper towels (or on a clean tea towel that you don't mind staining) and pat dry.

4 Pour the salad dressing over the spinach and toss well. Divide the spinach evenly among 4 plates. Sprinkle each salad with ½ cup (125 mL) blackberries and 1 tsp (5 mL) minced shallot.

TEEN ALERT

The Center for Young Women's Health at Children's Hospital Boston recommends that teenage girls eat 3 cups (750 mL) of dark green vegetables per week, or about ½ cup (125 mL) every day, not only for the rich nutrient base, but also for the vitamin K needed to build healthy bones.

PER SERVING: 127 CALORIES, 5 G TOTAL FAT, 0.4 G SATURATED FAT, 0 G TRANS FAT, 97 MG SODIUM, 17.9 G CARBOHYDRATE, 7 G FIBRE, 41.5 G SUGARS, 4 G PROTEIN

DIABETES FOOD CHOICE VALUES PER SERVING: 1 CARBOHYDRATE, ½ MEAT AND ALTERNATIVES, 1 FAT

Spinach Salad with Apple

A version of this recipe appeared in my first cookbook back in 1998. I had just finished shooting three seasons of Harrowsmith Country Life.

I really wanted to call that book Bite Me!*, but my publishers at the time were not impressed. Shocked and appalled would be a better description. They felt that it was really too rude even for me, and we settled on* Lick the Spoon! *Almost 12 years later, a book came out called* Bite Me, *which, apparently, hasn't offended anyone. I always knew I was ahead of the times.*

MAKES 4 SERVINGS | ONE SERVING = ONE PLATEFUL

CREAMY MAPLE DRESSING

- 1/4 cup (60 mL) low-fat mayonnaise
- 2 tbsp (30 mL) apple cider vinegar (see page 12)
- 1 tbsp (15 mL) pure maple syrup (see page 14)

SPINACH SALAD

- 8 cups (2 L) lightly packed baby spinach
- 1 large sweet red pepper
- 1 Honeycrisp apple, scrubbed and patted dry
- 1/4 cup (60 mL) coarsely chopped walnuts
- 8 thin slices red onion

1 For the dressing, whisk together the mayonnaise, vinegar, and maple syrup in a small bowl. Set aside.

2 For the salad, rinse the spinach under cold running water. Place in a salad spinner and spin-dry, or pat dry on paper towels. Place in a large bowl.

3 Julienne the red pepper, discarding the seeds. (See page 18 for instructions on how to julienne. Just in case you can't be bothered, it means to cut into really thin slices.) Add the pepper to the spinach.

4 Cut the apple into quarters and remove the core. Cut each quarter into 4 slices. Set aside. (The apple slices won't turn brown by the time you need them, unless your mom calls and you end up talking on the phone for an hour.)

5 Add the dressing to the spinach and red pepper and toss well. Divide the salad evenly among 4 plates. (I like the way this salad looks on large white or black plates.)

6 Divide the apple slices evenly among the 4 salads. Sprinkle each salad with 1 tbsp (15 mL) chopped walnuts, then top with 2 slices of red onion. Serve right away and get ready for your guests to ask for seconds—oops, there aren't any!

PER SERVING: 162 CALORIES, 8.6 G TOTAL FAT, 0.6 G SATURATED FAT, 0 G TRANS FAT, 206 MG SODIUM, 18.8 G CARBOHYDRATE, 4 G FIBRE, 7.9 G SUGARS, 4 G PROTEIN

DIABETES FOOD CHOICE VALUES PER SERVING: 1 CARBOHYDRATE, 1/2 MEAT AND ALTERNATIVES, 1 1/2 FAT

Asian-Style Chicken and Watercress Soup

This mildly spicy soup is a great appetizer for a cold winter night. It contains immune-enhancing shiitake mushrooms and garlic, plus ginger and red pepper flakes to help you breath better, all in one bowl.

MAKES 6 CUPS (1.5 L) | ONE SERVING = 3 CUPS (750 ML) AS A MAIN COURSE, 1½ CUPS (375 ML) AS AN APPETIZER

INGREDIENTS

- 4 large cloves garlic
- 8 oz (250 g) shiitake mushrooms, rinsed, drained, and patted dry
- 8 oz (250 g) skinless, boneless chicken thighs (about 2 or 3 small thighs)
- 4 cups (1 L) watercress
- 1 cup (250 mL) boiling water
- 1 tbsp (15 mL) miso paste (see page 14)
- 1 tbsp (15 mL) canola oil
- 3 cups (750 mL) lowest-sodium chicken broth (85 mg sodium per cup/250 mL; see page 7)
- 1 tbsp (15 mL) finely chopped fresh ginger
- 1 tsp (5 mL) red pepper flakes
- ½ cup (125 mL) thinly sliced green onions
- ½ cup (125 mL) chopped fresh cilantro (optional)

1 Mince the garlic and set aside. Remove the stems from the shiitake mushrooms (reserve them for stock or discard). Thinly slice the mushrooms caps and set aside.

2 Wash your hands. Cut the chicken into 1-inch (2.5 cm) pieces and set aside on a clean plate. Wash your hands and cutting board really well. (I keep a separate cutting board to use for raw meat and fish.)

3 Swish the watercress in a clean sink of cold water to make sure there isn't any sand or dirt clinging to it. Place in a salad spinner and spin-dry, or pat dry on paper towels. Chop the watercress coarsely and set aside.

4 Mix together the boiling water and miso paste in a small bowl, and set aside.

5 Heat a large saucepan over medium heat. Add the oil, then the mushrooms. Let the mushrooms cook until they're lightly browned, 3 to 5 minutes; no bumping them around, just leave them alone. Add the garlic and sauté for 1 minute.

6 Add the broth and bring to a boil. Add the chicken. Reduce the heat to a simmer and cook, uncovered, until the chicken is no longer pink inside, 5 to 7 minutes. Add the watercress, miso mixture, ginger, and red pepper flakes. Cook, stirring, until the watercress is wilted, about 2 minutes.

7 Ladle the soup into deep, Asian-style soup bowls. Sprinkle each portion with green onions and cilantro (if using).

PER MAIN-COURSE SERVING (3 CUPS/750 ML): 385 CALORIES, 16.6 G TOTAL FAT, 3.3 G SATURATED FAT, 0.3 G TRANS FAT, 552 MG SODIUM, 25.3 G CARBOHYDRATE, 6 G FIBRE, 8.7 G SUGARS, 34 G PROTEIN

DIABETES FOOD CHOICE VALUES PER MAIN-COURSE SERVING (3 CUPS/750 ML): 1½ CARBOHYDRATE, 4½ MEAT AND ALTERNATIVES, ½ FAT

Watercress-Grapefruit Salad with Orange Dressing

A terrific blend of peppery greens with tart-sweet notes coming from the grapefruit and dried cranberries, this salad is beautiful to look at and fabulous to eat. It's good enough for company, but don't save it for special occasions; for heart health, eat it once a week.

MAKES 4 SERVINGS | ONE SERVING = ONE PLATEFUL

1 For the salad, swish the watercress in a clean sink of cold water to make sure there isn't any sand or dirt clinging to it. Place in a salad spinner and spin-dry, or pat dry on paper towels. Chop the watercress into 2-inch (5 cm) pieces. Place in a large bowl and set aside.

2 Scrub the grapefruit. Peel the fruit and cut into segments (see page 24). Set aside.

3 For the dressing, whisk together the oil, orange juice concentrate, vinegar, and honey in a small bowl.

4 Pour the dressing over the watercress and toss well. Divide the watercress evenly among 4 plates.

5 Divide the grapefruit evenly among the salads. Sprinkle each salad with 1 tbsp (15 mL) dried cranberries.

PER SERVING: 105 CALORIES, 3.8 G TOTAL FAT, 0 G SATURATED FAT, 0 G TRANS FAT, 8 MG SODIUM, 18.5 G CARBOHYDRATE, 2 G FIBRE, 14 G SUGARS, 1 G PROTEIN

DIABETES FOOD CHOICE VALUES PER SERVING: 1 CARBOHYDRATE, 1 FAT

WATERCRESS-GRAPEFRUIT SALAD

1 bunch watercress

1 large red grapefruit

¼ cup (60 mL) dried cranberries

ORANGE DRESSING

1 tbsp (15 mL) canola oil

1 tbsp (15 mL) frozen orange juice concentrate, thawed (see page 13)

1 tbsp (15 mL) apple cider vinegar (see page 12)

1 tsp (5 mL) honey

WORDS FROM THE WISE

Sir Francis Bacon (1561 – 1626), British scientist, statesman, and philosopher, claimed that watercress could restore "a youthful bloom to women." If that means no wrinkles, sign me up.

HEALTH BITE

Grapefruit contains compounds that may interfere with certain prescription drugs. Check with your doctor.

Watercress 101

Mention watercress and most people conjure up visions of a dainty afternoon tea, but this major player in the leafy green band is more than just a sandwich filler.

Gram for gram, watercress contains more vitamin C than oranges, more calcium than milk, and more iron than spinach. This peppery-tasting green is also rich in cancer-fighting beta-carotene. And 1 cup (250 mL) has only 4 itty-bitty calories, so watercress will make a huge salad for 8 calories, and serve a small town for only 100 calories.

Buy It, Store It

Watercress is sold in bunches. Choose a bright green bunch that's free of any slimy leaves. Avoid bunches that have any yellow leaves, are wilted, or have more stems than leaves. Think perky green with lots of leaves.

Once you get your little treasure home, eat it. Watercress doesn't like living in your fridge, so get it onto your plate ASAP.

Watercress and Egg Salad for One

Once a week I hard-cook—not hard-boil (see sidebar)—several eggs to have on hand for a snack, for a main-course salad, or to put in a sandwich.

Eggs really are nature's perfect little package. They are loaded with vitamins, minerals, and choline (which has been shown to play a strong role in brain development and function). One egg provides half your daily requirement of choline. It also contains 70 calories and 6 grams of protein, and provides your body with 6% of its daily recommended intake of iron.

According to Canada's Food Guide, two hard-cooked eggs equal one serving of Meat and Alternatives.

Eggs got a lot of heat years ago when the Food Fear du Jour was cholesterol. Yes, eggs do contain cholesterol, but the major dietary contributors to our cholesterol levels are actually saturated fats and trans fats.

There are people who are sensitive to cholesterol in foods and need to watch their diets more closely, but the majority of healthy adults can eat eggs.

MAKES 1 SERVING

CREAMY GARLIC DRESSING

1 clove garlic

1 tbsp (15 mL) low-fat mayonnaise

1 tbsp (15 mL) fresh lemon juice

WATERCRESS SALAD

1 bunch watercress

2 hard-cooked omega-3 eggs, peeled and coarsely chopped (see below)

1 green onion, thinly sliced

1 For the dressing, mince the garlic and set aside.

2 For the salad, swish the watercress in a clean sink of cold water to make sure there isn't any sand or dirt clinging to it. Place in a salad spinner and spin-dry, or pat dry on paper towels. Chop the watercress into 2-inch (5 cm) pieces. Place on a large plate.

3 Sprinkle the watercress with the eggs and green onion.

4 Whisk together the mayonnaise, lemon juice, and garlic in a small bowl. Drizzle the dressing over the salad.

PER SERVING: 205 CALORIES, 14 G TOTAL FAT, 3.2 G SATURATED FAT, 0 G TRANS FAT, 260 MG SODIUM, 6.7 G CARBOHYDRATE, 1 G FIBRE, 0.9 G SUGARS, 14 G PROTEIN

DIABETES FOOD CHOICE VALUES PER SERVING: ½ CARBOHYDRATE, 2 MEAT AND ALTERNATIVES, 1½ FAT

HOW TO

Never hard-boil an egg; it toughens them up, plus it leaves a dark ring around the yolk. Here is the best method I know for hard-cooking eggs, direct from the experts at Egg Farmers of Canada:

1 Place cold eggs in a single layer in a saucepan. Cover with cold water to come at least 1 inch (2.5 cm) above the top of the eggs.

2 Cover the saucepan and bring quickly to a boil over high heat. Immediately remove the saucepan from the heat. Let the eggs stand in the hot water for 18 to 23 minutes, depending on how creamy you like your yolks. (I let mine stand for 20 minutes.)

3 Drain the eggs and immediately run cold water over them until they're cooled. (Hard-cooked eggs can be stored, covered, in the fridge for up to 1 week.)

TO MARKET, TO MARKET

My favourite time on the culinary calendar is when the local farmers market opens at my neighbourhood civic centre. Come hell or high water, I leap out of bed on that Tuesday morning of the third week in May. I arrive sans makeup, with my trusty reusable bags or bundle buggy, and sprint across the lawn to discover the week's treasures.

I'm there rain or shine with my change purse, shopping, chatting, learning what's coming into season, and getting ideas about how to cook some unusual fruit or vegetable. It's like going to Foodie Disney World — no rides, but thrills nonetheless.

Sometimes I play *Plan Your Dinner Party Around What's Available*; other times I just let the smells and sights dictate the entire week's menus.

One of the best parts about buying local, just-picked produce is that because it's so incredibly fresh, it's more nutrient dense and lasts much longer in your fridge.

If you're a newbie to shopping at a farmers market, here are some tips to help you navigate Playland.

Before you leave home:

- Pack a cooler and a cold source like ice packs. Those just-picked blackberries will become smoosh if you don't take care of them on the way home.
- Bring small change and small bills. Don't expect a farmer to be thrilled giving you change for a twenty when you only spent about 50¢ on some radishes.
- Pack your own bags. Embracing a farmers market isn't just about the freshness and flavours of homegrown, it's also about keeping our environment green. Put your money where your mouth is and bring your own bags.
- A buggy, a wagon, or a teenager are all great to take with you for the heavy stuff. Sure, the teen may grumble, but after the first whiff of a cinnamon bun from the bakeshop vendor, he'll be putty in your hands.
- Arrive early to avoid disappointment. I missed the first crop of asparagus the one morning I slept in.

When you arrive:

- Take a walkabout before you get caught up in farmers market flurry. Circle the market to see what's available, what looks fantastic, and who has the best price.
- Buy the heavy stuff first. That way you won't squish the tomatoes with your Hubbard squash.
- Experiment with fruits and veggies you've never tried before. Most farmers are only too happy to share a recipe or cooking tip.
- Become a regular and get to know your farmers. I love chatting with my heirloom tomato guy from Thiessen Farms in Jordan Station, Ontario. The morning his heirloom tomatoes appear, I'm in tomato heaven. Like all real farmers he is knowledgeable about the variety he's selling, has tips on storage and handling, and can give you serving ideas. (For more information, check out thiessenfarms.blogspot.com.)

The day the farmers pack up their treasures and head home for the winter was always a sad one for me until I discovered local, all-season markets. In Toronto, we have the St. Lawrence Market and my new favourite community market, the market at Artspace Wychwood Barns. Lucky Vancouverites have Granville Island Public Market all year round, but then they don't really *have* winter, do they?

heirloom tomatoes

10

Herbs and Spices:
A Little Bit Goes a Long Way

I don't add salt to my cooking. I use salt three times in this entire book and all three times it's added for a function. (No prizes, but see if you can spot the three recipes with salt in them.) I add flavour to my cooking with herbs and spices. They are my salt.

Don't be shocked when you see the amount of herbs and spices I use in my recipes. I love the way they add pizzazz to food, but I *really* love the way they can add good years to our long-term health.

GOOD FOR YOU

Herbs and spices are treasure troves of antioxidants, which can block the formation of harmful compounds that are associated with aging.

Rosemary, thyme, oregano, basil, mint, cinnamon, cloves, and turmeric—plus my favourite, allium-garlic—are all very rich in these disease-lowering antioxidants, and you'll find my recipes all teem with them.

THE POWER OF HERBS

Adding herbs like fresh or dried oregano to dishes boosts your body's ability to fight bad bacteria. Gram for gram, oregano is believed to have the most powerful antioxidant activity of any food. But before you add 2 cups of oregano to your spaghetti sauce, think frequency rather than quantity.

OREGANO
ROSEMARY
PARSLEY
BASIL

Quick and Easy Greek Salad

With most provinces offering locally grown hothouse cucumbers and grape tomatoes year round, you can start making this colourful salad before the field cucumbers and tomatoes are even planted.

MAKES 4 CUPS (1 L) | ONE SERVING = 1 CUP (250 ML)

1 Wash, drain, and dry the tomatoes and cucumber.

2 Cut the tomatoes in half and place in a salad bowl.

3 Cut the cucumber lengthwise into quarters, then slice into pieces about the same size as the tomato halves. Add to the salad bowl, along with the basil, olives, and oregano.

4 Drizzle the salad with the oil and vinegar, and toss well. Sprinkle the cheese over the salad and toss again.

PER SERVING: 109 CALORIES, 8.3 G TOTAL FAT, 2.8 G SATURATED FAT, 0 G TRANS FAT, 303 MG SODIUM, 6.9 G CARBOHYDRATE, 2 G FIBRE, 2.8 G SUGARS, 4 G PROTEIN

DIABETES FOOD CHOICE VALUES PER SERVING: ½ CARBOHYDRATE, ½ MEAT AND ALTERNATIVES, 1½ FAT

INGREDIENTS

2 cups (500 mL) grape tomatoes
½ unpeeled English cucumber
¼ cup (60 mL) fresh basil chiffonade (see page 18)
8 kalamata olives, pitted and chopped (see page 23)
2 tsp (10 mL) finely chopped fresh oregano
1 tbsp (15 mL) extra virgin olive oil
1 tbsp (15 mL) red wine vinegar
½ cup (125 mL) crumbled goat's milk feta cheese (see page 14)

WORDS FROM THE WISE

James Hargrove, associate professor of food and nutrition at the University of Georgia in the US, says, "Because herbs and spices have a very low calorie content and are relatively inexpensive, they're a great way to get a lot of antioxidant and anti-inflammatory power into your diet."

And Diane Hartle, of the UGA College of Pharmacy, says this: "If you set up a good herb and spice cabinet and season your food liberally, you could double or even triple the medicinal value of your meal without increasing the caloric content."

Grilled Ratatouille Salad

Ratatouille is a marriage of heart-healthy veggies, immune-enhancing herbs, and cholesterol-lowering eggplant. Perfect.

Don't worry about the exact sizes of the vegetables for this salad; it will taste great no matter what size they are.

MAKES 8 TO 9 CUPS (2 TO 2.25 L) | ONE SERVING = 1 CUP (250 ML)

1 For the grilled veggies, preheat the barbecue to high. Peel the garlic cloves but do not mince. Wrap the garlic loosely in a piece of foil and set aside.

2 Since there are a lot of veggies, you'll have to cook them in batches. Put the eggplant, onions, and the garlic, in its cute little foil package, on the grill. Reduce the heat to medium-high.

3 Close the lid and grill the eggplant and onions, turning once, until they are slightly blackened on both sides, 8 to 10 minutes. (No, there isn't any fat on them. And no, they won't stick if your grill is clean.) Remove the eggplant first and place in a large bowl. Top with the cooked onions. (There is a method to my madness; keep reading.) Leave the garlic on the grill.

4 Put the red peppers, zucchini, and mushroom caps on the grill, arranging the mushrooms gill side up.

5 Grill the peppers and zucchini, turning once, until they are slightly blackened on both sides, 6 to 10 minutes. Remove the peppers and zucchini and place on top of the onions.

6 Watch the garlic; it takes 15 to 20 minutes to cook. How's it doing? Is it soft yet? If so, take it off the grill and set aside.

7 Flip the mushrooms and grill them until they are tender, 8 to 12 minutes. Remove the mushrooms and place on top of the zucchini. (Layering the vegetables is going to help them soften up without the aid of oil.)

GRILLED VEGGIES

3 large cloves garlic
1 lb (500 g) baby eggplants (about 3), cut into ½-inch (1 cm) slices
2 onions, cut into ½-inch (1 cm) slices
2 sweet red peppers, seeded and quartered
2 zucchini, quartered lengthwise
3 portobello mushrooms, stems removed

BELLS AND WHISTLES

⅔ cup (160 mL) thinly sliced sun-dried tomatoes (not packed in oil; see below)
⅓ cup (80 mL) fresh basil chiffonade (see page 18)
2 tbsp (30 mL) capers, drained and rinsed (see page 12)
1 tbsp (15 mL) finely chopped fresh oregano
2 tbsp (30 mL) extra virgin olive oil

WHAT IS . . . ?

Sun-dried tomatoes come in two versions: packed in oil in a jar, or dry in a bag. We want the dry ones that come in a bag. Grocery Store Search: They're usually in the produce section of the supermarket.

8 Back in the kitchen, cut all the grilled veggies into 1-inch (2.5 cm) pieces. Put the veggies back in the bowl with the onions. Set aside while you prep the bells and whistles.

9 For the bells and whistles, add the sun-dried tomatoes, basil, capers, and oregano to the grilled veggies. Toss well.

10 By this time, the garlic will have cooled in its package. Remove it and place in a small bowl. Using a fork, smash up the garlic. Add the oil and blend well.

11 Add the garlic mixture to the salad and toss really well. Serve right away or let the salad sit at room temperature for up to 1 hour.

PER SERVING: 98 CALORIES, 4 G TOTAL FAT, 0.6 G SATURATED FAT, 0 G TRANS FAT, 110 MG SODIUM, 14.5 G CARBOHYDRATE, 5 G FIBRE, 7.4 G SUGARS, 3 G PROTEIN

DIABETES FOOD CHOICE VALUES PER SERVING: ½ CARBOHYDRATE, 1 FAT

MAKEOVERS

This grilled salad makes enough for two dinners. Eat half tonight, then tomorrow toss the leftovers with 2 cups (500 mL) cooked whole-grain fusilli pasta, sprinkle with 1 oz (30 g) finely grated Asiago cheese, and dinner is ready.

GIVE IT A TWIST

In the spring, substitute asparagus for the zucchini. Leave the spears whole, grill them until tender, then cut into 4 equal pieces and add to the salad.

Greek-Style Grilled Chicken

We live really close to the Greek neighbourhood along Danforth Avenue in Toronto. This chicken is a dead ringer for the grilled chicken you can get at most of the restaurants on the Danforth.

Serve it with Quick and Easy Greek Salad (page 227) and homemade Tzatziki (page 273). Make sure you're using the right size garlic clove to get the garlic flavour this recipe needs. See page 15 for a picture of different sizes of garlic cloves.

Feel free to double, triple, or quadruple this recipe, but you'll need a bigger bag or dish in which to marinate the chicken.

Marinating the chicken overnight will intensify its flavour, but for an even more pronounced hit of garlic, freeze it in the marinade for up to one month. Thaw the chicken overnight in the refrigerator before grilling.

MAKES 4 SERVINGS | ONE SERVING = 1½ TO 2 THIGHS

INGREDIENTS

- 6 large cloves garlic (or use Toppits Crushed Garlic Cubes; see page 137)
- 1 lemon
- 2 tbsp (30 mL) canola oil
- 1 tbsp (15 mL) dried oregano leaves
- ½ tsp (2.5 mL) cracked black pepper
- 1 lb (500 g) skinless, boneless chicken thighs (6 to 8 thighs)

1 Mince the garlic and set aside.

2 Wash and dry the lemon. Using a Microplane grater (see page 8), remove the zest from the lemon and set aside. With your palm, roll the lemon on the counter (this makes it yield more juice), then cut in half and squeeze out ¼ cup (60 mL) juice.

3 Whisk together the lemon juice, oil, oregano, and pepper. Add the lemon zest and garlic, and mix well.

4 Wash your hands. Place the chicken into a medium resealable plastic bag or a non-metallic baking dish. Wash your hands again. Pour in the marinade. If using a bag, gently press the air out and seal the bag. Massage the bag to help the marinade coat the chicken. If using a baking dish, make sure the marinade coats the chicken well. Cover the dish tightly.

5 Refrigerate for at least 60 minutes or up to 12 hours. If using a bag, massage it occasionally. If using a dish, turn the chicken occasionally.

GIVE IT A TWIST

Slice the grilled chicken into thin diagonal slices, and serve in a 100% whole-grain whole wheat pita with chopped tomatoes, grilled onions, and Tzatziki (see page 273).

6 Preheat an indoor grill or outdoor barbecue to medium. Remove the chicken from the fridge and let it sit at room temperature for 5 minutes.

7 Remove the chicken from the marinade, discarding the marinade. Grill the chicken, with the lid closed and turning the chicken occasionally, until the chicken is no longer pink inside and a meat thermometer inserted into each piece of chicken registers 165°F (74°C), 7 to 15 minutes.

8 Remove the chicken from the grill and let it sit on a clean plate for 5 minutes before serving.

PER SERVING: 243 CALORIES, 14.9 G TOTAL FAT, 3.2 G SATURATED FAT, 0 G TRANS FAT, 84 MG SODIUM, 2.9 G CARBOHYDRATE, 1 G FIBRE, 0.4 G SUGARS, 24 G PROTEIN

DIABETES FOOD CHOICE VALUES PER SERVING: 3½ MEAT AND ALTERNATIVES, 1 FAT, 1 EXTRA

WEEKEND WONDER

This is a great recipe to take up to the cottage, especially if you're a guest. Marinate the chicken in a resealable plastic bag and pack it in a cooler with a cold source like ice packs. When you arrive at the cottage, all you have to do is fire up the grill.

Jerk Marinade

Jerk is more than just a highly spiced combination of antioxidant-rich green onions, thyme, allspice, cinnamon, nutmeg, and hot spices; it's a process that doesn't work if you're in a hurry.

The chicken, fish, or tofu needs time to marinate, the grill needs to be clean and fired up, and that protein needs to cook slowly. All these elements need to be in place to make the end result spicy-sweet and full of flavour.

This jerk recipe is on the mild side so that kids and friends who are spicy-food-challenged can enjoy the fabulous flavours. If you want it spicy, you'll need to add your favourite hot sauce.

You really need a food processor to make this marinade (see page 8 to read why you should buy one).

MAKES ABOUT 1 CUP (250 ML)

INGREDIENTS

1 onion, quartered
4 green onions (green and white parts), quartered
1 tsp (5 mL) honey
1 tsp (5 mL) ground thyme
1 tsp (5 mL) ground allspice
1 tsp (5 mL) cinnamon
1 tsp (5 mL) cracked black pepper
½ tsp (2.5 mL) grated nutmeg
½ tsp (2.5 mL) red pepper flakes
3 tbsp (45 mL) lower-sodium soy sauce (see page 17)
1 tbsp (15 mL) canola oil
1 tbsp (15 mL) apple cider vinegar (see page 12)

1 Whirl all the ingredients in a food processor until they form a thick paste. (Refrigerate in an airtight container for up to three days.) Use to marinate poultry, fish, or tofu.

PER CUP (250 ML): 246 CALORIES, 15.3 G TOTAL FAT, 1.5 G SATURATED FAT, 0.3 G TRANS FAT, 1,757 MG SODIUM, 29 G CARBOHYDRATE, 7 G FIBRE, 10.9 G SUGARS, 6 G PROTEIN

DIABETES FOOD CHOICE VALUES PER CUP (250 ML): 1½ CARBOHYDRATE, 1 MEAT AND ALTERNATIVES, 2½ FAT

HEALTH BITE

Research done at the Department of Animal Sciences and Industry and the Food Science Institute at Kansas State University by Daniel Y. C. Fung, an expert on E. coli, has found that preparing food with garlic, oregano, cinnamon, cloves, and sage reduces the chances of E. coli and salmonella bacteria growing in the food.

Of course the best way to reduce the incidence of E. coli is to cook meat properly to the correct internal temperature.

Jerk Chicken

I lived on Queen Street East in Toronto when I was in The Second City comedy troupe. Every day I'd walk to The Old Fire Hall, SC's mainstage location at the time, and go right by a Caribbean restaurant called The Real Jerk, with its tantalizing smells. I was a starving actress and rarely went to a sit-down restaurant, and it killed me to just walk on by. It wasn't until about 15 years later that I got to taste the restaurant's specialty, Jerk Chicken. It was totally worth the wait.

MAKES 8 SERVINGS | ONE SERVING = 1½ TO 2 THIGHS

INGREDIENTS

Jerk Marinade (facing page)

2 lb (1 kg) boneless, skinless chicken thighs (12 to 16 thighs)

1 Pour the marinade into a large resealable plastic bag or a non-metallic baking dish. Wash your hands. Add the chicken to the bag or dish. Wash your hands again. If using a bag, gently press the air out and seal the bag. Massage the bag to make sure the marinade is coating the chicken. If using a baking dish, make sure the marinade coats the chicken well. Cover the dish tightly.

2 Refrigerate for at least 12 hours or up to 24 hours. If using a bag, massage it occasionally. If using a dish, turn the chicken occasionally and spoon the marinade over it occasionally.

3 Preheat an indoor grill or outdoor barbecue to medium-low. Remove the chicken from the fridge and let it sit at room temperature for 5 minutes.

4 Wash your hands. Remove the chicken from the marinade, discarding the marinade. Put the chicken on the barbecue. Wash your hands again. Grill the chicken, with the lid closed and turning the chicken often, until the chicken is no longer pink inside and a meat thermometer inserted into each piece of chicken registers 165°F (74°C), 20 to 35 minutes, depending on the thickness of the chicken.

5 Remove the chicken from the grill and let it sit on a clean plate for 5 minutes before serving.

MAKEOVERS

This recipe makes enough for eight people so, if you're not feeding a crowd, you can either cut the recipe in half or cook up the whole thing and serve the leftovers cold the next day. It's a fabulous make-ahead dish to take on a picnic or to the cottage.

GRILLING TIPS

For best grilling results, always start with a clean grill. Turn grill to high, preheat, and then brush to make sure any blackened bits have been removed.

PER SERVING: 213 CALORIES, 11 G TOTAL FAT, 2.9 G SATURATED FAT, 0 G TRANS FAT, 302 MG SODIUM, 3.6 G CARBOHYDRATE, 1 G FIBRE, 1.4 G SUGARS, 24 G PROTEIN

DIABETES FOOD CHOICE VALUES PER SERVING: 3½ MEAT AND ALTERNATIVES, 1 EXTRA

11

Mushrooms:
Not Your Average Little Balls of Fungi

Mushrooms may be little balls of fungi, but they carry a lot of clout. Four or five mushrooms contain a legion of B vitamins plus the minerals selenium, copper, potassium, iron, and zinc. Those same four or five mushrooms, depending on the variety, even offer 1 to 2 grams of fibre.

Mushrooms are the only vegetable that contains vitamin D, and the winner in this category is the shiitake mushroom. One serving of shiitakes supplies 48% of the recommended daily value for this important sunshine vitamin.

Mushrooms also contain antioxidants, those fearsome fighters against disease. The antioxidant specific to mushrooms is called L-ergothioneine. (Try saying that one fast four times in a row.) Shiitake, maitake, and oyster mushrooms have the highest levels of this powerful antioxidant, followed by portobello and cremini (brown) mushrooms, then white or button mushrooms.

MUSHROOM PRIMER

Most supermarkets have a dizzying array of mushrooms available these days. Here are some of my favourites, all of which are pictured on page 239:

WHITE (A.K.A. BUTTON)

These are those cute little mushrooms that everyone's familiar with, and a good choice for the rookie mushroom eater. They have a mild, woodsy flavour and can be sautéed, used in side dishes, or added to soups.

CREMINI

Sometimes described in stores as brown mushrooms, and usually about the same size as button mushrooms, these fungi are very popular. They have a rich, earthy flavour, and are delicious sautéed, baked, or added to rice, pasta, stews, or soups.

OYSTER

Oyster mushrooms are light grey in colour, with a velvety feel. They're extremely delicate and have a very mild flavour. Serve as a side dish rather than using them as an ingredient.

PORCINI

With their deep, rich flavour and a hint of smoke, these mushrooms are used mostly in Italian-style dishes, and are fabulous in a risotto. Look for dried porcini in larger grocery stores.

The bottom brown mushroom isn't fresh; the top one is.

PORTOBELLO

These are the really big mushrooms that look like small Frisbees. They have a deep, rich, earthy, meaty flavour and are great grilled or baked.

SHIITAKE

This is the superstar of the mushroom world. Shiitakes have a definite woodsy flavour and can be sautéed, stir-fried, or added to rice or pasta dishes. Cook only the caps because the stems are very tough. Save the stems for making soup stock. Shiitakes are also available dried.

BUY IT, STORE IT

Gills aren't just how fish breathe. Gills on a mushroom are the darker-coloured, fan-like strands on the underside of the mushroom cap.

In white and cremini (brown) mushrooms, the gills shouldn't be visible. For all other types of mushrooms, tight gills are the key. The more open the gills, the less fresh or firm the mushroom will be (see photo). Pick out mushrooms that look and feel firm, not mushy, and that are dry and free of spots.

Most stores offer brown paper bags for loose mushrooms. The paper allows the mushrooms to breathe, unlike plastic, which acts as a slime accelerator.

Mushrooms also come in pre-packaged containers. Check them out as best you can. If you're buying packaged mushrooms, leave them in the package until you use them. Once you open the package, store any leftovers in a paper bag.

Store mushrooms in the fridge and eat them within a couple of days of purchase. Depending on how fresh they are, they can last up to one week.

The Great Mushroom Cleaning Debate still rages. To wash or not to wash, that is the question. Tons of foodies will say *don't* wash mushrooms. But after talking to many mushroom experts, I wash them lightly under cold running water, let them drain in a colander, and then pat them dry. But I *only* do this just before I'm going to use them. Remember that "lightly wash" doesn't mean drowning or soaking them in a sinkful of water. All you really want to do is get the surface dirt off.

Marinated Mushrooms

A heart-healthy immune-enhancing hors d'oeuvre—imagine that! Serve these with a glass of red wine and feel extremely virtuous.

MAKES 40 MARINATED MUSHROOMS | ONE SERVING = 5 MUSHROOMS

1 Mince the garlic and set aside.

2 In a 4-cup (1 L) glass jar with a tight-fitting lid (I use a large glass canning jar), combine the vinegars, oil, maple syrup, basil, thyme, oregano, and 2 tbsp (30 mL) water. Shake well.

3 Wash the mushrooms gently under cold running water. Let them drain in a colander, then pat dry.

4 Add the garlic to the jar. Screw on the lid tightly and shake well.

5 Add the mushrooms to the jar. Screw on the lid tightly and roll the jar around to coat those little babies.

6 Marinate the mushrooms in the fridge for up to 3 days (any longer and they turn mushy). Give the jar a little shake and a roll a couple times a day, whenever you're in the fridge foraging for food.

7 To serve, drain the mushrooms well and either place on a serving plate lined with kale leaves or pile them in a bowl on their own. (Don't use lettuce to line the plate; the acid from the vinegar will make the leaves wilt really quickly, and then you'll have a plate of beautiful mushrooms lying on some dead-looking lettuce.) Serve with toothpicks.

PER SERVING: 51 CALORIES, 1.2 G TOTAL FAT, 0 G SATURATED FAT, 0 G TRANS FAT, 144 MG SODIUM, 9.4 G CARBOHYDRATE, 1 G FIBRE, 6.1 G SUGARS, 2 G PROTEIN

DIABETES FOOD CHOICE VALUES PER SERVING: ½ CARBOHYDRATE

INGREDIENTS

2 large cloves garlic
¼ cup (60 mL) apple cider vinegar (page 12)
¼ cup (60 mL) balsamic vinegar
¼ cup (60 mL) canola oil
1 tbsp (15 mL) pure maple syrup (see page 14)
1 tbsp (15 mL) dried basil leaves (don't use fresh; the leaves get slimy)
1 tbsp (15 mL) dried thyme leaves
1 tbsp (15 mL) dried oregano leaves
40 small cremini or white mushrooms

HEALTH BITE

Lab research has shown that mushroom extracts have anti-tumour properties, and can stimulate the immune system in animals.

king oyster
cremini
white
porcini
oyster
portobello
dried shiitake
fresh shiitake

Stuffed Mushrooms

In my final year of home economics at the University of British Columbia we had to take a demonstration class that required us to conduct a live 20-minute demonstration using a food of our choice. After much research, I settled on mushrooms.

In the early 1970s in Vancouver, while eating magic mushrooms was almost run-of-the-mill, eating regular mushrooms was considered exotic.

I practised preparing and cooking mushrooms for weeks, and by the end of that live demo, I was totally hooked on cooking in front of a crowd. Who knew that this class would be the beginning of my TV career as an on-camera professional home economist?

This is a spin on one of the recipes I demonstrated way back in the '70s when I was young and wrinkle-free.

MAKES 24 STUFFED MUSHROOMS | ONE SERVING = 1 MUSHROOM

INGREDIENTS

1 large clove garlic
24 medium to large cremini mushrooms
1 tbsp (15 mL) extra virgin olive oil
1 large shallot, diced
1/4 cup (60 mL) finely chopped walnuts
1 tbsp (15 mL) finely chopped fresh oregano
1/4 tsp (1 mL) cracked black pepper
2 oz (60 g) soft goat cheese, crumbled

1 Preheat the oven to 350°F (180°C). Line a 13- × 9-inch (3.5 L) metal baking pan with parchment paper. Place a wire rack on top of the parchment. (It's all about easy cleanup.)

2 Mince the garlic and set aside.

3 Wash the mushrooms gently under cold running water. Remove the stems, reserving both the stems and the caps. Let them drain in a colander, then pat dry.

4 Place the mushroom caps on the wire rack, gill side up, and set aside. Dice the mushroom stems and set aside.

5 Heat a large non-stick skillet over medium heat. Add oil, then the shallot, and sauté until the shallot is soft, 3 to 5 minutes.

6 Add the diced mushroom stems and garlic, and sauté until the mushrooms are tender, about 5 minutes.

7 Add the walnuts, oregano, and pepper, and sauté for 1 minute.

8 Remove the skillet from the heat and stir in the cheese.

9 Stuff each mushroom cap with 1 heaping teaspoon (7 mL) of the walnut mixture. You may have to pack it in. Bake until the filling is bubbly, about 20 minutes. Let cool slightly before serving.

PER STUFFED MUSHROOM: 25 CALORIES, 1.9 G TOTAL FAT, 0.5 G SATURATED FAT, 0 G TRANS FAT, 22 MG SODIUM, 1.3 G CARBOHYDRATE, 0 G FIBRE, 0.2 G SUGARS, 1 G PROTEIN

DIABETES FOOD CHOICE VALUES PER STUFFED MUSHROOM: ½ FAT, 1 EXTRA

HEALTH BITE

A study published in the International Journal of Cancer that looked at more than 2,000 women in China found that the women who ate more fresh and dried mushrooms had a lower risk for breast cancer. The risk was even lower for the women who also drank green tea every day.

Chicken Soup for Your Cold

Culinary myth or a fact? Chicken soup is good for a cold.

If you knew it was a fact, give yourself a pat on the back. It's true. The steam from "Grandma's Penicillin" helps you breathe better, and keeps you hydrated. The next time anyone in your family gets a cold, make this quick and easy soup.

Adults, if you need some zip, add some cayenne or your favourite hot sauce.

MAKES 10 CUPS (2.5L) | ONE SERVING = 2 CUPS (500 ML)

1 Bring the broth to a boil in a large pot over medium-high heat.

2 While the broth is coming to a boil, mince the garlic and set aside.

3 Dice the onion, and thinly slice the celery and carrots. Set aside.

4 Wash the mushrooms gently under cold running water. Let them drain in a colander, then cut them in half. Set aside.

5 By now the broth should be boiling. Add the garlic, onion, celery, carrots, mushrooms, and quinoa. Bring back to a boil. Reduce the heat to a simmer and cook, covered, for 12 minutes.

6 Meanwhile, wash your hands, then cut the chicken into 1-inch (2.5 cm) pieces. Wash your hands and cutting board really well. (I keep a separate cutting board to use for raw meat and fish.)

7 Add the chicken to the pot. Bring back to a boil. Reduce the heat to medium-low, stir well, and cover the pot. Cook gently until the chicken is no longer pink inside, about 8 to 10 minutes.

8 Stir in the frozen peas and parsley. Serve.

PER SERVING: 229 CALORIES, 2.5 G TOTAL FAT, 0 G SATURATED FAT, 0 G TRANS FAT, 249 MG SODIUM, 18.8 G CARBOHYDRATE, 4 G FIBRE, 7.2 G SUGARS, 33 G PROTEIN

DIABETES FOOD CHOICE VALUES PER SERVING: 1 CARBOHYDRATE, 4½ MEAT AND ALTERNATIVES

INGREDIENTS

6 cups (1.5 L) lower-sodium chicken broth (see page 7)

4 to 6 large cloves garlic

1 onion

2 stalks celery

2 large unpeeled carrots, scrubbed

8 oz (250 g) cremini mushrooms

¼ cup (60 mL) whole-grain quinoa (see page 152)

1 lb (500 g) skinless, boneless chicken breast

1 cup (250 mL) frozen peas

½ cup (125 mL) finely chopped parsley

LOAD IT UP

This recipe is also loaded with garlic to help fight viruses. The carrots and mushrooms are there to help your immune system work, and there is plenty of protein from the chicken and the quinoa to keep all systems nourished.

Chicken-Coconut Soup

You wouldn't think someone with Irish, Scots, and English roots would pick an Asian dish as their comfort food, but this soup is definitely mine.

Everyone deals with being sick in their own way. I want someone to check on me, make sure I'm still alive, and bring me tea and chicken-coconut soup.

When my partner, Scott, is sick, he wants to be left alone, in the dark.

When we were first together and I got sick, he looked after me the way he liked being looked after—he left me alone and in the dark. This was not even close to what I wanted, so when I got better, I wrote him a funny list of things to do the next time I got sick.

Sure enough, the next time I was in bed with a bad cold, Scott showed up at the bedroom door with chicken-coconut soup from our favourite Thai restaurant, and singing an Irish lullaby. That was on the list, too.

MAKES 4 CUPS (1 L) | ONE SERVING = 1 CUP (250 ML)

INGREDIENTS

- 1 cup (250 mL) lowest-sodium chicken broth (85 mg sodium per cup / 250 mL; see page 7)
- 1 cup (250 mL) sliced cremini or white mushrooms (6 to 8 medium)
- 2 tbsp (30 mL) fish sauce (see sidebar, next page)
- 1 tbsp (15 mL) finely grated fresh ginger
- ¼ tsp (1 mL) red pepper flakes
- 8 oz (250 g) skinless, boneless chicken breast
- 1 lime, scrubbed well and dried
- 1 cup (250 mL) light coconut milk (see below)
- 1 cup (250 mL) sliced green onions
- ¼ cup (60 mL) finely chopped fresh cilantro

QUICK TIP

I use Thai Kitchen's Lite Coconut Milk. It has 60% fewer calories from fat than regular coconut milk. Shake the can well before opening it. Pour any leftovers into a clean container and store in the fridge for up to three days.

1 Bring the broth to a simmer in a medium saucepan over medium-high heat.

2 Add the mushrooms, fish sauce, ginger, and red pepper flakes to the broth, and bring to a boil. Reduce the heat to a simmer and cook, covered, for 10 minutes.

3 Meanwhile, wash your hands, then cut the chicken across the grain into thin strips. Add the chicken to the saucepan. Wash your hands and cutting board really well. (I keep a separate cutting board to use for raw meat and fish.) Bring the broth mixture back to a boil. Reduce the heat to a simmer, and cook, covered, until the chicken is no longer pink inside, about 8 to 10 minutes.

CONTINUED . . .

4 Meanwhile, using a Microplane grater (see page 8), remove the zest from the lime. With your palm, roll the lime on the counter (this makes it yield more juice), then cut in half and squeeze out 2 tbsp (30 mL) juice.

5 Add the lime zest and juice, coconut milk, green onions, and cilantro to the saucepan. Heat the soup until it is piping hot, but do not let it boil. Stir, then ladle into soup bowls.

PER SERVING: 120 CALORIES, 3.2 G TOTAL FAT, 2.5 G SATURATED FAT, 0 G TRANS FAT, 729 MG SODIUM (SEE SIDEBAR), 5.8 G CARBOHYDRATE, 1 G FIBRE, 1.5 G SUGARS, 17 G PROTEIN

DIABETES FOOD CHOICE VALUES PER SERVING: 2½ MEAT AND ALTERNATIVES, 1 EXTRA

WHAT IS . . . ?

Fish sauce is a fishy-smelling, reddish-brown fermented sauce that's made from fish, salt, and water. It has a powerful punch and is an important ingredient in this recipe. It's also high in sodium, so a little goes a long way. There's 729 mg sodium in 1 cup (250 mL) of this amazing soup. Feel free to reduce the fish sauce by half and that 1 cup (250 mL) will contain only 392 mg sodium. Grocery Store Search: You'll find fish sauce in the Asian section of most large grocery stores. Once opened, store it in the fridge.

Mushrooms with Herbs

Here's my all-time favourite mushroom side dish. It's simple and goes really well with just about anything.

MAKES 2 CUPS (500 ML) — THE DREADED SHRINKAGE STRIKES AGAIN!
ONE SERVING = ½ CUP

1 Wash the mushrooms gently under cold running water. Let them drain in a colander, then pat dry and thinly slice.

2 Finely chop the thyme leaves, or whatever herb you picked.

3 Heat a large non-stick skillet over medium heat. Add the oil, then the mushrooms.

4 Now, here is your big mushroom challenge: don't touch them. Back away and take your wooden spoon with you. You want the mushrooms to brown. Every time you stir them you encourage the mushrooms to release some liquid, which will stew them. We want brown and flavourful, not pale and steamed. You still need to watch them so they don't burn, but only move them around occasionally.

5 When the mushrooms are starting to brown, after about 4 minutes, add the thyme. Cook until the mushrooms are tender and browned, another 4 to 6 minutes.

PER SERVING: 67 CALORIES, 4.3 G TOTAL FAT, 0.5 G SATURATED FAT, 0 G TRANS FAT, 9 MG SODIUM, 5.3 G CARBOHYDRATE, 1 G FIBRE, 2.1 G SUGARS, 3 G PROTEIN

DIABETES FOOD CHOICE VALUES PER SERVING: ½ MEAT AND ALTERNATIVES, 1 FAT, 1 EXTRA

INGREDIENTS

1 lb (500 g) cremini mushrooms

1 tbsp (15 mL) fresh thyme or rosemary (see page 25), or fresh oregano, or a combination

1 tbsp (15 mL) extra virgin olive oil

HOW TO

Overcrowding the skillet and bumping the mushrooms around, instead of letting them brown, will result in steamed, watery mushrooms, not fried, golden brown ones. Use a skillet large enough to hold the mushrooms in a single layer.

Mushroom-Smothered Chicken Thighs

The rustic flavours of chicken and rosemary mixed with earthy mushrooms make this dish perfect fall or winter comfort food. I prefer to use a salty ingredient that has some nutritional value instead of adding salt, which is why the olives can't be eliminated. If you don't like green ones, feel free to use black kalamata olives.

MAKES 4 SERVINGS | ONE SERVING = ONE PLATEFUL

1 Mince the garlic and set aside.

2 Whisk together the lemon juice and Dijon in a small bowl. Set aside.

3 Wash the mushrooms gently under cold running water. Let them drain in a colander, then pat dry. Slice them thinly and set aside.

4 Heat a large non-stick skillet over medium heat. Wash your hands. Add the chicken thighs to the skillet. Wash your hands again. Cook the thighs until they are browned on both sides, about 6 to 8 minutes.

5 While the chicken is doing its thing, finely chop the shallots and the rosemary and set aside. Coarsely chop the olives and set aside.

6 Remove the chicken from the skillet and place on a clean plate. Cover and set aside.

7 Add the mushrooms to the now-empty skillet and cook until they are browned, about 5 minutes. Don't be tempted to bump them around; just let them be. Two rules to live by: never wake a sleeping baby, and never bump a frying mushroom.

8 Add the shallots, rosemary, and garlic that have all been patiently waiting, and sauté for 1 minute. Add the pepper.

INGREDIENTS

4 large cloves garlic
2 tbsp (30 mL) fresh lemon juice
2 tsp (10 mL) grainy Dijon mustard
1 lb (500 g) cremini mushrooms
1 lb (500 g) skinless, boneless chicken thighs (6 to 8 thighs)
3 large shallots
2 tbsp (30 mL) fresh rosemary (see page 25)
8 green olives, pitted
1/4 tsp (1 mL) cracked black pepper

9 Return the chicken to the skillet, along with any juices that are on the plate. Pour the lemon juice mixture over the top and sprinkle with olives. Reduce the heat to a simmer and cook, covered, until the chicken is no longer pink inside and a meat thermometer inserted into each piece of chicken registers 165°F (74°C), about 15 to 20 minutes.

10 Using a slotted spoon, remove the chicken and the mushrooms to a clean bowl. Cover and set aside. Increase the heat to medium and boil the sauce until it has reduced by half, about 2 minutes.

11 Divide the chicken and mushrooms evenly among 4 plates, then spoon the sauce evenly over the top.

PER SERVING: 264 CALORIES, 11.6 G TOTAL FAT, 3 G SATURATED FAT, 0 G TRANS FAT, 288 MG SODIUM, 12.7 G CARBOHYDRATE, 1 G FIBRE, 2.4 G SUGARS, 28 G PROTEIN

DIABETES FOOD CHOICE VALUES PER SERVING: 1 CARBOHYDRATE, 4 MEAT AND ALTERNATIVES

Spring Mushroom Omelette for Two

When my son left for university, and after I stopped crying, I had to rethink the way I cooked. He could eat two to three servings of most things I cooked, so to wrap my head around "serves two" was a challenge, until I rediscovered the wonders of the omelette.

Oh, those nutrient-dense eggs—quick, easy, and economical. Eggs are the perfect answer to many dinner dilemmas.

Serve this power dinner with a green salad to make a quick and easy meal for two.

MAKES 2 SERVINGS | ONE SERVING = HALF AN OMELETTE

INGREDIENTS

4 oz (125 g) shiitake mushrooms
4 oz (125 g) oyster mushrooms
2 tbsp (30 mL) fresh sage leaves
4 omega-3 eggs (see page 13)
½ tsp (2.5 mL) cracked black pepper
1 tbsp (15 mL) extra virgin olive oil
1 large shallot, diced
½ sweet red pepper, seeded and diced
2 oz (60 g) soft goat cheese, crumbled
2 tsp (10 mL) snipped fresh chives

1 Wash the mushrooms gently under cold running water. Remove the stems and save them for the stockpot, or just give them the old heave-ho. Let the mushroom caps drain in a colander, then pat dry.

2 Cut the sage leaves into a chiffonade. (See page 18 for instructions on how to cut something into a chiffonade. Just in case you can't be bothered, it means to cut into very, very thin shreds.) Set aside.

3 Whisk together the eggs and ¼ cup (60 mL) water in a medium bowl. Whisk in the sage and cracked pepper and set aside.

4 Heat a large non-stick skillet over medium heat. Add the oil, then the shallot, and sauté until the shallot is lightly coloured, 2 to 3 minutes. Add the red pepper and sauté for 1 minute.

5 Add the mushrooms and cook, without moving them too much, until lightly browned, 4 to 5 minutes.

6 Pour the egg mixture evenly into the skillet. Cook, without stirring, until the edges start to look set, about 1 minute.

GIVE IT A TWIST

It may be called a spring omelette, but you could eat this all year. If you can't get chives at your local grocery store, use thinly sliced green onions instead.

HEALTH BITE

Two eggs are considered a protein source from the Meat and Alternatives food group of Canada's Food Guide.

7 Tip the pan and lift the outer edges of the omelette to allow the uncooked egg to run underneath. Reduce the heat to low and cook, covered, until the top of the omelette no longer looks raw and wet, 3 to 5 minutes.

8 Sprinkle the goat cheese evenly over the omelette and cook, covered, until the cheese has melted and the top of the omelette is cooked, about 3 to 5 minutes. Using the back of a spoon, spread the cheese out evenly so it covers the entire omelette.

9 Remove the skillet from the heat. Loosen the edges of the omelette with a rubber spatula and carefully fold the omelette in half—easy does it.

10 Slide the omelette out of the skillet onto a clean cutting board. Cut the omelette in half. Place one half on each of 2 plates and sprinkle each serving with chives.

PER SERVING: 349 CALORIES, 23.1 G TOTAL FAT, 8.2 G SATURATED FAT, 0 G TRANS FAT, 371 MG SODIUM, 19.6 G CARBOHYDRATE, 4 G FIBRE, 4.3 G SUGARS, 20 G PROTEIN

DIABETES FOOD CHOICE VALUES PER SERVING: 1 CARBOHYDRATE, 2½ MEAT AND ALTERNATIVES, 3 FAT

HEALTH BITE

Shiitake and oyster mushrooms contain polysaccharides and lentinan, which stimulate the growth and activity of immune cells.

12

Nuts:
You'd Be Nuts Not to Eat Them!

There was a time, many years ago, when we were afraid of all the fat in nuts. I am so glad that was then and this is now, because nuts have had their day in court and the verdict is in: you'd be nuts not to eat them!

All nuts contain vitamins, minerals, fibre, and those amazing disease-reducing antioxidants. They're also a protein source, making them a vegan or vegetarian alternative to meat.

The Nurses' Health Study, one of the largest and longest-running studies investigating the factors that affect women's health, found that frequent nut consumption was associated with a reduced risk of coronary heart disease.

Each variety of nut contains a unique nutrient profile, so mix them up. Include peanuts, walnuts, almonds, hazelnuts, pistachios, pecans, pine nuts, cashews, and Brazil nuts in your day. Every day. (And for all the type As: even though peanuts are technically legumes and pine nuts are seeds, they still get to stay on the list.)

But (there's always a butt), before you run out and eat an entire bag of your favourite nut, take heed.

Size matters. Always has. Always will.

Oh, yes, my lovelies, you can't eat any more than a small handful of nuts at a time or you'll end up with a big, old butt. Even though nuts are a nutrient-dense food, they're also calorie dense, so a little goes a long way.

That small handful works out to be about ¼ cup (60 mL). Yup, that's it! According to Canada's Food Guide a serving of nuts is a pitiful ¼ cup (60 mL), so don't go grazing at the nut bowl.

The best idea is to measure out ¼ cup (60 mL) nuts and put them in your own little dish. Sadly, this doesn't really work at a party, asking the hostess for your own bowl, having to explain, discussing your weight, and on and on ... Just think "small handful," grab some, and walk away. If you're trying to lose weight, you might even want to reduce the amount to 2 tbsp (30 mL), which is half of a really small handful.

PICTURED ON PAGE 254
YEAR ROUND

Chai-Roasted Almonds

The South Asian influence in cooking is not only a taste trend; it's a health trend, too. With the research on spices highlighting the benefits of the antioxidants they contain, this tasty recipe has a hit of health in every handful. (Don't you just love alliteration?!) Add the fact that almonds have been shown to lower cholesterol, and this really is a win-win snack.

MAKES 4 CUPS (1 L) | ONE SERVING = ¼ CUP (60 ML)

INGREDIENTS

- ¼ cup (60 mL) pure maple syrup (see page 14)
- 2 tbsp (30 mL) cinnamon
- 1 tbsp (15 mL) pure vanilla extract
- 2 tsp (10 mL) ground cardamom
- 1 tsp (5 mL) ground allspice
- ½ tsp (2.5 mL) ground cloves
- ½ tsp (2.5 mL) cracked black pepper
- 4 cups (1 L) whole raw almonds

1 Position a rack in the middle of the oven. Preheat the oven to 350°F (180°C). Line a large, rimmed baking sheet with parchment paper.

2 Whisk together the maple syrup, cinnamon, vanilla, cardamom, allspice, cloves, and pepper in a large bowl until slightly thickened and well combined.

3 Add the almonds and, using a rubber spatula, mix until the nuts are well coated with the maple syrup mixture.

4 Pour the nuts out onto the prepared baking sheet, spreading them out in a single layer.

5 Roast in the oven until the nuts are dry and crispy looking, 30 to 35 minutes. Check them halfway through cooking to see if they are overbrowning on the bottom. If they are, carefully pick up the edges of the parchment paper and roll the nuts around. If that sounds too weird or complicated, flip the nuts with a flipper and return the baking sheet to the oven.

6 Remove the nuts from the oven and let them cool completely on the baking sheet. They will crisp up as they cool. Toss to break up any nuts that stick together. These actually taste better the next day, after the flavours have melded together, but feel free to munch on a serving as soon as they're cool. (Store in an airtight container for up to 3 weeks.)

GIVE IT A TWIST

To make a totally decadent treat, toss 2 tbsp (30 mL) chopped dark chocolate (with at least 70% cocoa mass) with ¼ cup (60 mL) cooled Chai-Roasted Almonds.

PER SERVING: 206 CALORIES, 18.1 G TOTAL FAT, 1.7 G SATURATED FAT, 0 G TRANS FAT, 2 MG SODIUM, 8.5 G CARBOHYDRATE, 3 G FIBRE, 3.1 G SUGARS, 4 G PROTEIN

DIABETES FOOD CHOICE VALUES PER SERVING: ½ CARBOHYDRATE, ½ MEAT AND ALTERNATIVES, 3½ FAT

Chai-Roasted Almonds (left; *page 253**) and Sweet and Spicy Walnuts (right)*

Sweet and Spicy Walnuts

These walnuts are fabulous for a mid-afternoon snack when your body is crying out for protein. Better yet, munch a small handful along with a scrubbed, unpeeled apple. This great flavour combo gives you a hit of nutrient-dense, heart-healthy food.

Depending on how well you mix the maple syrup and the spices together, you may get the odd "Wow, these are so-o-o spicy!" They're not really, but it's all in the mixing, so make sure you blend the ingredients really well. And if you want a bigger spicy kick, increase the cayenne to 1 tsp (5 mL).

MAKES 4 CUPS (1 L) | ONE SERVING = ¼ CUP (60 ML)

INGREDIENTS

¼ cup (60 mL) pure maple syrup (see page 14)

1 tbsp plus 2 tsp (25 mL) ground cumin

1 tbsp plus 2 tsp (25 mL) ground coriander

1 tbsp (15 mL) paprika

1 tsp (5 mL) cracked black pepper

1 tsp (5 mL) cinnamon

½ tsp (2.5 mL) cayenne

4 cups (1 L) whole walnuts

1 Position a rack in the middle of the oven. Preheat the oven to 350°F (180°C). Line a large rimmed baking sheet with parchment paper.

2 Whisk together the maple syrup, and all the spices in a large bowl until slightly thickened and well combined.

3 Add the walnuts and, using a rubber spatula, mix until the nuts are well coated with the maple syrup mixture. Pour the nuts out onto the prepared baking sheet, spreading them out in a single layer.

4 Roast in the oven until the nuts are dry and crispy looking, 14 to 16 minutes. Check them halfway through cooking to see if they are overbrowning on the bottom. If they are, carefully pick up the edges of the parchment paper and roll the nuts around. If that sounds too weird or complicated, flip the nuts with a flipper and return the baking sheet to the oven.

5 Remove the nuts from the oven and let them cool completely on the baking sheet. They will crisp up as they cool. Toss to break up any nuts that stick together. These actually taste better the next day, after the flavours have melded together, but feel free to munch on a serving as soon as they're cool. (Store in an airtight container for up to 3 weeks.)

PER SERVING: 204 CALORIES, 18.2 G TOTAL FAT, 1.7 G SATURATED FAT, 0 G TRANS FAT, 4 MG SODIUM, 8.3 G CARBOHYDRATE, 2 G FIBRE, 3.1 G SUGARS, 4 G PROTEIN

DIABETES FOOD CHOICE VALUES PER SERVING: ½ CARBOHYDRATE, ½ MEAT AND ALTERNATIVES, 3½ FAT

MAKING OUR ROADS SAFER

Nuts are the perfect snack for the long drive home from work. Right around 4:00 pm. we all need a protein hit to help keep us alert. If I didn't eat the small bag of nuts that I always keep in my car, I would probably lose it on my way home during rush hour when some insane idiot of a driver cuts me off in the merge lane on the highway.

That hit of health keeps me not so short-fused as to run someone off the road (who may, in fact, deserve to be driven off the road, but I don't want to go to prison). Yes, for the sake of humanity we all need to keep a bag of nuts in the car.

YEAR ROUND
KID FRIENDLY

Peanut Butter-and-Apple French Toast for One

It's late and you just got in the door. You're starving. You go to pick up the phone to call for pizza, or worse, you start foraging in the cupboard for cookies.

STOP! Hang up the phone, or back away from the cupboard. Here's a quicker — and healthier — solution.

Peanut butter is an inexpensive source of protein and two B vitamins (niacin and folate), and teamed with apple in a French-toasted sandwich, it makes a great nutrient-dense dinner. One sandwich is one serving, so dust off your math skills and start multiplying to figure out how to serve more.

Eating this with a glass of 100% orange juice helps your body absorb the iron in this vegetarian dinner sandwich.

MAKES 1 SERVING

INGREDIENTS

1 omega-3 egg (see page 13)
2 tbsp (30 mL) skim milk or fortified organic soy beverage
1/4 tsp (1 mL) cinnamon
2 slices 100% whole-grain whole wheat bread (see sidebar)
2 tbsp (30 mL) natural peanut butter (see page 14)
1/2 unpeeled apple, scrubbed, cored, and thinly sliced
Canola oil or non-stick baking spray
Pure maple syrup (optional)

1 Whisk together the egg, milk, and cinnamon in a wide shallow bowl.

2 Spread each slice of bread with 1 tbsp (15 mL) peanut butter. Top 1 slice with apple slices. Cover with the second slice of peanut-buttered bread, peanut butter side down. Press down lightly to make sure the apple doesn't fall out.

3 Heat a small non-stick skillet over medium heat.

4 While the skillet is heating, place the sandwich in the egg mixture. Let it soak up half of the egg mixture, then flip it over and let it soak up the rest of the egg mixture.

5 Grease the skillet lightly with oil or spray lightly with baking spray.

HEALTH BITE

According to Canada's Food Guide, one egg plus 2 tbsp (30 mL) peanut butter adds up to one serving from the Meat and Alternatives food group.

HEALTH BITE

Peanuts contain folate, which can help lower levels of blood-vessel-damaging homocysteine.

6 Place the egg-dipped sandwich in the skillet and reduce the heat to medium-low. Cook until the sandwich is browned on the underside, about 5 minutes. Carefully flip the sandwich and gently press down. Continue cooking until browned on the second side and all of the egg is cooked, about 5 minutes.

7 Remove the sandwich from the skillet, cut it in half, and serve with a little maple syrup (if using) or just eat it plain.

HOW TO

This works better with bread that's starting to go a little stale, as opposed to really fresh bread. Slightly drier bread absorbs the egg mixture better.

PER SERVING (WITHOUT SYRUP): 481 CALORIES, 23.1 G TOTAL FAT, 3.5 G SATURATED FAT, 0 G TRANS FAT, 421 MG SODIUM, 51.7 G CARBOHYDRATE, 8 G FIBRE, 10.8 G SUGARS, 22 G PROTEIN

DIABETES FOOD CHOICE VALUES PER SERVING (WITHOUT SYRUP): 3 CARBOHYDRATE, 2 MEAT AND ALTERNATIVES, 3½ FAT

After-School Cookies

These chewy, peanutty cookies aren't overly sweet. The chocolate hit comes from natural cocoa powder (see page 12 to read more about cocoa powder).

As the name suggests, this is a great cookie to serve to your kids with a glass of milk when they get home from school.

MAKES 36 COOKIES | ONE SERVING = 2 COOKIES (OF COURSE, YOU CAN ALWAYS EAT JUST 1 COOKIE, BUT I'M TRYING TO BE REALISTIC)

INGREDIENTS

- 3/4 cup (185 mL) natural peanut butter (see page 14)
- 1/3 cup (80 mL) canola oil (be sure to measure accurately; see page 21)
- 1 omega-3 egg (see page 13)
- 1 cup (250 mL) packed dark brown sugar
- 1 tsp (5 mL) pure vanilla extract
- 1/4 cup (60 mL) natural cocoa powder (see page 12)
- 1 cup (250 mL) whole wheat flour
- 2 tbsp (30 mL) wheat germ
- 1/2 tsp (2.5 mL) baking soda
- 1/2 tsp (2.5 mL) cinnamon

HOW TO

I always use electric beaters when I make cookies. If you prefer to mix the batter the old-fashioned way, make sure you stir it really, really well.

1 Position a rack in the middle of the oven. Preheat the oven to 350°F (180°C). Line a large baking sheet with parchment paper.

2 Using electric beaters, beat together the peanut butter and oil in a medium bowl. Beat in the egg until the mixture is thick. Beat in the brown sugar. Add 1/4 cup (60 mL) water and the vanilla and gently beat in.

3 Gently beat in the cocoa powder. (Don't crank up the beaters or you'll be wearing cocoa powder. Just warning you.) Set aside.

4 Stir together the flour, wheat germ, baking soda, and cinnamon in a medium bowl. Stir the flour mixture into the peanut butter mixture (the dough will be fairly stiff).

5 Form teaspoonfuls (5 mL) of batter into balls, or use a mini-scoop (see page 11), and place on the prepared baking sheet. Dip the tines of a fork in flour and gently press down on each cookie to make a waffle-weave pattern.

6 Bake until golden brown, 10 to 12 minutes. Let the cookies cool slightly on the baking sheet before removing them to a wire rack to cool completely. (Store the cookies in an airtight container for up to 1 week, or freeze for up to 2 months.)

PER SERVING: 168 CALORIES, 9.4 G TOTAL FAT, 1.3 G SATURATED FAT, 0 G TRANS FAT, 85 MG SODIUM, 19.4 G CARBOHYDRATE, 2 G FIBRE, 11.2 G SUGARS, 4 G PROTEIN

DIABETES FOOD CHOICE VALUES PER SERVING: 1 CARBOHYDRATE, 1/2 MEAT AND ALTERNATIVES, 1 1/2 FAT

From left, clockwise: Triple-Oat Cookies (page 174), Pumpkin-Date Spice Cookies (page 190), Chocolate Chip Cookies (page 282), After-School Cookies (facing page), Go-Big-or-Go-Home Chocolate Chip Cookies (page 283), and Triple-Chocolate Brownie Cookies (page 284)

13

Onions, Garlic, Shallots, Leeks, and Chives: *The Whole Darned Allium Family*

The 2015 Foodie Oscars: A Screenplay

The ballroom of the Waldorf-Astoria in New York City. A large crowd comprising the who's who of the foodie world fills the room. Sitting at large round tables laden with fabulous foods, everyone is eating and drinking. There is a sense of expectancy in the air.

A hologram of Julia Child makes its way to the podium.

JULIA CHILD

Hello-o-o-o. I would like to thank George Lucas and the people at Industrial Light and Magic for helping me be here tonight. I haven't looked this good in years.

Laughter in the audience as the camera pans the crowd. Martha Stewart is frozen in a half smile, Bobby Flay is cutting into a steak, Gordon Ramsay is smelling his plate, and Rachael Ray is **really** ***smiling.***

JULIA CHILD

I have loved this category since my days in Paris. So, here are the nominees for this year's Foodie Oscar for Best Performance by a Must-Have Ingredient in Your Kitchen.

Julia clears her throat.

Apocalypse Soon, starring Sodium.

Cut to Emeril Lagasse sprinkling a salt shaker.

Billy Bonkers and the Glucose Factory, starring Sugar.

Cut to Paula Deen eating a cupcake.

All in the Allium Family, starring Onions, Garlic, Shallots, Leeks, and Chives.

Cut to Jamie Oliver giggling like a teenager on his first date.

And last but not least, *The Curious Case of Benjamin Butter,* starring—you guessed it—my favourite ingredient, Butter.

Julia opens the envelope.

And the Foodie Oscar for Best Performance by a Must-Have Ingredient in Your Kitchen goes to ... *All in the Allium Family!*

Wild cheering from the crowd. The camera pans and we see Susur Lee and Alice Waters high-fiving each other as Jamie Oliver sprints toward the stage.

VOICE-OVER

Accepting the Foodie Oscar for Best Performance by a Must-Have Ingredient in Your Kitchen is the UK's Jamie Oliver.

JAMIE OLIVER

Wow! This was really a tough category. I'd just like to say thanks to the members of the Academy for their wise decision. Let's give a shout-out to my friends Onions, Garlic, Shallots, Leeks, and Chives. They can help fight heart disease, give your immune system a much-needed leg up, lower blood glucose levels, and protect against cancer. Thank you, everyone. Eat your allium! Cheers!

Fade to black.

Caramelized Onions

Don't let anyone tell you that fried onions are the same as caramelized ones. Sure, they're both cooked in a skillet with some fat, but the similarities end there.

Caramelized onions are cooked slowly to allow their natural sugars to turn a dark golden brown, which gives the onions a sweetness and a flavour that quick-fried onions just can't compete with.

Serve caramelized onions with any grilled meat or poultry, or as a condiment for my Hockey-Night-in-Canada Burgers on page 295.

MAKES 1 CUP (250 ML) — REMEMBER THE SHRINKAGE FACTOR
ONE SERVING = 1/4 CUP (60 ML)

INGREDIENTS

1 tbsp (15 mL) extra virgin olive oil

4 onions, thinly sliced

1 Heat a large non-stick skillet over medium heat. Add the oil, then the onions.

2 Cook, stirring occasionally, until the onions are very soft and golden brown, 30 to 45 minutes, reducing the heat to low if the onions start to brown too much.

HEALTH BITE

I am such a fan of onions, garlic, shallots, leeks, and chives that one or more of these members of the allium family are present and accounted for in most of the savoury dishes in this book.

PER SERVING: 75 CALORIES, 3.5 G TOTAL FAT, 0.8 G SATURATED FAT, 0 G TRANS FAT, 4 MG SODIUM, 10 G CARBOHYDRATE, 2 G FIBRE, 5 G SUGARS, 1 G PROTEIN

DIABETES FOOD CHOICE VALUES PER SERVING: 1/2 CARBOHYDRATE, 1 FAT

Leek, Parsnip, and Apple Soup

Apples give this soup its mild, sweet taste. According to my friend and taste-tester extraordinaire Marianne, this is a parsnip soup for people who don't like parsnips.

You can't taste the potassium, folate, or fibre, but they're definitely there, upping the nutrition ante.

MAKES 7 CUPS (1.75 L) | ONE SERVING = ABOUT 1¼ CUPS (310 ML)

1 Heat a large saucepan over medium heat. Add the oil, then the leeks, and sauté for 5 minutes.

2 Add the parsnips, apples, thyme, and coriander, and sauté for 1 minute.

3 Add the broth and juice, and bring to a boil. Reduce the heat to a simmer and cook, covered, until the parsnips are very tender, 20 to 25 minutes.

4 Use a hand-held immersion blender (see page 8) to purée the soup in the saucepan until smooth. (Or purée the soup in a blender, about 2 cups / 500 mL at a time, until smooth.)

5 Ladle into soup bowls. (The soup can be refrigerated in an airtight container for up to 2 days, or frozen for up to 3 months. To serve, thaw the soup, then reheat it before serving.)

PER SERVING: 203 CALORIES, 5.6 G TOTAL FAT, 1 G SATURATED FAT, 0 G TRANS FAT, 119 MG SODIUM, 36.3 G CARBOHYDRATE, 6 G FIBRE, 17.1 G SUGARS, 4 G PROTEIN

DIABETES FOOD CHOICE VALUES PER SERVING: 2 CARBOHYDRATE, 1 FAT

INGREDIENTS

- 2 tbsp (30 mL) extra virgin olive oil
- 3 leeks (white and pale green parts only), thinly sliced (see page 23)
- 4 large unpeeled parsnips, scrubbed and cut into ½-inch (1 cm) slices (4 cups / 1 L)
- 2 Idared apples, scrubbed, cored, and cut into 1-inch (2.5 cm) chunks (2 cups / 500 mL)
- 1 tsp (5 mL) dried thyme leaves
- ½ tsp (2.5 mL) ground coriander
- 3 cups (750 mL) lower-sodium chicken or vegetable broth (see page 7)
- 1 cup (250 mL) natural apple juice (see page 12)

HEALTH BITE

Pectin, a soluble fibre in the whole apple, also helps reduce cholesterol, which in turn reduces your chances of developing heart disease.

Fennel and Spanish Onion Slaw

My voice agent, Donna Trimble, is a fabulous cook. Donna and I are always exchanging recipes and cooking ideas. One time she served me a version of this salad. I loved it so much, I made it a part of my own dinner repertoire. The next time I had her over, I totally forgot she had given me the recipe, and served it to her. She has never let me forget that marvellous menopausal moment.

And yes, this recipe includes salt. For anyone keeping score, that's three times I've used it in the entire book. See if you can find the other recipes.

MAKES 6 CUPS (1.5 L) | ONE SERVING = ½ CUP (125 ML)

INGREDIENTS

1 large fennel bulb

1 small Spanish onion

1 lemon

2 tbsp (30 mL) extra virgin olive oil

¼ tsp (1 mL) salt

1 Cut the fluffy green bits off the top of the fennel. (For those who like to be in the know, they're called fronds.) Cut the fennel bulb in half and thinly slice it using a food processor or a mandoline (see pages 8 and 11 for why you need these must-have tools). Or use a really sharp knife and some patience. You should have 4 to 5 cups (1 to 1.25 L), depending on the size of the fennel bulb. Place the fennel in a large bowl.

2 Repeat the process with the onion. You should have about 2 cups (500 mL) thinly sliced onion. Add the onion to the bowl.

3 Scrub and dry the lemon. Using a Microplane grater (see page 8), remove the zest. With your palm, roll the lemon on the counter (this makes it yield more juice), then cut in half and squeeze out ¼ cup (60 mL) juice.

4 Add the lemon zest and juice, olive oil, and salt to the salad and toss well. Cover and refrigerate for 2 hours before serving. (Salad will keep for up to 3 days in the fridge.)

SALAD DAYS

This salad is slightly crunchy after 2 hours, and becomes a softer, pickled salad after 12 hours. Either way, it's great. Also, the salad shrinks as it marinates in the fridge, so there will be less of it the following day than there was 2 hours after making it. As usual, blame it on shrinkage.

PER SERVING: 32 CALORIES, 2.3 G TOTAL FAT, 0.3 G SATURATED FAT, 0 G TRANS FAT, 60 MG SODIUM, 2.8 G CARBOHYDRATE, 1 G FIBRE, 0.6 G SUGARS, 0 G PROTEIN

DIABETES FOOD CHOICE VALUES PER SERVING: ½ FAT, 1 EXTRA

14

Oranges, Grapefruit, Lemons, and Limes: *Make Dinner More A-Peeling*

Citrus fruits are loaded with immune-enhancing vitamin C, which we need to consume every day.

Vitamin C has many functions in our bodies. It helps keep our gums healthy, aids in the absorption of iron, and helps in the formation of our connective tissue.

Eating citrus fruits is important, but their peel may, in fact, be the most important part of them.

According to a small case study at the University of Arizona, consuming the peel of oranges, lemons, and limes, which contains d-Limonene, may lower your chances of developing skin cancer.

I use the zest or the thin outer peel from citrus fruits in many of the recipes in this book. It's not just a pretty garnish; it's an important element in the disease-lowering effects of the recipes.

To remove the zest from citrus fruit, scrub the fruit well and dry it first, then use your Microplane grater (see page 8 to find out why you need one).

Citrus Salad with Orange-Honey Dressing

January in Canada is not for the faint-hearted. It can be bitterly cold, with snow up to your armpits, or you could be floating in a sea of rain. To make matters worse, it's pretty bleak in the produce department, too.

Sure, there are still local apples, root vegetables, and squash to buy, which are all great if you like the idea of being a pioneer. Then, right around the middle of the month, when you're thinking you'd give up chocolate for a Ruby Red grapefruit, the seasonal oranges and grapefruit arrive. Hallelujah for imported citrus!

MAKES 2 CUPS (500 ML) | ONE SERVING = ½ CUP (125 ML)

INGREDIENTS

2 tbsp (30 mL) frozen orange juice concentrate, thawed (see page 13)

1 tbsp (15 mL) honey, or your choice of sweetener to taste

1 large orange, scrubbed well and dried

1 lime, scrubbed well and dried

1 large red grapefruit, scrubbed well and dried

1 Whisk together the orange juice concentrate and honey in a medium bowl.

2 Using a Microplane grater (see page 8), remove 1 tsp (5 mL) zest from the orange and 2 tsp (10 mL) zest from the lime. Add the zest to the bowl.

3 Peel the grapefruit and orange and cut into segments (see page 24). Add the grapefruit and orange segments to the bowl and toss well.

PER SERVING: 80 CALORIES, 0.2 G TOTAL FAT, 0 G SATURATED FAT, 0 G TRANS FAT, 1 MG SODIUM, 19.2 G CARBOHYDRATE, 2 G FIBRE, 16.5 G SUGARS, 1 G PROTEIN

DIABETES FOOD CHOICE VALUES PER SERVING: 1 CARBOHYDRATE

GET AHEAD

You can make this salad a day ahead, but store the zest in the fridge in a separate container and add it to the salad just before serving.

FOR THE LOVE OF CITRUS

Looking for a green salad starring citrus fruit? Check out my January Salad on page 198.

HEALTH BITE

Grapefruit contains compounds that may interfere with certain prescription drugs. Check with your doctor.

15

Yogurt:
The Good Bacteria

There was a time when yogurt was a plain, tangy, watery milk product that you bought at a health food store. Now, every grocery store in town has a yogurt section, and you need a manual to figure out who's who.

YOGURT PRIMER

So, what's with all the hype about yogurt?

All yogurts are made with good-for-your-gastrointestinal-tract bacteria — the kind of bacteria that helps your immune system work at its best. For my regular everyday-eating yogurt, I choose one that has the words *lactobacillus acidophilus* and / or *bifidus bacteria* on the label. I usually pick plain, without any added sugars, and add either my own fruit, or some honey and cinnamon at serving time.

WHICH ONE'S BEST FOR YOU?

Read the labels. Check out the fat content first. Best bets in the health department are non-fat to lower-fat yogurts. Try to stay under 2 to 3 grams of saturated fat per serving.

Too many yogurts have too much in the way of added sugars. Some brands have as much as 2 tbsp (30 mL) added sugars per serving. Choose a yogurt that's labelled "original," "natural," or "plain." But double-check the ingredient list, as some of those also contain added sugars. Bottom line: read the ingredient list to check if the manufacturer has added sugar or anything that ends in "-ose," which will be a type of sugar.

THE YOGURT OF MY DREAMS

You can wade through the yogurt section if you like, but I've found my favourite. I'd heard about a type of yogurt that had zero fat and was thick and creamy, loaded with protein, and a great source of calcium, from my friend Michale, who lives in L.A. Thanks to Liberté, a Quebec-based company, Canada finally has this fabulous style of yogurt, and all my yogurt dreams have come true.

I used to make my own thickened yogurt, sometimes called yogurt cheese, for dips, desserts, and toppings for fruit. Now I can use thickened yogurt any old time I want. I just open a container of Liberté's plain 0% fat Greek-style yogurt, and I'm good to go. If you still want to make your own thickened yogurt, go for it (the recipe's on page 272). But I'm going to buy Liberté's yogurt forever and ever. (And just for the record: no one paid me to write any of this.)

Thickened Yogurt

It's easy to make your own Greek-style yogurt. Just make sure to choose a yogurt that doesn't contain any gelatin (check the label). Try Astro's BioBest no-gelatin yogurt, or Liberté's regular non-fat, no-gelatin yogurt. I use thickened yogurt in Tzatziki on the next page and in Light Lemony Mousse on page 321.

MAKES 2 CUPS (500 ML) | ONE SERVING = 2 TBSP (30 ML)

INGREDIENTS

3 coffee filters

1 container (24 oz / 650 g) plain non-fat or low-fat yogurt, with no gelatin added

1 Either the night before you need the thickened yogurt or the morning before you need it, line a wire-mesh strainer with the coffee filters, fanning them out to cover the whole strainer. Set the strainer over a bowl.

2 Pour the yogurt into the strainer, cover, and refrigerate for at least 6 hours. The liquid (whey) will drip out into the bowl, leaving the thickened yogurt in the strainer.

3 Discard liquid and store yogurt in a covered container for up to 5 days.

PER SERVING: 20 CALORIES, 0 G TOTAL FAT, 0 G SATURATED FAT, 0 G TRANS FAT, 24 MG SODIUM, 3.3 G CARBOHYDRATE, 0 G FIBRE, 1.6 G SUGARS, 2 G PROTEIN

DIABETES FOOD CHOICE VALUES PER SERVING: ½ MEAT AND ALTERNATIVES, 1 EXTRA

HEALTH BITE

Yogurt contains calcium, the mineral we need to build strong bones. But we need vitamin D to help absorb calcium. This calcium-vitamin D combo is found in milk, but most brands of yogurt don't contain vitamin D. So, don't depend on yogurt for this important fat-soluble vitamin.

Tzatziki

Attention, all vampires! You're not *going to like this sauce at all.*

Tzatziki is a Greek condiment that's usually made with thickened yogurt, cucumber, and lots of garlic. (I omit the cucumber in my recipe because I prefer a smoother texture.) Never eat this before a hot date, a public meeting, or a sports event—just warning you.

Tzatziki is great spooned over grilled fish or poultry (like my Greek-Style Grilled Chicken on page 230), as a dip for raw veggies, or drizzled over grilled asparagus (see sidebar on page 42).

MAKES 1 CUP (250 ML) | ONE SERVING = 2 TBSP (30 ML)

INGREDIENTS

3 to 4 cloves garlic

1 cup (250 mL) plain 0% fat Greek-style yogurt (or Thickened Yogurt, facing page)

GIVE IT A TWIST

Garlic lovers, go ahead and add as many cloves as you want.

1 Mince the garlic.

2 Stir together the yogurt and garlic in a small bowl. Serve right away or cover and store in the fridge for up to 3 days. The longer it sits, the stronger the taste.

PER SERVING (MADE WITH PLAIN 0% FAT GREEK-STYLE YOGURT): 20 CALORIES, 0 G TOTAL FAT, 0 G SATURATED FAT, 0 G TRANS FAT, 16 MG SODIUM, 1.4 G CARBOHYDRATE, 0 G FIBRE, 0.8 G SUGARS, 3 G PROTEIN

DIABETES FOOD CHOICE VALUES PER SERVING (MADE WITH PLAIN 0% FAT GREEK-STYLE YOGURT): ½ MEAT AND ALTERNATIVES, 1 EXTRA

16

Chocolate:
Because There's Always Room

You'd have to have been living under a rock for the past several years not to know that dark chocolate is good for you.

Yay! We can eat chocolate totally guilt free ... can't we?

Well, candy companies would like you to think so, but the truth is that not all chocolate is good for you. And even the type that is, you can't pig out on.

GOOD FOR YOU

Chocolate contains antioxidant compounds called flavanols, specifically proanthocyanidins, which are also found in blueberries, cranberries, apples, purple grape juice, cinnamon, and red kidney beans. It appears that these compounds may be responsible for many of the cardiovascular health benefits of chocolate, including reducing blood pressure, improving insulin sensitivity, and preventing LDL, the "big bad guy" type of cholesterol, from becoming worse.

But before you start chowing down on your daily dark chocolate, remember size matters. You can't eat an entire 8 oz (250 g) chocolate bar and expect to be healthier. Chocolate has calories and your body recognizes calorie overload, plus it's a whiz at math:

TOO MANY CALORIES IN + NOT ENOUGH CALORIES OUT = WEIGHT GAIN

If you can afford the extra calories, you can have 1 oz (30 g) of dark chocolate daily. That's right, just one little old ounce a day is all you get.

Size matters, portions matter, and so does the brand you choose.

CHOCOLATE PRIMER

That rich, dark chocolate bar starts life as a pod on a cacao tree. The pods are filled with about 40 white, pulp-covered seeds called cocoa beans.

The beans are fermented, dried, cleaned, and roasted, then winnowed, a process that separates the shells from the nibs. These nibs are the very essence of chocolate and are the best bang for your antioxidant buck (see page 12 for more on cocoa nibs).

The nibs are then ground and milled into a dark brown paste that contains cocoa liquor (but not the drinkable kind), cocoa butter, and cocoa solids. The cocoa solids are processed into cocoa powder. Chocolate manufacturers create their signature flavours by blending cocoa powder, cocoa liquor, and cocoa butter in different ratios, along with other ingredients like milk and sugar.

solid chocolate
chocolate chips
cocoa beans
cocoa nibs
natural cocoa
powder

So far, so good, but there's a catch. Cocoa manufacturers traditionally ferment the beans to maximize their flavour. They use high heat to roast them, then add an alkaline to improve the colour, texture, and flavour. This process is called Dutching. The big problem is that Dutching reduces the total flavanol content by two-thirds. And it's the flavanols that are responsible for the long-term health effects of eating dark chocolate. (For more on cocoa powder, see page 12.)

Some chocolate manufacturers label their products with the percentage of cocoa used in the finished product. Keep in mind that the percentage of cocoa *isn't* an indicator of flavanol content. That "75% cocoa mass" on the label doesn't mean that the bar is made up of 75% flavanols (although higher cocoa mass content may also indicate a higher flavanol content).

So, what kind of chocolate should you buy?

Select a brand that processes its beans in a way that keeps the flavanol content high. As this book went to press, Mars, the maker of Dove chocolate, was the leader in this area, but other companies that process their beans so the flavanol content is high include Swiss manufacturer Barry Callebaut; Naturex, a French company; and Hershey's (whose extra-dark chocolate and natural cocoa powder are high in antioxidants). My personal favourite chocolate is Dove Dark; I love the flavour and I know that its flavanol content is high.

When it comes to health and chocolate, the bottom line is if the chocolate hasn't been processed in a way that protects those valuable antioxidants, it doesn't matter if the chocolate fairies sprinkled pixie dust on it: you're better off having a flavanol-rich apple instead.

HEALTH BITE

If heart health is your number-one concern, then skip milk chocolate and white chocolate altogether. They have little or no antioxidants in them.

YEAR ROUND
KID FRIENDLY

They'll-Never-Guess-the-Secret-Ingredient Chocolate Mousse

I discovered a non-dairy chocolate mousse at the Whole Foods Market in Toronto on February 12, 2004. Yes; perhaps sadly, I made a note of it in my foodie journal: Dear Diary, finally found a moose I can eat!

I loved that mousse so much, I made daily trips to the store for another hit of chocolate creaminess. About 40 bucks later, I read the ingredient list and came up with this recipe.

The secret ingredient? Soft silken tofu. Heart-healthy tofu, in a chocolate mousse? Who knew an ingredient other than heavy cream and eggs could whip up a mousse into fluffy lightness?

But here's some sage advice from a mom: whatever you do, don't tell anyone about the silken tofu part of the recipe. Plant the T-word in anyone's brain and they just won't eat this mousse. They may not even try it. So, just serve it and see what happens. And let me know — I love tofu stories.

MAKES 2 CUPS (500 ML) | ONE SERVING = ½ CUP (125 ML)

INGREDIENTS

One 12 oz (340 g) package soft silken tofu (see below)
5 oz (150 g) really good dark chocolate with at least 70% cocoa mass (see sidebar on page 313)
3 tbsp (45 mL) honey
½ tsp (2.5 mL) pure vanilla extract (please don't use the artificial kind; it really affects the final flavour, and not in a good way)

WHAT IS . . . ?

The only type of tofu that works in this recipe is soft silken tofu, which is made with extra-thick soy milk, then strained through silk. It's often sold in a Tetra Pak carton and will likely be in the health-food section of your grocery store. Although for some strange reason, my local grocery store stocks it in the soup aisle. My advice? Ask someone before you start trudging around aimlessly trying to out-guess the Grocery Store Gods. The brand I use is Mori-Nu.

1 Using an immersion blender (see page 8 to read why you need one), purée the silken tofu in a deep narrow container until it's really smooth. (Or whirl the tofu in a blender until smooth.)

2 Melt the chocolate and honey together in a metal bowl set over a saucepan of gently boiling water. Stir often until the chocolate is almost melted, then remove the bowl from the heat and stir until completely melted. (Or, for the unorthodox and not faint of heart, place the chocolate and honey in a microwaveable bowl and microwave on medium for 20 seconds. Stir well. If the chocolate isn't melting, microwave it in 5-second increments until the chocolate starts to melt, then stir until it's completely melted. But be warned: if you overheat the chocolate, it will burn and wreck the recipe.)

CONTINUED . . .

CONTINUED FROM PAGE 278

3 Let the chocolate mixture cool until it's just warm but still liquid, 2 to 5 minutes.

4 Add the cooled, melted chocolate to the tofu, and using the immersion blender, purée until smooth. (Or add the chocolate to the blender and whirl until smooth.)

5 Add the vanilla. Purée until well blended.

6 Pour into a 3-cup (750 mL) bowl, then cover and refrigerate until chilled and thickened, about 2 hours. (Mousse can be refrigerated for up to 3 days.)

PER SERVING: 289 CALORIES, 15 G TOTAL FAT, 6.8 G SATURATED FAT, 0 G TRANS FAT, 1 MG SODIUM, 38.1 G CARBOHYDRATE, 3 G FIBRE, 31.3 G SUGARS, 6 G PROTEIN

DIABETES FOOD CHOICE VALUES PER SERVING: 2½ CARBOHYDRATE, ½ MEAT AND ALTERNATIVES, 3 FAT

YEAR ROUND
KID FRIENDLY

Double-Chocolate Banana Muffins

These muffins are a spin on my family's favourite Banana Chocolate Chip Muffins from Ultimate Foods for Ultimate Health ... and don't forget the chocolate! *They now have natural cocoa powder and wheat germ, making them a whole-grain muffin that's yummier and more heart healthy than before.*

Be warned: each muffin contains 6 grams of fibre, which is about six times more than a commercial muffin, so don't go pigging out and eat half a dozen. To put it mildly, about 12 to 24 hours later, you'll be in for a big surprise!

MAKES 12 MUFFINS | ONE SERVING = 1 MUFFIN

INGREDIENTS

- 1 cup (250 mL) whole wheat flour
- 3/4 cup (185 mL) wheat bran
- 3/4 cup (185 mL) ground flaxseed (see page 13)
- 1/4 cup (60 mL) natural cocoa powder (see page 12)
- 2 tbsp (30 mL) wheat germ
- 2 tbsp (30 mL) cinnamon
- 1½ tsp (7.5 mL) baking powder
- 1 tsp (5 mL) baking soda
- 1/4 cup (60 mL) chocolate chips with at least 60% cocoa mass or chocolate chunks with at least 70% cocoa mass
- 1½ cups (375 mL) mashed very overripe bananas (about 3 large or 4 small bananas; see below)
- 3/4 cup (185 mL) packed dark brown sugar
- 1/2 cup (125 mL) 1% plain yogurt
- 1/4 cup (60 mL) skim milk
- 1 omega-3 egg (see page 13)

1 Preheat the oven to 400°F (200°C). Line a 12-cup muffin pan with paper liners.

2 Whisk together the flour, wheat bran, flaxseed, cocoa powder, wheat germ, cinnamon, baking powder, and baking soda in a large bowl. Stir in the chocolate chips.

3 In a medium bowl, beat together the mashed bananas, brown sugar, yogurt, milk, and egg. The mashed bananas really need to be mixed in well.

4 Add the banana mixture to the flour mixture and mix just until combined.

5 Divide the batter evenly among the muffin cups (I use a 1/4-cup / 60 mL ice-cream scoop with a release lever). Bake until a toothpick comes out clean, 20 to 25 minutes. Let the muffins cool in the pan on a wire rack for 5 minutes. Remove the muffins and let them cool completely on the wire rack. (Store the muffins in an airtight container for up to 2 days, or freeze them for up to 2 months.)

WHAT IS . . . ?

A very overripe banana is the kind that's so dark brown, mushy, and soft you wouldn't eat it raw because it can barely stand up straight when it's peeled. This is absolutely the best banana for baking. Freeze overripe bananas, then thaw them before making these muffins.

PER SERVING: 208 CALORIES, 5.8 G TOTAL FAT, 1.6 G SATURATED FAT, 0 G TRANS FAT, 168 MG SODIUM, 37.7 G CARBOHYDRATE, 6 G FIBRE, 18.9 G SUGARS, 6 G PROTEIN

DIABETES FOOD CHOICE VALUES PER MUFFIN: 2 CARBOHYDRATE, 1 FAT

PICTURED ON PAGE 259
YEAR ROUND
KID FRIENDLY

Chocolate Chip Cookies

These are big, buttery-tasting chocolate chip cookies that aren't even made with butter. They bake up skinny and slightly chewy, like a cross between a flat florentine and a regular chocolate chip cookie. My friend Joanne says they taste like "More, please!"

MAKES 42 COOKIES (USING 2 TSP / 10 ML MINI-SCOOP)
ONE SERVING = 2 COOKIES

INGREDIENTS

- ½ cup (125 mL) unsalted non-hydrogenated margarine
- ½ cup (125 mL) packed dark brown sugar
- ¼ cup (60 mL) granulated sugar
- 1 omega-3 egg (see page 13)
- 1 tsp (5 mL) pure vanilla extract
- ¾ cup (185 mL) whole wheat flour
- ½ cup (125 mL) large-flake rolled oats
- ¼ cup (60 mL) oat bran
- 1 tbsp (15 mL) wheat germ
- ½ tsp (2.5 mL) baking soda
- ¼ cup (60 mL) chocolate chips with at least 60% cocoa mass or chocolate chunks with at least 70% cocoa mass

1 Position the oven rack in the middle of the oven. Preheat the oven to 375°F (190°C). Line a large baking sheet with parchment paper.

2 Cream the margarine in a medium bowl. Beat in the brown and granulated sugars until well blended.

3 Add the egg and vanilla, and beat until the batter turns a light beige and is light and fluffy.

4 Beat in the flour, oats, oat bran, wheat germ, and baking soda. Stir in the chocolate chips until well distributed. Drop the batter by rounded teaspoonfuls (10 mL), or use a mini-scoop (see page 11), onto the prepared baking sheet, spacing the cookies about 1 inch (2.5 cm) apart. Bake until light golden brown, 8 to 10 minutes.

5 Let the cookies cool slightly on the baking sheet before removing them and letting them cool completely on a wire rack. (Store the cookies in an airtight container for up to 1 week, or freeze for up to 2 months.)

PER SERVING: 111 CALORIES, 6 G TOTAL FAT, 1.2 G SATURATED FAT, 0 G TRANS FAT, 33 MG SODIUM, 13.8 G CARBOHYDRATE, 1 G FIBRE, 8.1 G SUGARS, 2 G PROTEIN

DIABETES FOOD CHOICE VALUES PER SERVING: 1 CARBOHYDRATE, 1 FAT

HEALTH BITE

If you're taking blood thinners, don't go on a chocolate binge. There's some evidence that there may be an interaction between these drugs and high levels of dark chocolate consumption. Check with your doctor.

PICTURED ON PAGE 259
YEAR ROUND
KID FRIENDLY

Go-Big-or-Go-Home Chocolate Chip Cookies

Adding the wheat germ helps make these very crunchy, not-too-sweet chocolate chip cookies a whole-grain treat.

MAKES TWENTY 3-INCH (8 CM) COOKIES | ONE SERVING = 1 COOKIE

1 Position a rack in the middle of the oven. Preheat the oven to 350°F (180°C). Line a large baking sheet with parchment paper.

2 Beat together the canola oil and the brown and granulated sugars. The mixture will look like wet sand.

3 Add the egg and vanilla, and beat until the batter turns a light beige and is light and fluffy.

4 Stir in the flour, wheat germ, baking soda, and cinnamon, mixing thoroughly. Add the All-Bran Buds and chocolate chips to the batter and stir in thoroughly. The dough will be very stiff, so feel free to mix it with your hands.

5 Drop the batter by rounded tablespoonfuls (20 mL), about 1½ inches (4 cm) apart, onto the prepared baking sheet. Press down lightly on each heap of batter (for all you Type As out there, you want the cookies to be about ½ inch / 1 cm thick). Bake until the edges of the cookies are starting to turn golden brown but their centres are still soft, 10 to 12 minutes.

6 Let the cookies cool slightly on the baking sheet before removing them and letting them cool completely on a wire rack. (Store the cookies in an airtight container for up to 4 days, or freeze for up to 2 months.)

PER COOKIE: 141 CALORIES, 8 G TOTAL FAT, 1.6 G SATURATED FAT, 0 G TRANS FAT, 50 MG SODIUM, 17.1 G CARBOHYDRATE, 2 G FIBRE, 10.1 G SUGARS, 2 G PROTEIN

DIABETES FOOD CHOICE VALUES PER COOKIE: 1 CARBOHYDRATE, 1½ FAT

INGREDIENTS

- ½ cup (125 mL) canola oil (be sure to measure accurately; see page 21)
- ½ cup (125 mL) packed dark brown sugar
- ¼ cup (60 mL) granulated sugar
- 1 omega-3 egg (see page 13)
- 1 tsp (5 mL) pure vanilla extract
- 1¼ cups (310 mL) whole wheat flour
- 1 tbsp (15 mL) wheat germ
- ½ tsp (2.5 mL) baking soda
- ½ tsp (2.5 mL) cinnamon
- ½ cup (125 mL) Kellogg's All-Bran Buds
- ½ cup (125 mL) chocolate chips with at least 60% cocoa mass or chocolate chunks with at least 70% cocoa mass

GIVE IT A TWIST

Try adding 1 tbsp (15 mL) orange zest (see page 18) for a different flavour spin.

HOW TO

I use electronic beaters when I make these cookies, up to the point of adding the All-Bran Buds and chocolate chips; then it's elbow grease all the way. But if you're an exercise nut (or a purist), feel free to mix the entire recipe with a wooden spoon.

PICTURED ON PAGE 259
YEAR ROUND
KID FRIENDLY

Triple-Chocolate Brownie Cookies

I've been trying to make my own two-bite brownie ever since they appeared on supermarket shelves several years ago. My regular brownie recipe just didn't hold up in those teeny-tiny muffin tins. After three creative attempts, I threw in the towel.

I've always thought that combining cocoa powder, cocoa nibs, and chocolate chips was a really great idea, so when I started working on this recipe I had a stroke of genius: why not try for the two-bite brownie as a cookie? Even if they didn't look great, I'd bet my membership in the Royal Society of Chocolate Lovers that they'd still taste great.

I was right. And on my first try!

So here, in my humble, card-carrying chocoholic opinion, is my next award-winning cookie, with the heart-healthy benefits of canola oil, natural cocoa powder, cocoa nibs, and dark chocolate.

MAKES 32 COOKIES (USING 2 TSP/10 ML MINI-SCOOP)
ONE SERVING = 2 COOKIES

INGREDIENTS

- 3/4 cup (185 mL) packed dark brown sugar
- 6 tbsp (90 mL) canola oil
- 2 tbsp (30 mL) honey
- 1 omega-3 egg (see page 13)
- 2 tsp (10 mL) pure vanilla extract
- 1/2 cup (125 mL) natural cocoa powder (see page 12)
- 3/4 cup (185 mL) whole wheat flour
- 1/4 cup (60 mL) cocoa nibs (see page 12)
- 1/4 cup (60 mL) chocolate chips with at least 60% cocoa mass or chocolate chunks with at least 70% cocoa mass
- 2 tbsp (30 mL) wheat germ
- 1/4 tsp (1 mL) baking soda

1 Position a rack in the middle of the oven. Preheat the oven to 375°F (190°C). Line a large baking sheet with parchment paper.

2 Beat together the brown sugar, oil, honey, egg, and vanilla in a medium bowl using electric beaters until the batter is creamy, about 3 minutes.

3 Beat in the cocoa powder *gently*. Warning: turn those beaters to full throttle and you'll be a cocoa-covered mess in seconds. Start beating on low speed, then increase the speed once the cocoa has been incorporated. Beat for 1 minute.

4 Stir together the flour, cocoa nibs, chocolate chips, wheat germ, and baking soda in a medium bowl. Add the flour mixture to the cocoa mixture, and blend until well mixed, about 1 minute. The batter will be really sticky.

5 Drop the batter by rounded teaspoonfuls (10 mL), or use a mini-scoop (see page 11), onto the prepared baking sheet, spacing the cookies about 1 inch (2.5 cm) apart. Bake until the outside of the cookies is crunchy looking and they have puffed up, 8 to 10 minutes. Don't overbake these morsels. There aren't a lot of things that taste worse than burnt chocolate; okay, I can name three, but that's for another day. My oven bakes these perfectly in exactly 9 minutes.

6 Let the cookies cool slightly on the baking sheet before removing them and letting them cool completely on a wire rack. (Store the cookies in an airtight container for up to 1 week, or freeze for up to 2 months.)

PER SERVING: 154 CALORIES, 8.2 G TOTAL FAT, 1.9 G SATURATED FAT, 0 G TRANS FAT, 24 MG SODIUM, 19 G CARBOHYDRATE, 2 G FIBRE, 12.3 G SUGARS, 2 G PROTEIN

DIABETES FOOD CHOICE VALUES PER SERVING: 1 CARBOHYDRATE, 1½ FAT

COOKIE EAT-A-THON

Reality tester Simone in Edmonton said her husband nearly ate all 32 cookies the afternoon she made them.

THE TREAT DILEMMA

I don't know when it happened, but it definitely did, and no one emailed the announcement to me. Shocking!

I get announcements and emails about everything, from new products on the market to the state of the male reproductive organ, but no one ever sent me the one about needing treats every day or we'll die.

When I was growing up — and I'm not even that old — you got a treat because it was a very, very special occasion. Santa was here, or someone in your immediate family had been knighted by the Queen. It had to be big news to warrant a treat.

You got a chocolate bar, a candy cane, or if you were really, really lucky, an extremely cold pop out of one of those old pop machines that were in every local corner store. Nowadays, you get a treat just for getting up in the morning. Okay, maybe some mornings you *deserve* a treat for that, but most days, I don't think so.

The problem is, we are constantly surrounded by treats. You can be standing at the grocery checkout and have a buggy filled with fruits and vegetables, then out of the blue the thought of having a cold pop, a bag of chips, and a chocolate bar seems like a brilliant idea. It feels like you're running the junk food gauntlet: just make it past the checkout and you'll be fine. Brian Wansink, PhD, the author of *Mindless Eating: Why We Eat More Than We Think*, has proven again and again that what we see, we eat. See treats, eat treats.

Ever had a Beaver Tail? A Beaver Tail is deep-fried bread dough sprinkled with icing sugar. It's the true definition of a treat: high sugar, high fat, empty calories, and can I please have three more?

No, but you can have just one, as long as you're in Ottawa skating down the Rideau Canal. If you can skate the 7.8-kilometre (5-mile) Skateway in hideous, cold February weather during Ottawa's annual Winterlude festival where they feature the treat, you deserve one — and 20 bucks for a cab ride home. Heck, you can have a treat just for showing up with your skates, tuque, and smile.

Perhaps there should be a warning on treats: *This food may contribute to a shortened lifespan. Eat with caution and indulge only occasionally or you'll end up with a large gut and clogged arteries.*

But if warnings really worked, I guess I wouldn't have taken that running leap off the stairs at my school as a dare when I was 11. And I wouldn't have torn all the ligaments in my ankle. And I wouldn't have had ankle surgery in my early twenties. And I wouldn't be wearing sensible shoes instead of cute high heels for the rest of my life. Yes, it's true that some warnings don't really work until after the fact.

Bottom line: indulge in a treat once in a while, and try to have a little foresight.

The Ultimate Healthy Chocolate Treat

I love chocolate.

I also love chocolate and something crunchy. These cereal-based goodies are a spin on a treat that was popular when I was a kid. I revised the recipe from one in Ultimate Foods for Ultimate Health ... and don't forget the chocolate! *They're easy to make and easy to eat.*

The Ultimate Healthy Chocolate Treat may become my true claim to fame. It tastes fabulous, and may help lower your cholesterol at the same time. Factor in the whole fibre and GI-tract thing and—bingo, bango, boom—it's a winner.

Just a heads-up, though: one little treat contains 6 grams of fibre. For anyone keeping score, that's a ton of fibre for a treat. Actually, it's a ton of fibre for anything.

To put it into perspective, each of these treats has the same amount of fibre as a regular bowl of high-fibre cereal. Now, you wouldn't have two bowls of high-fibre cereal, but you might want to have two of these babies. So, think twice before you go on a chocolate treat rampage.

I felt obligated to warn you.

MAKES 24 TREATS | ONE SERVING = 1 TREAT

INGREDIENTS

3 cups (750 mL) Kellogg's All-Bran Buds

2 cups (500 mL) Nature's Path Organic Flax Plus Multibran cereal

8 oz (250 g) really good dark chocolate with at least 70% cocoa mass (see sidebar, page 313), chopped into ½-inch (1 cm) chunks

1 Line your kitchen counter with 1 sheet of waxed paper about 24 inches (60 cm) long.

2 Mix together the All-Bran Buds and Multibran cereal in a large bowl.

CONTINUED ...

CONTINUED FROM THE PREVIOUS PAGE

3 Place the chocolate in a large heavy saucepan. Place the saucepan over medium-low heat and start stirring. Do not leave the stove. I don't care if the phone rings, your dog is barking at the wind, or your partner comes home with a raise; you are working with chocolate, and for the love of Pete, priorities, please!

4 As soon as the chocolate starts to melt, reduce the heat to low. (If you are using an electric stove, you may even have to take the saucepan off the element for a minute.) Keep stirring gently and let the chocolate melt slowly. When it is almost all melted, remove the saucepan from the heat. Stir until the chocolate is completely melted and shiny.

5 Pour the chocolate over the cereals and stir well. Let the mixture cool slightly, then drop heaping tablespoonfuls (20 mL) of the mixture onto the waxed paper. You should get 24 heaps.

6 Here comes the hard part: let the treats cool until they are set and firm enough to pick up, at least 1 hour. Walk away. Console yourself by licking the saucepan, remembering that all foods eaten over the sink don't really count as calories. And if you buy that one, how about the chances of the Toronto Maple Leafs winning the Stanley Cup anytime soon?

7 When the treats are firm, store them in an airtight container for up to 1 week (as if they'll last that long).

PER TREAT: 95 CALORIES, 3.9 G TOTAL FAT, 1.9 G SATURATED FAT, 0 G TRANS FAT, 83 MG SODIUM, 17.2 G CARBOHYDRATE, 6 G FIBRE, 8.2 G SUGARS, 2 G PROTEIN

DIABETES FOOD CHOICE VALUES PER TREAT: 1 CARBOHYDRATE, 1 FAT

Chocolate Monkey Smoothie

I was in Grade 6 when the hippies hit Vancouver. My parents were convinced that hippie food and hippie beliefs would lead us all down the road to cultural disaster and political anarchy. As for myself? I dreamed of having flowers in my hair, and eating all the hippie foods I could find.

One of my family's favourite activities was going for a ride. This wasn't some far-out drug-induced trip; this was literally all of us, in the car, going for a ride around town.

By the time I was 12, it felt like being shot out of a cannon would be less painful than being seen with Mommy and Daddy. So, the only reason I went along was because we usually ended up at Peter's Ice Cream.

I'll never forget the day that my dad drove the long way to the ice cream place, taking us up Fourth Avenue to stare at the local hippie commune. I was mortified. I ducked behind the front seats so no one would know I was with these gauche oglers. My dad even drove around the block a couple of times to get a really good look.

For the life of me, I can't remember why a Chocolate Monkey and being a hippie have always been wrapped up together in the same memory. But for all the flower children my parents gawked at, here's my spin on a classic from the '60s.

MAKES ABOUT 3 CUPS (750 ML), DEPENDING ON THE SIZE OF THE BANANAS AND HOW POWERFUL YOUR BLENDER IS | ONE SERVING = ABOUT 1½ CUPS (375 ML)

INGREDIENTS

2 very ripe bananas

1 cup (250 mL) ice cubes (about 4)

1 cup (250 mL) skim milk

2 tbsp (30 mL) natural peanut butter (see below)

2 tbsp (30 mL) natural cocoa powder (see page 12)

2 tbsp (30 mL) skim milk powder (see page 17)

2 tbsp (30 mL) honey, or your choice of sweetener to taste

1 Put all the ingredients in a blender and whirl until smooth. While I love my food processor (see page 8 for why it's great for lots of other recipes), I always use a blender for this, as it makes a much smoother smoothie.

2 Pour into 2 glasses, dividing evenly.

HEALTH BITE

As much as I would love you to use natural peanut butter, I'm sure a lot of you don't, so the brand you're using probably has sugar in it. Check the label, and if it is sweetened, skip adding the honey or sweetener of your choice. The peanut butter will probably make it sweet enough without the added carbs and sugars from the honey. (See page 14 for more information on natural peanut butter.)

PER SERVING: 354 CALORIES, 9 G TOTAL FAT, 1.5 G SATURATED FAT, 0 G TRANS FAT, 108 MG SODIUM, 61.3 G CARBOHYDRATE, 4 G FIBRE, 42.3 G SUGARS, 14 G PROTEIN

DIABETES FOOD CHOICE VALUES PER SERVING: 4 CARBOHYDRATE, 2 MEAT AND ALTERNATIVES, ½ FAT

Old-Fashioned Hot Cocoa

One of my pet peeves is how the terms "cocoa" and "hot chocolate" get bandied around as if they were one and the same thing.

No, no, no, no, no!

Hot chocolate is made from melted chocolate, and cocoa is made from—wait for it!—cocoa powder.

Natural cocoa powder is higher in flavanols (those powerful antioxidants that can help reduce your blood pressure) than regular cocoa powder. Read more about how to spot natural cocoa powder on page 12.

MAKES 1 SERVING

INGREDIENTS

2 tbsp (30 mL) natural cocoa powder (see page 12)

2 tbsp (30 mL) agave syrup (see below) or honey, or your choice of sweetener to taste

1 cup (250 mL) skim milk or fortified organic soy beverage, divided

1 In a glass measuring cup and using a cocoa whisk (see page 11), whisk together the cocoa powder, agave, and a little of the milk to make a smooth paste.

2 Pour the rest of the milk into a small saucepan and heat over medium heat until it starts to steam. (Or heat in a microwaveable mug in the microwave on low until steamy.)

3 Whisk in the cocoa mixture until there aren't any lumps.

4 Heat over medium heat until steaming. (Or microwave on low until hot.)

PER SERVING: 250 CALORIES, 1 G TOTAL FAT, 0.6 G SATURATED FAT, 0 G TRANS FAT, 127 MG SODIUM, 51 G CARBOHYDRATE, 2 G FIBRE, 45 G SUGARS, 11 G PROTEIN

DIABETES FOOD CHOICE VALUES PER SERVING: 3½ CARBOHYDRATE, ½ MEAT AND ALTERNATIVES

WHAT IS . . . ?

Agave syrup is made from the same plant that's responsible for that alcoholic truth serum tequila. Agave has a couple of interesting characteristics: it's sweeter than honey or granulated sugar, so you use less, and it has a lower glycemic index (GI) than regular sugar. (See page 188 for more information on the glycemic index.)

LIGHTEN UP

To reduce the total amount of carbs to 42 g and the sugars to 31 g, use an unsweetened organic soy beverage for this. My brand of choice is Canadian Natur-a.

Chai-Infused Cocoa

This spiced hot cocoa was inspired by the flavourful South Asian tea called chai. It has the antioxidant powers of natural cocoa powder, cinnamon, cloves, allspice, and cardamom to help ward off colds and warm up your soul.

MAKES 2 CUPS (500 ML) | ONE SERVING = 1 CUP (250 ML)

1 Pour 1⅔ cups (410 mL) milk into a small saucepan. Add the green cardamom pods, black cardamom seeds, peppercorns, allspice, and cloves.

2 Heat over medium heat until the milk starts to steam. Cover the saucepan and reduce the heat to low. Steep the milk and spices together for 10 minutes.

3 In a glass measuring cup and using a cocoa whisk (see page 11), whisk together the cocoa powder, sugar, cinnamon, and remaining milk.

4 Whisk the cocoa mixture into the hot milk. Whisk until frothy. Strain into 2 mugs and serve.

PER SERVING: 188 CALORIES, 1.2 G TOTAL FAT, 0.6 G SATURATED FAT, 0 G TRANS FAT, 128 MG SODIUM, 33.5 G CARBOHYDRATE, 2 G FIBRE, 25 G SUGARS, 11 G PROTEIN

DIABETES FOOD CHOICE VALUES PER SERVING: 2 CARBOHYDRATE

INGREDIENTS

2 cups (500 mL) skim milk or fortified organic soy beverage, divided
6 whole green cardamom pods
4 whole black cardamom seeds
½ tsp (2.5 mL) whole black peppercorns
½ tsp (2.5 mL) whole allspice
½ tsp (2.5 mL) whole cloves
¼ cup (60 mL) natural cocoa powder (see page 12)
2 tbsp (30 mL) granulated sugar, or your choice of sweetener to taste
1 tsp (5 mL) cinnamon

GIVE IT A TWIST

For a more intense spice flavour, crush the green cardamom pods, black cardamom seeds, peppercorns, allspice, and cloves together with a mortar and pestle before adding them to the milk.

HEALTH BITE

Fibre in hot cocoa? Yes, cocoa has fibre in it. Who knew?

17

Fast Food:
Just Stop It!

If I had one wish, it wouldn't be to win $1 million, or even for world peace. My wish would be that fast food go back to being a treat, not everyday fare. I'll be the first to admit how corny that sounds, but I'm afraid for the future of our kids. We need to step up to the plate (pun intended) and start making changes to our diets — for our children's sake.

I know we're all really busy.

I know there doesn't seem to be enough time in the day to make dinner.

I know that a lot of us are struggling to find babysitters or daycare, or are busy driving our kids to hockey, soccer, gymnastics, and band. But we need to make time for a sit-down dinner with our children, our teens, or whoever happens to be at home.

The question may be, what's for dinner? But fast food isn't the answer.

A detour to the drive-through or calling for takeout doesn't cut it. We've gotten used to overly salty, overly fatty, overly mediocre food, and we need to put on the brakes. I'm not saying that you have to stop eating out altogether (although I'd be really happy if you did), but at least limit it to just once a month.

You thought I was going to say once a week, didn't you? If you eat out more than three times a week, start limiting that to once a week, then go from there. The more you eat out, the higher your fat, sodium, and junk food meter rises, and the faster your long-term health goes down.

Rent Morgan Spurlock's documentary *Super Size Me*. It follows Mr. Spurlock as he eats fast food, and only fast food, for one month. Not only did the lean Mr. Spurlock gain 24 ½ lb (11.1 kg) in 30 days, but his body mass increased by 13%, his cholesterol went off the charts, and he developed fatty liver disease. And that weight he gained in one month? It took him 14 months to lose it, and who knows how long to reverse the damage done to his body.

Okay, most of you will agree that we need to eat more home-cooked meals. But what's quick and easy that the kids will eat?

A large majority of the recipes in this book are both quick and easy. Some require you to plan ahead; others can be made in advance, then served different ways.

I have labelled the recipes my kid tasters loved, but my kid tasters may not have the same palate as your children, so use this only as a guideline.

Get your family involved. Have them share kitchen duties with you.

Here are some family- and kid-friendly recipes that are easy to fix, taste great, and can be a springboard to making healthier choices. Because the bottom line is, our kids deserve healthier choices.

YEAR ROUND
KID FRIENDLY

Hockey-Night-in-Canada Burgers

Every family has its own traditions. Some families go camping every May Two-Four long weekend, some go to church every Sunday. And my family? We watch Hockey Night in Canada *every Saturday night.*

As far back as I can remember, my dad would make hamburgers and we'd be allowed to watch the game. Didn't matter if you were sick, or had a previous engagement or a new boyfriend: you ate Dad's hamburgers and watched the game.

Since I grew up in Vancouver, the game started around 5:00 p.m. Dad would fire up the frying pan, heat up scones or hamburger buns from McPherson's bakery, burn a batch of onions, and get the fixings ready. Dad's 100% beef burgers had so much guck on them you needed at least 16 serviettes. If we were really lucky, we got potato chips on the side!

So, in honour of my father (who is, of course, the best dad ever), here's my version of homemade burgers.

MAKES 8 BURGERS | ONE SERVING = 1 BURGER

INGREDIENTS

4 cloves garlic
3 large shallots
2 tbsp (30 mL) fresh rosemary (see page 25)
1 tbsp (15 mL) chili powder
1 tsp (5 mL) paprika (try smoked paprika; it's excellent)
1 tsp (5 mL) cracked black pepper
3 tbsp (45 mL) ketchup (preferably organic)
2 tsp (10 mL) Worcestershire sauce
1 lb (500 g) extra-lean ground beef
1 lb (500 g) extra-lean ground turkey
Eight 100% whole wheat hamburger buns (or 100% whole-grain whole wheat buns, if you can find them)

1 Get out a large plate for the burgers.

2 Process the garlic, shallots, and rosemary in a food processor until finely minced. (If you don't have a food processor, use a knife to very finely chop the ingredients, then read why you need a food processor on page 8.)

3 Add the chili powder, paprika, pepper, Worcestershire sauce, and ketchup to the food processor and process until a thick paste forms. (Or mix everything together in a large bowl.)

CONTINUED ...

KID ZONE

If your kids are into plain, eliminate the chili powder and cracked black pepper, and reduce the rosemary to 1 tbsp (15 mL).

HEALTH BITE

Using half extra-lean ground beef and half extra-lean ground turkey reduces the amount of saturated fat in these burgers.

CONTINUED FROM THE PREVIOUS PAGE

4 Scrape the paste out into a large bowl. Wash your hands and add the ground beef and turkey. Use your hands or a large spoon to mix the ingredients together really well.

5 Form the ground meat mixture into 8 even-sized patties. Place them on that large plate you set out in Step 1 so you don't cross-contaminate your kitchen as you go to get a plate out of the cupboard. (The uncooked burgers can be covered and refrigerated for up to 6 hours.)

6 Wash your hands again, then preheat the barbecue to medium. Grill the burgers, flipping them often to prevent them blackening, until a meat thermometer inserted horizontally into each burger registers 160°F (71°C), 12 to 15 minutes.

7 Just before the burgers are ready, split the buns and toast on the barbecue until golden brown. Serve the burgers in the buns, with all your favourite fixings, or try my recipe for Caramelized Onions (page 263).

PER BURGER (WITHOUT THE BUN OR FIXINGS): 217 CALORIES, 9.4 G TOTAL FAT, 3.3 G SATURATED FAT, 0 G TRANS FAT, 114 MG SODIUM, 6.3 G CARBOHYDRATE, 1 G FIBRE, 1.6 G SUGARS, 17 G PROTEIN

DIABETES FOOD CHOICE VALUES PER SERVING (WITHOUT THE BUN OR FIXINGS): ½ CARBOHYDRATE, 2½ MEAT AND ALTERNATIVES, ½ FAT

MAKEOVERS

Don't have enough people in your house to eat eight burgers? No problem. As long as you use ground meat that hasn't previously been frozen, you can freeze the uncooked patties. Wrap them individually and store them in the freezer for up to three months. Grill them straight from the freezer over medium heat, flipping them often to prevent them from blackening, until a meat thermometer inserted horizontally into each burger registers 160°F (71°C), 20 to 25 minutes.

HEALTH BITE

This high-end, gourmet burger is lean, juicy, and full of flavour. Better still, the rosemary, garlic, and shallots help reduce the carcinogens that are produced when you blacken protein on a grill. So the next time you crank up the barbecue, make sure you have these potent antioxidant-rich ingredients on hand, and flip the burgers often to prevent them from blackening.

My Mom's Mini Meat Loaf, Circa 1960

My mother fixed a great meat loaf. On one of my visits home to Vancouver, I asked her how she made her specialty. Turns out it was based on advice columnist Ann Landers's meat loaf recipe. I went looking through my mom's recipe tin and found it. So, with a humble salute to Miss Landers and my mom, here's my version of that classic recipe, baked in muffin tins.

MAKES 16 MINI MEAT LOAVES | ONE SERVING = 2 MINI MEAT LOAVES

INGREDIENTS

Non-stick baking spray
2 slices 100% whole-grain whole wheat bread
2 large shallots
6 large cloves garlic
½ tsp (2.5 mL) ground sage
½ tsp (2.5 mL) paprika
¼ tsp (1 mL) cracked black pepper
One 5.5 oz (156 mL) can tomato paste
½ cup (125 mL) ketchup (preferably organic)
1 omega-3 egg (see page 13)
2 tbsp (30 mL) Worcestershire sauce
1 lb (500 g) extra-lean ground beef
1 lb (500 g) extra-lean ground turkey

1 Preheat the oven to 350°F (180°C). Lightly spray two 12-cup muffin pans with non-stick baking spray. Set aside.

2 Break the bread up into chunks and place in a food processor (see page 8 to read why you need a food processor) or blender. Pulse until soft breadcrumbs form. (You should have about 1½ cups/375 mL.) Place the breadcrumbs in a large bowl.

3 If you're using a food processor, add the peeled shallots and garlic to the processor, and pulse until minced. Or mince the shallots and garlic with a knife. Add the shallots and garlic to the breadcrumbs.

4 Add the sage, paprika, pepper, tomato paste, ketchup, egg, and Worcestershire sauce, and mix well.

5 Wash your hands. Add the ground beef and turkey to the bowl, and mix well using your hands or a large spoon. Wash your hands again. Spoon the meat mixture into 16 of the muffin cups, dividing evenly. Lightly press down on the meat mixture in each cup. Fill the empty muffin cups with water. Bake until a meat thermometer inserted in the centre of each mini meat loaf registers 160°F (71°C), 50 to 55 minutes.

6 Remove the pans from the oven and let the meat loaves rest for 10 minutes. A perfect time to mash the potatoes, because you *have* to have mashed potatoes with meat loaf.

PER SERVING: 260 CALORIES, 10.2 G TOTAL FAT, 3.4 G SATURATED FAT, 0 G TRANS FAT, 177 MG SODIUM, 13.3 G CARBOHYDRATE, 2 G FIBRE, 5.2 G SUGARS, 19 G PROTEIN

DIABETES FOOD CHOICE VALUES PER SERVING: 1 CARBOHYDRATE, 2½ MEAT AND ALTERNATIVES, ½ FAT

YEAR ROUND
KID FRIENDLY

Good-for-You Chicken Fingers

Kids love chicken fingers, but unfortunately, most commercial brands are on the not-so-good-for-you list. They contain bad fats, too much sodium, and unrecognizable ingredients.

In my pursuit of a healthier chicken finger, I've tried many different versions, but it wasn't until I made a recipe from the Ontario Apple Growers' website (onapples.com) that I knew I was on to something.

I think the recipe developer, Nicole Young, made a great choice when she used chili sauce to help the crumbs stick to the chicken. After experimenting with endless spice combos, here, at long last, is a healthy and delicious recipe for chicken fingers that I've based on Nicole's original recipe.

CHICKEN FINGERS: MAKES 4 SERVINGS | ONE SERVING = 3 TO 4 CHICKEN FINGERS
DIPPING SAUCE: MAKES ½ CUP (125 ML) | ONE SERVING = 2 TBSP (30 ML)

CHICKEN FINGERS

- 1 lb (500 g) skinless, boneless chicken breast
- 2 cups (500 mL) Nature's Path Organic Flax Plus Multibran cereal or other whole-grain cereal flakes
- 1 tbsp (15 mL) paprika
- 1½ tsp (7.5 mL) onion powder
- ½ tsp (2.5 mL) garlic powder
- ½ tsp (2.5 mL) ground sage
- ½ tsp (2.5 mL) dried oregano leaves
- ½ tsp (2.5 mL) dried basil leaves
- ½ tsp (2.5 mL) cracked black pepper
- ¼ cup (60 mL) chili sauce

DIPPING SAUCE

- ¼ cup (60 mL) low-fat creamy Caesar or ranch dressing
- ¼ cup (60 mL) low-fat plain yogurt

ACCOMPANIMENTS

Carrot and celery sticks, and cherry or grape tomatoes

KID ZONE

For a plainer version, omit the paprika, sage, and pepper, and reduce the amount of onion powder to ½ tsp (2.5 mL).

1 Preheat the oven to 400°F (200°C). Line a large rimmed baking sheet with parchment paper.

2 Wash your hands and cut the chicken breasts lengthwise into chunky, finger-width strips. Try to make them all the same size for even cooking. Set aside on a clean plate.

3 Wash your hands and cutting board really well. (I keep a separate cutting board to use for raw meat and fish.)

4 In a food processor (see page 8), or in a bowl and using a potato masher, crush the cereal until it looks like small crumbs.

5 Mix together the cereal, paprika, onion powder, garlic powder, sage, oregano, basil, and pepper in a medium bowl.

6 Pour the chili sauce into a shallow bowl.

CONTINUED ...

CONTINUED FROM PAGE 298

7 Dip the chicken fingers in the chili sauce. Don't overcoat them with the sauce; you just want a light coating. Roll the chicken fingers in the cereal mixture until completely coated. Discard any leftover crumb mixture and chili sauce.

8 Arrange the chicken fingers in a single layer on the prepared baking sheet. Bake until the chicken fingers are no longer pink inside and the crumb coating is browned, about 20 minutes depending on size.

9 While the chicken fingers are baking, make the dipping sauce by mixing together the salad dressing and yogurt in a small bowl.

10 Divide the chicken fingers evenly among 4 plates. Serve with the dipping sauce and raw veggies.

PER SERVING (WITHOUT DIPPING SAUCE OR RAW VEGGIES): 240 CALORIES, 3 G TOTAL FAT, 0.6 G SATURATED FAT, 0 G TRANS FAT, 144 MG SODIUM, 18.7 G CARBOHYDRATE, 4 G FIBRE, 7.3 G SUGARS, 30 G PROTEIN

DIABETES FOOD CHOICE VALUES PER SERVING (WITHOUT DIPPING SAUCE OR RAW VEGGIES): 1 CARBOHYDRATE, 4 MEAT AND ALTERNATIVES

PER SERVING (DIPPING SAUCE): 43 CALORIES, 3 G TOTAL FAT, 1 G SATURATED FAT, 0 G TRANS FAT, 189 MG SODIUM, 3 G CARBOHYDRATE, 0 G FIBRE, 2 G SUGARS, 1 G PROTEIN

DIABETES FOOD CHOICE VALUES PER SERVING (DIPPING SAUCE): 1 EXTRA, ½ FAT

MONEY SAVER

I don't use onion or garlic powder very often, so I buy small amounts of each at my local bulk store; it costs all of 10¢.

MAKEOVERS

My sister-in-law Valorie had a brilliant idea for any leftover chicken fingers. Make a main-meal wrap by tucking a serving of cooked chicken fingers inside a 100% whole wheat or whole-grain whole wheat tortilla, along with lettuce, tomatoes, and some of the dipping sauce.

PIZZA? MAKE MINE HOMEMADE

I loved my Grade 8 Home Economics class, I loved my unit — the four-person kitchen we cooked in — and I loved my teacher, Mrs. Favaro. She knew everything there was to know about food.

Every class was exciting. We made weird date balls that you cooked in a frying pan, some kind of cooked egg thing — and pizza.

With my English, Scots, and Irish roots, I was mesmerized by pizza. It was the most exotic food ever to cross my lips, and I practically flew home with the recipe, ready to wow my family:

MAIRLYN: Mom, we made pizza at school today and I got an A. Can I make it for dinner? It's the best thing I've ever had in my life. Wait and see!
MOM: No.
MAIRLYN: But Mom, it was the best thing ever!
MOM: No.
MAIRLYN: — But Mom!!!
MOM: No!
MAIRLYN: BUT! MOM!!!
MOM: NO!!!
MAIRLYN: WHY???
MOM: Because it's Italian food, and we don't eat Italian food.
MAIRLYN: WHAT?

What kind of goofy answer was that? My mother was nuts. I'd always had my suspicions, but now I had proof.

We don't eat Italian? My self-serving teenage brain went into high gear and I campaigned tenaciously for pizza for months. I was relentless. Any opportunity to sneak in an Italian reference became my new favourite hobby. Watching *Hockey Night in Canada*: *Hey, did you know that Phil Esposito is Italian?* Leaving for school: *Ciao*. And my showstopper: *Sophia Loren has big boobs because she eats spaghetti.*

My mother finally caved in after months of benign Italian references, but I always thought it was the mention of Sophia's "attributes" that sent her over the edge. At last I got to whip up a pizza made with baking powder biscuit dough, tomato sauce, and cheese.

My family's first taste sent them into overdrive, and I was commissioned to make this Italian food of the gods every week. Yup, I had them right where I wanted them.

Basic Whole Wheat Pizza Dough

This pizza crust sure beats the heck out of baking powder biscuit dough. The only glitch? You need a large food processor for this recipe.

If you want to make more than one pizza, go ahead and make two batches of dough, and double the toppings.

MAKES 1 PIZZA CRUST

STARTER

- ¼ cup (60 mL) warm water (105°F to 115°F / 40°C to 46°C)
- 1 tbsp (15 mL) whole wheat flour
- One 0.30 oz (8 g) package or 2¼ tsp (11 mL) traditional active dry yeast

DOUGH

- 1½ cups (375 mL) plus up to ¼ cup (60 mL) more whole wheat flour, divided
- ½ tsp (2.5 mL) salt (Salt?! Yes, it serves a function in the dough, so don't omit it.)
- ½ cup (125 mL) warm water (105°F to 115°F / 40°C to 46°C)
- 1 tbsp (15 mL) extra virgin olive oil or canola oil

1 For the starter, using either a mini-whisk or a fork, whisk together the water, flour, and yeast in a small bowl. Cover and leave in a warm place until foamy, 5 to 10 minutes.

2 For the dough, place 1½ cups (375 mL) flour and the salt in the bowl of the food processor. Pulse 3 times. Once the starter is foamy, stir it, then pour it into the food processor.

3 Add the warm water and the oil. Pulse several times until the dough starts to come together. Process for 1 minute.

4 Add 1 tbsp (15 mL) flour and pulse for 20 seconds. Add another 1 tbsp (15 mL) flour and process for 1 minute. The dough will have formed into a ball.

5 If the ball of dough is very sticky, add up to 2 tbsp (30 mL) additional flour and process until a ball of dough forms.

6 Remove the dough from the food processor and knead it on a lightly floured counter until the dough looks smooth, about 2 minutes.

7 Remove the blade from the food processor and return the ball of dough to the bowl of the food processor. Cover and leave in a warm place to proof for 1¼ hours. "Proof?" It's chef-speak for letting the dough rise and double in size. (I use the microwave for this step: Microwave 1 cup / 250 mL water in a microwaveable bowl on high for 1½ minutes. Leave the bowl of water in the microwave. Place the dough in the bowl of the food processor but don't cover it. Place the food processor bowl in the microwave alongside the bowl of hot water and close the door. Leave to proof for about 45 minutes.)

8 When the dough has doubled in size, remove it from the food processor bowl. Use to make the pizzas on pages 304 and 305.

PER PIZZA CRUST (WITHOUT TOPPINGS): 945 CALORIES, 19.2 G TOTAL FAT, 2.6 G SATURATED FAT, 0 G TRANS FAT, 1,191 MG SODIUM, 155.3 G CARBOHYDRATE, 16 G FIBRE, 7.3 G SUGARS, 32 G PROTEIN

DIABETES FOOD CHOICE VALUES PER PIZZA CRUST (WITHOUT TOPPINGS): 9 CARBOHYDRATE, 1 MEAT AND ALTERNATIVES, 3 FAT

GET AHEAD

While the dough is proofing, preheat the pizza stone (see below). No pizza stone? Use a regular pizza pan, but preheat the oven to 450°F (230°C) for at least 10 minutes before baking your pizza to make sure the oven is really, really hot.

MY FAVOURITE PIZZA TOYS

PIZZA STONE: A large flat piece of earthenware on which to bake a pizza. Using a pizza stone produces an evenly cooked, crispy crust. Put the stone in a cold oven, then preheat the oven to 450°F (230°C). Place the uncooked pizza on the hot stone and follow the cooking time in the recipe.

BAKER'S PEEL: A long-handled wooden paddle used to slide pizza on and off a pizza stone.

PIZZA WHEEL OR PIZZA CUTTER: A sharp, rolling wheel that neatly cuts the pizza (and a finger if it gets in the way; I have a small scar on my thumb to prove it).

YEAR ROUND
KID FRIENDLY

Tex-Mex Pizza

Lower the fat content of this nachos-style pizza by choosing low-fat cheese.

MAKES 8 SLICES | ONE SERVING = 1 SLICE

1 Position a rack in the middle of the oven. If using a pizza stone, place it on the middle rack about 45 minutes before you plan to bake the pizza, and preheat the oven to 450°F (230°C). (If using a regular pizza pan, preheat the oven for 10 minutes.)

2 If using frozen corn, place it in a colander and rinse under hot water until thawed. Place the thawed corn on paper towels and pat dry. Place the fresh or thawed corn in a medium skillet and cook over medium heat until the kernels are slightly blackened, 6 to 8 minutes. Set aside.

3 Shape and stretch or roll the pizza dough into a 12-inch (30 cm) disc.

4 Dust your kitchen counter lightly with cornmeal. Place the disc of dough on top, press down lightly, then shake off any excess cornmeal and transfer the dough to either a baker's peel (if you're using a pizza stone) or a regular pizza pan.

5 Spread the refried beans evenly over the pizza crust. Spread the salsa evenly over the beans. Sprinkle the pizza evenly with blackened corn and green onions. Sprinkle evenly with cheese.

6 If using a pizza stone, carefully slide the pizza off the baker's peel and onto the stone. If it won't slide, use a flipper to loosen an edge, then slide it onto the stone. If using a regular pan, place it in the oven.

7 Bake until the crust is golden brown and the cheese has melted, 12 to 15 minutes. Using the baker's peel, slide the pizza off the stone; or remove the pizza pan from the oven. Slide the pizza onto a clean cutting board. Sprinkle evenly with cilantro. Using a pizza wheel or sharp knife, cut the pizza into 8 slices.

PER SLICE: 213 CALORIES, 6.8 G TOTAL FAT, 3.2 G SATURATED FAT, 0 G TRANS FAT, 432 MG SODIUM, 28.9 G CARBOHYDRATE, 3 G FIBRE, 2.5 G SUGARS, 11 G PROTEIN

DIABETES FOOD CHOICE VALUES PER SLICE: 2 CARBOHYDRATE, 1 MEAT AND ALTERNATIVES, ½ FAT

INGREDIENTS

1 cup (250 mL) fresh or frozen corn kernels
1 recipe for Basic Whole Wheat Pizza Dough (see page 302)
Cornmeal for dusting
¾ cup (185 mL) low-fat canned refried beans
½ cup (125 mL) mild, medium, or hot fresh salsa (from the deli)
2 green onions, thinly sliced
1 cup (250 mL) shredded Monterey Jack cheese
¼ cup (60 mL) lightly packed chopped fresh cilantro

Kid-Friendly Cheese Pizza with Homemade Sauce

Personalize your pizza by adding sliced sweet peppers, onion, mushrooms, fresh herbs, and broccoli florets. Make the sauce while the dough is proofing.

MAKES 8 SLICES | ONE SERVING = 1 SLICE

SAUCE

1 clove garlic
¼ cup plus 2 tbsp (90 mL) canned crushed tomatoes
1 tsp (5 mL) dried basil leaves
¼ tsp (1 mL) dried oregano leaves

CRUST

1 recipe for Basic Whole Wheat Pizza Dough (see page 302)
Cornmeal for dusting

TOPPINGS

⅔ cup (160 mL) shredded light mozzarella cheese
¼ cup (60 mL) grated Asiago cheese

1 Position a rack in the middle of the oven. If using a pizza stone, place it on the middle rack about 45 minutes before you plan to bake the pizza, and preheat the oven to 450°F (230°C). (If using a regular pizza pan, preheat the oven for 10 minutes.)

2 For the sauce, mince the garlic. Mix together the tomatoes, basil, and oregano in a small bowl. Stir in the garlic. Set aside.

3 For the crust, shape and stretch or roll the pizza dough into a 12-inch (30 cm) disc.

4 Dust your kitchen counter lightly with cornmeal. Place the disc of dough on top, press down lightly, then shake off any excess cornmeal and transfer the dough to either a baker's peel (if you're using a pizza stone) or a regular pizza pan.

5 Spread sauce evenly over the pizza crust. Sprinkle evenly with the cheeses.

6 If using a pizza stone, carefully slide the pizza off the baker's peel and onto the stone. If it won't slide, use a flipper to loosen an edge, then slide it onto the stone. If using a regular pan, place it in the oven.

7 Bake until the crust is golden brown and the cheese has melted, 12 to 15 minutes. Using the baker's peel, slide the pizza off the stone; or remove the pizza pan from the oven. Slide the pizza onto a clean cutting board. Using a pizza wheel or sharp knife, cut the pizza into 8 slices.

PER SLICE: 166 CALORIES, 5.2 G TOTAL FAT, 2 G SATURATED FAT, 0 G TRANS FAT, 288 MG SODIUM, 21.1 G CARBOHYDRATE, 2 G FIBRE, 1.4 G SUGARS, 8 G PROTEIN

DIABETES FOOD CHOICE VALUES PER SLICE: 1½ CARBOHYDRATE, ½ MEAT AND ALTERNATIVES, 1 FAT

18

Throwing a Dinner Party without Losing Your Mind

I love having dinner parties.

Don't get me wrong. I'm no Martha Stewart, but my idea of a great time is sharing a meal with friends. I love the planning and the cooking. I even love the grocery shopping and the setting-the-table part. I especially love the cocktails and the wine!

When I first started entertaining, I was famous for my Mary Tyler Moore parties: they were all tremendously awful. I'd either have too many people and not enough food, or attempt some spectacular, flaming entrée and start a small kitchen fire.

Even worse, the people I'd invite wouldn't have anything in common with each other and the night would be so boring even I'd want to leave.

Through years of trial and error, I finally figured out how to win at entertaining:

- Keep the numbers manageable: invite no more than six to eight people. Anything over eight is called catering.
- Invite people who know each other or have common interests—or who are so much fun, all you have to do is laugh.
- Keep the menu simple and only experiment on guests when it's an official taste-testing evening.

By following these simple rules, I've actually become pretty good at dinner parties.

While I was writing this book, my publisher was in town, so I invited him to dinner to try some of my new creations. My partner was away, but my son, Andrew, was home from university, so I thought we would have a nice, casual dinner.

I went to my local farmers market early that morning with one of my neighbours, Diva #1 (see page 164), and created my menu based on what was available. Even I was impressed.

I decided on Arugula with Roasted Beets and Goat Cheese (page 200) even though they didn't have any arugula; dandelion greens would be tart enough to handle the sweetness of the beets. I had spotted some fresh oyster mushrooms, so I decided to make my Spring Mushroom Omelette for Two (page 248) for the main course (increasing the quantities so Andrew wouldn't starve), along with Whole-Grain Irish Soda Bread (page 185). I thought I had some frozen blueberries, so I went with Baked Blueberries with Oat Topping (page 335) for dessert.

I came home from the market with my treasures. First I roasted the candy cane beets and made the dessert. The beets took an extra long time to get tender in the oven and ended up becoming candied beets. Well, they did have a higher sugar content than regular beets, but they'd be okay. I realized I didn't have any cultivated blueberries, so I ended up using some wild ones that had been in my freezer since—well, I wasn't sure how long they had been in there. I didn't even remember buying them, but the snowy ice on them would melt and they'd be fine.

I picked up Robert, and after we had visited Nick Rundall, Whitecap's vice-president, and his wife Katherine Govier, a well-known Canadian writer, we headed home.

We were later than I thought. I was a little flustered, but we did make it home. As I went to make the Irish soda bread, I realized I had forgotten to pick up whole wheat flour on the way home, so I ditched the bread idea, and Robert and I prepared the salad together.

But the salad didn't taste as good as it usually does. Those candied beets gave it a very different flavour, and the dandelion greens were so bitter they sucked the spit right out your mouth. However, the dressing was fabulous, as was the wine Robert had brought.

Hopefully the main course would be better. I love the omelette recipe, and with the farm-fresh eggs, local oyster mushrooms, and just-picked asparagus I'd bought, it would be perfection.

Now, the truth is, despite my love of wine and cocktails, I'm a lightweight in the drinking department. I had a bad experience with alcohol in Germany in the 1970s and that was it for me. Maybe it was because I was nervous, but against my better judgment, I thought another glass of wine was a *really* good idea.

We started fixing the Spring Mushroom Omelette for Two. Halfway through I realized that I'd used all the goat cheese on the salad so there wasn't enough for the omelette. Had I not been slightly inebriated—doesn't take much—I would have used one of the four different cheeses I had in the fridge. But my alcohol-riddled brain couldn't improvise, so we whipped up a slightly burned cheese omelette that was entirely free of cheese. My son decided he didn't like the look of it and microwaved a piece of frozen lasagna.

The omelette was awful. I hadn't bought enough oyster mushrooms, and without the cheese it was flat and sort of tasteless. Ketchup may have saved it, but you don't serve ketchup to your publisher. Andrew's lasagna smelled great.

I had another glass of wine and served dessert.

Never use wild blueberries in a crisp. Under the oat topping was a congealed blob of purple goo.

By this point, telling Robert that all these recipes were going to be in the book seemed insane even to looped-on-three-glasses-of-wine me.

The dinner plodded along as I talked about any inane thing that popped into my head. By the time the evening wound down, I knew I couldn't drive Robert back to his hotel, so I searched through my wallet to give him the cab fare back.

You can't go far on five bucks. My son had just got his learner's licence and I was fairly sure he wasn't allowed to drive with two other people in the car, especially when one of them was hammered. Feeling like a complete loser, I gave Robert three bucks and walked him to the subway.

When I got back home, my son critiqued the evening: "Mom, it's a good thing your publisher is such a nice guy, 'cause dinner was terrible."

Yes, it was endlessly terrible. I was mortified. My saving grace was that Robert knew me well enough to dismiss it as a blip, because if this had been my let's-try-to-get-a-book-deal night, I would have ended up bookless.

On a positive note, all those recipes have since been fixed and now include tips on how not to wreck them.

And I've added one more rule to my winning-at-dinner-parties list:

You are your own liquor control board: never, ever get inebriated at your own dinner party.

FOUR SEASONS, FOUR MENUS

If you're a newbie at entertaining, it can be daunting figuring out what to cook and how to have everything ready at the right time.

Move over, Martha! Here are four dinners, each tailor-made for a different season, which are good enough for company, but simple to prepare.

Each menu includes a game plan that's easy to follow and which makes fixing dinner for company a cinch.

The wine lists for each dinner feature wines from British Columbia and Ontario chosen by chef Jen Mattka, an honours graduate of Toronto's George Brown College Chef School. Jen was a chef at the G8 summit in Muskoka, Ontario, in June 2010, and the same month was featured as Chef of Merit in Toronto's *Main Street Magazine.*

MENU

Spring

SPRING'S IN THE AIR DINNER FOR FOUR

Carrot-Apricot Soup (page 312)

Spring Asparagus and Shrimp with Lemon Pasta (page 40)

Crustless Orange-Ricotta Cheesecake with Chocolate Glaze (page 313)

•

WINE LIST

To drink with the main course:

Konzelmann Sauvignon Blanc Reserve 2008 (Ontario)

or

White Bear Wines Sauvignon Blanc 2008 (British Columbia)

SPRING MENU GAME PLAN

THE DAY BEFORE:

- Put the wine in the fridge
- Make the soup (page 312) and store it in the fridge
- Make the cheesecake (page 313), without the glaze, and store it overnight in the fridge
- Transfer the shrimp from freezer to fridge to thaw

THE DAY OF:

- Prepare all the ingredients for the pasta dish (page 40), place them in separate bowls, and refrigerate, covered, until cooking time:
    - Mince the garlic
    - Dice the shallots
    - Wash and cut the asparagus
    - Pit and chop the olives
    - Drain and rinse the capers
    - Zest and juice the lemons
    - Mince the parsley

AT LEAST 1 HOUR BEFORE:

- Make the chocolate glaze and finish the cheesecake (page 313). Leave it, uncovered, on the counter for up to 1 hour before serving time
- Remove the mandarin oranges from the fridge and drain well. Cover and refrigerate until serving time

WHEN EVERYONE'S ARRIVED:

- Heat the soup
- Put a large pot of water on to boil for the pasta. When the water boils, add the pasta
- Garnish the soup and serve

AFTER YOU'VE EATEN THE SOUP:

- Make the pasta dish (all your ingredients are prepped and ready, so play out your fantasy of being a TV cooking show host)
- Serve the pasta (don't forget the parsley garnish)
- Enjoy the first fabulous wine

AFTER YOU'VE EATEN THE PASTA:

- Slice and plate the cheesecake, garnishing it with the mandarin oranges

Carrot-Apricot Soup

Apricots are a great source of beta-carotene and add sweetness to this easy soup. Factor in the carrots, and you get a double whammy of beta-carotene to help stimulate your body's immune system—a big plus during spring's cold-and-flu season. (Read more about beta-carotene on page 107.)

MAKES ABOUT 5 CUPS (1.25 L) | ONE SERVING = 1¼ CUPS (310 ML)

1 Mince the garlic and set aside.

2 Coarsely chop the onion. The onion is going to get puréed eventually, so don't go crazy—just a rough chop is good. Set aside.

3 Slice the carrots into ½-inch (1 cm) thick coins. Set aside.

4 Heat a large saucepan over medium heat. Add the oil, then the onion, and sauté until the onion is slightly golden brown, about 4 minutes.

5 Add the garlic and sauté for 1 minute. Add the carrots and pepper, and sauté for 2 minutes.

6 Add the broth and apricots, and bring to a boil. Reduce the heat to a simmer and cook, covered, until the carrots are very tender, about 30 minutes.

7 Use a hand-held immersion blender (see page 8) to purée the soup in the saucepan until smooth. (Or purée the soup in a blender, about 2 cups / 500 mL at a time, until smooth.)

8 Ladle into soup bowls. (The soup can be refrigerated in an airtight container for up to 2 days, or frozen for up to 3 months. To serve, thaw, then reheat before serving.)

PER SERVING: 88 CALORIES, 2.9 G TOTAL FAT, 0.4 G SATURATED FAT, 0 G TRANS FAT, 186 MG SODIUM, 12.2 G CARBOHYDRATE, 2 G FIBRE, 8.1 G SUGARS, 4 G PROTEIN

DIABETES FOOD CHOICE VALUES PER SERVING: ½ CARBOHYDRATE, ½ MEAT AND ALTERNATIVES

INGREDIENTS

4 cloves garlic
1 onion
4 large unpeeled carrots, scrubbed
1 tbsp (15 mL) extra virgin olive oil
¼ tsp (1 mL) cracked black pepper
4 cups (1 L) lower-sodium chicken or vegetable broth (see page 7)
8 dried apricots, cut in half

GLAM IT UP

How's this for a classy garnish? Whisk ¼ cup (60 mL) plain non-fat yogurt in a small bowl until smooth. Dollop 1 tbsp (15 mL) on each portion of soup. With a sharp knife, draw a line through the yogurt and swirl it slightly. Sprinkle with finely chopped parsley.

And reality tester Liz, in Toronto, sprinkled a garnish of cinnamon over the soup when she made it.

Crustless Orange-Ricotta Cheesecake with Chocolate Glaze

The perfect dinner party dessert is either easy to prepare or can be made ahead. This cheesecake fits the latter category but it's quite simple, too. Come dessert time, all you to need to do is slice it and serve.

You need to buy extra-smooth light ricotta for this cheesecake. I use Silani brand extra-smooth light ricotta. If you can't find it, whirl regular light ricotta in the food processor until it's smooth before using in the recipe.

MAKES 12 SLICES | ONE SERVING = 1 SLICE

1 The day before you want to serve the cheesecake, put the unopened can of mandarin oranges in the fridge.

2 That same day, preheat the oven to 350°F (180°C). Line the base of an 8-inch (2 L) springform pan with a circle of parchment paper, and the sides with a strip of parchment paper. Set aside.

3 Scrub and dry the orange. Using a Microplane grater (see page 8), remove the zest from the orange and measure out 1 tbsp (15 mL). Set aside.

4 Beat the cream cheese in a large bowl only until it's smooth. Don't go crazy; too much beating will add too much air, which results in a ton of cracks in the finished cheesecake.

5 Add the ricotta, sugar, and flour to the bowl, and beat gently until smooth. Gently beat in the eggs, yogurt, orange juice concentrate, and orange zest until just combined. Pour the mixture into the prepared pan, spread to the sides of the pan, and spread the top level.

6 Bake for 50 minutes. When the timer goes off, turn off the oven and let the cheesecake sit for 10 minutes in the oven with the door closed. Remove the cheesecake from the oven and let it cool completely. Cover and refrigerate in the pan overnight.

CONTINUED ...

INGREDIENTS

1 can (11 oz/284 mL) mandarin orange segments in light syrup

CHEESECAKE

1 orange

Two 8 oz (250 g) packages light cream cheese, at room temperature

1 cup (250 mL) extra-smooth light ricotta (see above)

3/4 cup (185 mL) granulated sugar

3 tbsp (45 mL) all-purpose flour

2 omega-3 eggs (see page 13)

1/4 cup (60 mL) low-fat vanilla yogurt

1/4 cup (60 mL) frozen orange juice concentrate, thawed (see page 13)

GLAZE

2 oz (60 g) dark chocolate with at least 70% cocoa mass (see below)

2 tbsp (30 mL) frozen orange juice concentrate, thawed (see page 13)

CHOCOLATE DREAMS

I use 12 squares of a 100 g Dove Dark 71% cocoa mass chocolate bar, which at 66 g works out to be a tad more than needed. Whoops!

CONTINUED FROM PAGE 313

7 The next day, remove the cheesecake from the fridge. If there is any moisture on the top, gently lay a piece of paper towel on top to absorb it. Release the sides of the pan and remove the cheesecake.

8 Now for the trickiest part of the whole recipe: carefully peel off the parchment paper from the sides and base of the cheesecake, then place the cheesecake on a flat serving plate. If the top of the cheesecake is cracked, just flip the cheesecake onto the plate so it's upside down, and carefully peel the parchment paper off the base.

9 For the glaze, break the chocolate into small pieces and place it in a small saucepan. Add the orange juice concentrate. Place over low heat and stir until melted. (Or, for the unorthodox and not faint of heart, place the chocolate and orange juice concentrate in a microwaveable bowl and microwave on medium for 20 seconds. Stir well. If the chocolate isn't melting, microwave it in 5-second increments until the chocolate starts to melt, then stir until it's completely melted. But be warned: if you overheat the chocolate, it will burn and wreck the recipe.)

10 Pour the glaze over the top of the cheesecake and, using a metal spatula, spread it right to the edges. Let the glaze set at room temperature for at least 30 minutes. If you aren't serving the cheesecake within 1 hour, refrigerate it, uncovered, until 1 hour before serving time.

11 Open the can of mandarin oranges and drain well. Refrigerate until ready to serve.

12 Just before serving, cut the cheesecake into 12 even-sized slices and place each slice on a dessert plate. Spoon some mandarin orange segments alongside each slice. (Any leftover cheesecake can be refrigerated, covered, for up to 3 days.)

PER SERVING: 240 CALORIES, 9.9 G TOTAL FAT, 6.6 G SATURATED FAT, 0.3 G TRANS FAT, 251 MG SODIUM, 30.5 G CARBOHYDRATE, 1 G FIBRE, 25.1 G SUGARS, 8 G PROTEIN

DIABETES FOOD CHOICE VALUES PER SERVING: 2 CARBOHYDRATE, 1 MEAT AND ALTERNATIVES, 1½ FAT

HEALTH BITE

Whether you enjoy a glass of wine, a bottle of beer, a cocktail, or a shot of Scotch on the rocks, alcohol can be part of a healthy diet. The key is how much and how often you imbibe.

Drinking any alcohol, beer, wine, or spirits is a double-edged sword. One drink a day for a woman, as long as she's getting enough folate in her diet (from spinach, lentils, asparagus, avocado, peanuts, peas, and oranges, to name just seven sources), can be beneficial for heart health; two drinks a day, and her chances of developing breast cancer go up.

Men, your daily limit is two drinks before you up your chances of developing cancer.

And don't even think about stockpiling your daily limits and knocking them all back on a Friday night. Moderation is the key.

MENU

Summer

ODE TO THE BERRY DINNER FOR FOUR

Marinated Olives (page 318)

Blueberry and Tomato Summer Salad (page 78; omit the arugula)

Grilled Salmon Fillets with Raspberry Salsa (page 319)

Light Lemony Mousse (page 321)

•

WINE LIST

To drink with the main course:

Cave Spring Cellars Chardonnay 2008 (Ontario)

or

Inniskillin Pinot Blanc 2009 (British Columbia)

SUMMER MENU GAME PLAN

THE DAY BEFORE:

- Put the wine in the fridge
- Make the olives (page 318)
- If you are making Thickened Yogurt (page 272) for the mousse, prep it now (or buy plain 0% fat Greek-style yogurt)
- Make the lemon curd for the mousse (page 321) and refrigerate, covered, until assembly time
- Make the Cheater's Candied Lemon Peel (sidebar, page 321)

THE DAY OF:

- Finish making the mousse (page 321), spoon it into individual dessert dishes, and refrigerate, covered, until serving time
- Wash the strawberries for the dessert garnish and let them dry on paper towels
- Put the olives in a serving bowl and set aside at room temperature
- Prepare all the ingredients for 4 blueberry and tomato salads (page 78), omitting the arugula (see page 79 for a picture and remember that the recipe on page 78 serves one):
    - Wash the blueberries, remove any stems, and let dry on paper towels on the counter, or anywhere but in the fridge
    - Wash the tomatoes and let them dry on paper towels (never store tomatoes in the fridge; it's grounds for a quick trip to Culinary Hell)
- Prepare all the ingredients for the salmon (page 319) and refrigerate, covered, until cooking time:
    - Wash the baby greens, spin-dry, wrap in a clean tea towel, and put in a plastic bag
    - Make the raspberry marinade (page 319) and place in a resealable bag or a non-metallic dish
    - Make the raspberry salsa (page 319; remove from the fridge 1 hour before serving)
    - Cut the salmon into 4 pieces

WHEN EVERYONE'S ARRIVED:

- Remember to remove the raspberry salsa from the fridge
- Thirty minutes before you want to serve the main course, add the salmon to the marinade
- Preheat the barbecue to high
- Assemble the salads, complete with oil, vinegar, and crumbled feta cheese, and serve

AFTER YOU'VE EATEN THE SALAD:

- Grill the salmon
- Plate the salmon on top of the baby greens, spoon over the raspberry salsa, and serve
- Enjoy your glass of wine

AFTER YOU'VE EATEN THE SALMON:

- Garnish the mousse with strawberries and Cheater's Candied Lemon Peel, and serve

Marinated Olives

This is a really great appetizer that goes with any pre-dinner cocktail. For the best flavour make them the day before, but they're still fabulous made at least 6 hours ahead.

Look for pickling spice in the spice aisle of your supermarket.

MAKES 2 CUPS (500 ML) | ONE SERVING = 6 OLIVES

INGREDIENTS

1 large clove garlic

1 lemon

2 cups (500 mL) kalamata olives with pits

¼ cup (60 mL) really good extra virgin olive oil

2 tbsp (30 mL) pickling spice

1 tsp (5 mL) red pepper flakes

1 Mince the garlic and set aside.

2 Scrub and dry the lemon. Using a Microplane grater (see page 8), remove the zest from the lemon and measure out ½ tsp (2.5 mL).

3 Put the lemon zest in a 3-cup (750 mL) glass jar with a tight-fitting lid (I use a glass canning jar), along with the olives, oil, pickling spice, red pepper flakes, and garlic. Screw the lid on tightly and roll the jar around until the olives are coated all over with the oil mixture.

4 Refrigerate the olives for at least 12 hours. (If you're in a hurry, the olives still taste amazing after about 6 hours.) Roll the jar often. Whenever I make these, I give the jar a roll every time I open the fridge. Just part of the exciting foodie life I live.

5 Remove the jar from the fridge about 1 hour before serving so the oil isn't too thick (it's described as "viscous" in the culinary world). Roll the jar a few times. Using a slotted spoon remove the olives from the jar and place in a serving bowl, leaving as much of the oil in the jar as possible. We want to eat olives, not olives dripping in oil. (Store any leftover olives, in their oil, in the fridge for up to 3 days.)

PER SERVING: 64 CALORIES, 5.7 G TOTAL FAT, 0.2 G SATURATED FAT, 0 G TRANS FAT, 396 MG SODIUM, 3.4 G CARBOHYDRATE, 0 G FIBRE, 0 G SUGARS, 1 G PROTEIN

DIABETES FOOD CHOICE VALUES PER SERVING: 1 FAT, 1 EXTRA

Grilled Salmon Fillets with Raspberry Salsa

Reality tester Michale is a fan of both salmon and raspberries, but thought I'd lost my mind when I combined the two. She was sure that this recipe was going to be terrible. Reluctantly, she made it, then phoned me from her cottage in Muskoka, Ontario, to tell me how fabulous it was. She had served it to company and it had gotten raves.

MAKES 4 SERVINGS | ONE SERVING = ONE PLATEFUL

RASPBERRY MARINADE

1 lime, scrubbed well and dried

1 tbsp (15 mL) canola oil

1 tbsp (15 mL) grainy Dijon mustard

1½ cups (375 mL) fresh raspberries, rinsed, drained, and patted dry

One 13 oz (370 g) skinless salmon fillet

RASPBERRY SALSA

1 lime, scrubbed well and dried

¼ cup (60 mL) finely chopped fresh cilantro

2 green onions, thinly sliced

1 tsp (5 mL) red pepper flakes

1 tsp (5 mL) extra virgin olive oil

1½ cups (375 mL) fresh raspberries, rinsed, drained, and patted dry

GARNISH

8 cups (2 L) lightly packed mixed baby greens, washed and spun dry

1 For the marinade, roll the lime on the counter with your palm (this makes the lime yield more juice), then cut it in half and squeeze out 2 tbsp (30 mL) juice.

2 Whisk together the lime juice, oil, and Dijon in a medium bowl. Add the raspberries and crush them lightly. Pour the marinade into a large resealable plastic bag or a non-metallic baking dish.

3 Wash your hands and cut the salmon into 4 even-sized pieces. Add the salmon to the bag or dish. Wash your hands and cutting board really well. (I keep a separate cutting board to use for raw meat and fish.)

4 If using a bag, gently press the air out and seal the bag. Massage the bag to make sure the marinade is coating the salmon. If using a baking dish, make sure the marinade coats the salmon well. Cover the dish tightly. Refrigerate for 30 minutes.

5 Meanwhile, for the salsa, using a Microplane grater (see page 8), remove the zest from the lime and set aside. Again with your palm, roll the lime on the counter, then cut it in half and squeeze out 2 tbsp (30 mL) juice.

6 Mix together the lime zest and lime juice, cilantro, green onions, red pepper flakes, and oil in a large bowl. Add the raspberries and toss gently. Set aside.

CONTINUED . . .

7 When the salmon has marinated for 30 minutes, preheat the barbecue to high. Remove the salmon from the bag or dish, discarding the marinade. Avoid the temptation to pour the marinade over the fish while it's grilling; the marinade has had raw fish in it, so it needs the old heave-ho.

8 Place the salmon on the grill, close the lid, and reduce the heat to medium. Grill until the salmon releases easily from the grill, 3 to 5 minutes. Flip the salmon over. Close the lid and cook until the pieces are opaque and start to flake when prodded, with no raw-looking parts inside, 3 to 5 minutes, depending on the thickness of the fillet. Salmon needs to be *just* cooked; overcooking will dry it out. A meat thermometer inserted into each piece of fish should register 158°F (70°C).

9 To serve, divide the greens evenly among 4 plates. Place a piece of grilled salmon on top of each portion of greens and spoon one-quarter of the salsa over the greens and fish.

PER SERVING (MADE WITH ATLANTIC FARMED SALMON): 253 CALORIES, 13.7 G TOTAL FAT, 2.3 G SATURATED FAT, 0 G TRANS FAT, 100 MG SODIUM, 12.7 G CARBOHYDRATE, 5 G FIBRE, 3.7 G SUGARS, 21 G PROTEIN

DIABETES FOOD CHOICE VALUES PER SERVING (MADE WITH ATLANTIC FARMED SALMON): ½ CARBOHYDRATE, 3 MEAT AND ALTERNATIVES, 1 FAT

PER SERVING (MADE WITH WILD SOCKEYE SALMON): 240 CALORIES, 11.6 G TOTAL FAT, 1.7 G SATURATED FAT, 0 G TRANS FAT, 89 MG SODIUM, 12.7 G CARBOHYDRATE, 5 G FIBRE, 3.7 G SUGARS, 22 G PROTEIN

DIABETES FOOD CHOICE VALUES PER SERVING (MADE WITH WILD SOCKEYE SALMON): ½ CARBOHYDRATE, 3 MEAT AND ALTERNATIVES, ½ FAT

GENTLY DOES IT

Do not wash fresh berries until you use them, and never soak them. Rinse and drain them well in a colander, let dry on paper towels, and use them right away. For more on berries, see Berries: Antioxidants to the Rescue! (page 67).

Light Lemony Mousse

Okay, I know: this recipe looks long. But the mousse can be made almost completely ahead of time. It's low in calories and fat but high in flavour, and always gets raves.

And don't be shocked and appalled, but there's a little bit of butter in this recipe. Butter? Yes, company's coming and butter goes under the Treat or Special Occasion category.

You need to make 2 cups (500 mL) Thickened Yogurt (see page 272; or buy a 500 mL container of plain 0% fat Greek-style yogurt) and prepare the Light Lemon Curd first.

MAKES 2 CUPS (500 ML) | ONE SERVING = ½ CUP (125 ML)

LIGHT LEMON CURD

- ¾ cup (185 mL) granulated sugar
- 1½ tbsp (22.5 mL) cornstarch
- 6 tbsp (90 mL) fresh lemon juice (about 2 large lemons)
- 1 omega-3 egg (see page 13)
- 1 tbsp (15 mL) unsalted butter

LEMONY MOUSSE

- 2 cups (500 mL) Thickened Yogurt (see page 272) or plain 0% fat Greek-style yogurt
- 4 whole fresh strawberries, or berries or fruit of your choice, rinsed, dried, and sliced
- Cheater's Candied Lemon Peel (see below)

1 At least 1 day before you want to serve the mousse, make the light lemon curd. Place a wire-mesh strainer over a medium bowl and set aside.

2 With your palm, roll the lemons on the counter (this makes them yield more juice), then cut in half and squeeze out the juice.

3 Whisk together the sugar, cornstarch, lemon juice, and egg in a small saucepan over medium-low heat. Cook, whisking constantly, until the mixture comes to a boil.

4 Reduce the heat to a gentle boil and cook, whisking constantly, for 3 minutes to cook the cornstarch.

5 Remove the saucepan from the heat. Add the butter and stir until melted.

6 Pour the hot lemon mixture through the strainer that you set aside in Step One. Why strain it? The egg-yolk anchor, called the chalaza, becomes rubbery and needs to be removed, and straining does the trick.

7 Pour the strained lemon mixture into a heatproof container, cover tightly, and refrigerate for up to 1 week.

GLAM IT UP

Cheater's Candied Lemon Peel is a great way to garnish the mousse. Scrub and dry 1 lemon. Using a Microplane grater (see page 8), remove the zest. Toss the lemon zest with 2 tsp (10 mL) granulated sugar in a small bowl. Spread out on a large plate and set aside to dry for at least 3 hours, or up to 1 day.

CONTINUED ...

8 For the lemon mousse, spoon the thickened yogurt into a medium bowl and whisk lightly so it's the consistency of a firm whipped cream.

9 Gently whisk the lemon curd into the thickened yogurt until well combined. Divide evenly among 4 dessert bowls. Cover and refrigerate until ready to serve, or up to 24 hours.

10 Just before serving, garnish each serving of mousse with sliced strawberries. Sprinkle evenly with Cheater's Candied Lemon Peel.

PER SERVING: 308 CALORIES, 7.3 G TOTAL FAT, 4.1 G SATURATED FAT, 0.2 G TRANS FAT, 111 MG SODIUM, 55.6 G CARBOHYDRATE, 1 G FIBRE, 44.6 G SUGARS, 10 G PROTEIN

DIABETES FOOD CHOICE VALUES PER SERVING: 3½ CARBOHYDRATE, ½ MEAT AND ALTERNATIVES, 1½ FAT

FEEDING A CROWD?

If you want the Light Lemony Mousse to serve eight, I've done the math for you.

Follow the recipe for Light Lemon Curd (previous page) using the following quantities:

- 1½ cups (375 mL) granulated sugar
- 3 tbsp (45 mL) cornstarch
- ¾ cup (185 mL) fresh lemon juice (3 to 4 large lemons)
- 2 omega-3 eggs
- 2 tbsp (30 mL) unsalted butter

Stir the lemon curd into 4 cups (1 L) Thickened Yogurt or plain 0% fat Greek-style yogurt. Use 8 strawberries for the garnish and sprinkle with Cheater's Candied Lemon Peel (sidebar, page 321) made with the zest of 2 lemons and 4 tsp (20 mL) granulated sugar.

MENU

Fall

A HARVEST DINNER FOR FOUR

Mulled Cranberry Juice (page 325)

Spinach Salad with Pears and Walnuts (page 213)

Braised Chicken with Savory and Dried Cherries (page 326)

Side-Dish Quinoa (page 153)

Quickie Sweet Potatoes (page 328)

Don't-Forget-to-Leave-Room-for-Chocolate Cake! (page 329)

Blueberry-Honey Sauce (page 183)

•

WINE LIST

To drink with the main course:

Rosehall Run Pinot Noir 2007 (Ontario)

or

Sandhill Syrah 2008 (British Columbia)

FALL MENU GAME PLAN

THE DAY BEFORE:

- Make the cake (page 329; icing it once cool, if desired), cover, and store overnight at room temperature
- Make the Blueberry-Honey Sauce (page 183; if using), cover, and refrigerate overnight
- Make the sweet potatoes, cover, and refrigerate
- Wash and spin-dry the spinach for the salad, wrap in a clean tea towel, and refrigerate in a plastic bag
- Make the salad dressing, cover, and refrigerate

THE DAY OF:

- Mince the garlic and dice the shallots for the chicken dish (page 326), cover, and refrigerate in separate bowls until cooking time
- Mix together the herbs and spices for the chicken dish and set aside on the counter
- Mix together the apple juice mixture for the chicken dish, cover, and refrigerate until cooking time

ONE HOUR BEFORE:

- Make the Mulled Cranberry Juice (page 325; its aromas when your guests arrive will be fabulous)
- Remove the Blueberry-Honey Sauce (if using) from the fridge

WHEN EVERYONE'S ARRIVED:

- Serve the mulled cranberry juice
- Assemble the salads (page 213; you need to wash and slice the pears just before serving so they won't go brown)
- Serve the salads (you can start cooking the quinoa just before you serve the salad but I like a pause in a dinner menu, so I usually wait until everyone has finished their salads before I start the quinoa)

AFTER YOU'VE EATEN THE SALAD:

- Start cooking the quinoa (page 153) and set the timer for 18 minutes
- Make the chicken dish (page 326; all your ingredients are prepped so make like a TV cooking star)
- When the timer goes off, check the quinoa (if it's done, fluff with a fork, cover, and set aside; even if the chicken takes another 20 minutes, the quinoa will be fine)
- Reheat the sweet potatoes in the microwave, or in a saucepan over medium-low heat
- Serve the main course
- Enjoy the fabulous wine and conversation

AFTER YOU'VE EATEN THE MAIN COURSE:

- Cut the cake and plate it with the sauce and icing sugar (if using; see photo on page 330)
- Serve the cake

Mulled Cranberry Juice

I have always been a fan of hot apple cider. Like any true foodie I love experimenting with different variations on a theme. So, here's my spin on the popular Thanksgiving drink, this time made with cranberry juice, but mind you, not 100% cranberry juice. Pure cranberry juice is very, very, very, very tart. It's so tart, it will dry out your mouth. Buy a 100% juice blend for this recipe, but not cranberry cocktail, which has a lot of added sugar.

MAKES 8 CUPS (2 L) | ONE SERVING = 1 CUP (250 ML)

INGREDIENTS

One 1.6-quart (1.89 L) bottle 100% cranberry juice blend
1 orange, scrubbed and cut into 8 thin slices
6 cinnamon sticks, broken in half
½ tsp (2.5 mL) whole allspice
½ tsp (2.5 mL) whole cloves

1 Pour the cranberry juice into a medium saucepan and add the orange slices, cinnamon sticks, allspice, and cloves.

2 Bring to a boil over high heat. Reduce heat to a simmer and cook, covered, for at least 30 minutes or up to 2 hours (the longer, the better).

3 Pour 1 cup (250 mL) into each mug, pouring through a mini-strainer to make sure the spices don't end up in the drink. Add 1 orange slice to each mug, if desired.

PER SERVING: 142 CALORIES, 0 G TOTAL FAT, 0 G SATURATED FAT, 0 G TRANS FAT, 34 MG SODIUM, 35.3 G CARBOHYDRATE, 0 G FIBRE, 33.7 G SUGARS, 0 G PROTEIN

DIABETES FOOD CHOICE VALUES PER SERVING: 2 CARBOHYDRATE

FEEDING A CROWD?

If I'm having a bunch of people over, I love to make this in my slow cooker. I save valuable stovetop space and the house is filled with fabulous smells when everyone arrives.

HOW TO

If you have some cheesecloth, wrap the whole allspice and cloves in a small square and tie with butcher's string before adding to the juice. That way you don't have to worry about the allspice and cloves getting into the mugs. I let the cinnamon sticks just float free.

Braised Chicken with Savory and Dried Cherries

One word: yum!

This is a winning combination of sweet, tangy, and spicy. It's a fabulous dinner for any special occasion or just for an ordinary day.

Don't be tempted to make this dish if you have no savory in your pantry. If you've never bought savory, run to your nearest bulk store (you'll likely be going there anyway to get the dried cherries), and buy just a little bit. You need it, this recipe needs it, and you will become a convert after trying it.

You also need a large non-stick skillet with a lid for this recipe.

MAKES 4 SERVINGS | ONE SERVING = ONE PLATEFUL

INGREDIENTS

- 4 cloves garlic
- 4 large shallots
- 1 tsp (5 mL) dried savory (see left)
- ½ tsp (2.5 mL) cracked black pepper
- ¼ tsp (1 mL) red pepper flakes (optional)
- ¼ tsp (1 mL) ground allspice
- ½ cup (125 mL) natural apple juice (see page 12)
- 2 tbsp (30 mL) balsamic vinegar
- 2 tbsp (30 mL) Ribena (see page 16)
- 1 lb (500 g) skinless, boneless chicken thighs (6 to 8 thighs)
- 2 tsp (10 mL) extra virgin olive oil
- ½ cup (125 mL) tart dried cherries

1 Mince the garlic and set aside. Dice the shallots and set aside.

2 Mix together the savory, black pepper, red pepper flakes (if using), and allspice in a small bowl. Set aside.

3 Whisk together the apple juice, balsamic vinegar, and Ribena in a small glass measuring cup. Set aside.

4 Heat a large non-stick skillet over medium heat. Wash your hands. Add the chicken and cook until browned on both sides, 6 to 8 minutes. Remove the chicken from the skillet and place on a clean plate. Cover and set aside. Wash your hands again.

5 Add the oil to the skillet. Add the shallots and sauté until they start turning brown, about 2 minutes. Add the garlic and sauté for 1 minute.

6 Add the spice mixture and sauté for 30 seconds.

7 Pour in the apple juice mixture, making sure you scrape up all the little browned bits stuck to the bottom of the skillet. Return the chicken to the skillet, along with any juices from the plate. Sprinkle the dried cherries over the chicken.

8 Bring to a boil. Reduce heat to a simmer and cook, covered, until the chicken is no longer pink inside and a meat thermometer inserted into each piece of chicken registers 165°F (74°C), about 20 minutes. Turn the chicken over halfway through the cooking time.

9 Remove the chicken from the skillet to a clean plate, cover, and keep warm. Increase the heat under the skillet to medium and boil the sauce until it has reduced by about half, 3 to 5 minutes.

10 Divide the chicken among 4 plates. Spoon the sauce over the top, dividing evenly.

PER SERVING: 350 CALORIES, 11.5 G TOTAL FAT, 2.9 G SATURATED FAT, 0 G TRANS FAT, 161 MG SODIUM, 35.3 G CARBOHYDRATE, 5 G FIBRE, 20 G SUGARS, 25 G PROTEIN

DIABETES FOOD CHOICE VALUES PER SERVING: 2 CARBOHYDRATE, 3 MEAT AND ALTERNATIVES

YEAR ROUND
KID FRIENDLY

Quickie Sweet Potatoes

This easy recipe is a favourite from Ultimate Foods for Ultimate Health ... and don't forget the chocolate!

You can make this a day ahead and reheat it in the microwave just before serving.

MAKES 2 CUPS (500 ML) | ONE SERVING = ½ CUP (125 ML)

INGREDIENTS

2 medium sweet potatoes

2 to 3 tbsp (30 to 45 mL) frozen concentrated orange juice, thawed (see page 13)

1 Scrub the sweet potatoes and prick them in several places with a fork. Wrap the potatoes loosely in paper towels. Microwave on high until tender, 10 to 12 minutes, or roast whole in a 350°F (180°C) oven until soft, about 45 minutes to 1 hour.

2 Put the sweet potatoes in a medium bowl and set aside for 5 minutes. This little "sweet potato rest time" makes it easier to remove the skin, which just happens to be the next step.

3 Peel the sweet potatoes, discarding the skin.

4 Add 2 tbsp (30 mL) orange juice concentrate and mash the sweet potatoes until smooth.

5 Taste the sweet potato mash. If you'd like a more intense orange flavour, add the remaining orange juice concentrate and mash again.

PER SERVING (MADE WITH 2 TBSP/30 ML ORANGE JUICE CONCENTRATE): 71 CALORIES, 0 G TOTAL FAT, 0 G SATURATED FAT, 0 G TRANS FAT, 36 MG SODIUM, 16.7 G CARBOHYDRATE, 2 G FIBRE, 6.2 G SUGARS, 1 G PROTEIN

DIABETES FOOD CHOICE VALUES PER SERVING (MADE WITH 2 TBSP/30 ML ORANGE JUICE CONCENTRATE): 1 CARBOHYDRATE

Don't-Forget-to-Leave-Room-for-Chocolate Cake!

This is my go-to cake for birthdays and any special occasion when it has to be chocolate. It's been on my top-ten list for years and deserves to be showcased again.

Although the cake has a luscious, lick-the-bowl icing, for this menu I omit the icing. Instead, I sprinkle each square of cake with a little icing sugar and set it on a puddle of Blueberry-Honey Sauce (page 183). See picture on page 330.

MAKES ONE 13- × 9-INCH (33 × 23 CM) CAKE; CUTS INTO 30 SQUARES
ONE SERVING = ONE 2-INCH (5 CM) SQUARE

CAKE

Non-stick baking spray
1 cup (250 mL) whole wheat flour
2/3 cup (160 mL) all-purpose flour
1½ cups (375 mL) granulated sugar
2/3 cup (160 mL) natural cocoa powder (see page 12)
1½ tsp (7.5 mL) baking soda
1 cup (250 mL) fortified organic chocolate soy beverage
One 4½ oz (128 mL) jar strained prunes baby food
1/4 cup (60 mL) canola oil (be sure to measure accurately; see page 21)
1 omega-3 egg (see page 13)
1 tbsp (15 mL) pure vanilla extract
2 tsp (10 mL) fresh lemon juice

ICING (OPTIONAL)

6 tbsp (90 mL) fortified organic chocolate soy beverage
1 oz (30 g) unsweetened dark chocolate with at least 70% cocoa mass (read the label)
2 tbsp (30 mL) unsalted non-hydrogenated margarine
2½ cups (625 mL) icing sugar
1/3 cup (80 mL) natural cocoa powder (see page 12)

GARNISH (OPTIONAL)

Blueberry-Honey Sauce (see page 183)
Sifted icing sugar

1 For the cake, preheat the oven to 350°F (180°C). Lightly spray the base and sides of a 13- × 9-inch (3.5 L) metal baking pan with baking spray, or line the base and sides of the pan with parchment paper. Set aside.

2 Whisk together the whole wheat and all-purpose flours, sugar, cocoa powder, and baking soda in a large bowl.

3 Add the soy beverage, baby food, oil, egg, vanilla, and lemon juice.

4 Using electric beaters on low speed (or a wire whisk), beat the ingredients together for 1 minute, scraping the bowl often.

5 Increase the speed of the electric beaters to medium and beat (or whisk like your life depends on it) for 2 minutes.

6 Scrape the batter into the prepared pan and smooth the top level. Bake until a toothpick inserted in the centre of the cake comes out clean, 30 to 35 minutes.

7 Let the cake cool in the pan on a wire rack for 10 minutes, then remove the cake from the pan and let cool completely on the wire rack.

CONTINUED . . .

CONTINUED FROM PAGE 329

8 For the icing (if using), place the soy beverage, chocolate, and margarine in a small microwaveable bowl. Heat on medium-low for 45 seconds. Stir well. Repeat until the chocolate is *almost* melted. Stir until the chocolate is completely melted and the mixture is smooth. The key here is to under-do it. Scorched chocolate is ruined chocolate, and in some countries that's considered a sin. (Or melt the ingredients in a small saucepan over low heat.)

9 Pour the melted chocolate into a medium bowl; don't lick this, it's unsweetened. Add the icing sugar and cocoa powder and beat until the icing is smooth. If it's too thick to spread, add a little more chocolate soy beverage until it's a spreadable consistency. When you're finished, lick the beaters, if desired.

10 If you're using the icing, place the cooled cake on a flat platter. Spread the icing evenly over the top and sides of the cake. Lick the bowl if you must! Serve right away or, once the icing has set, cover the cake and store at room temperature overnight, remembering that tomorrow it will taste even better. Cut into 2-inch (5 cm) squares to serve.

11 If you're serving the cake without icing, cut the cake into 2-inch (5 cm) squares. Spoon a puddle of blueberry-honey sauce (if using) onto each of 4 dessert plates and place a square of cake on each puddle. Sift a little icing (if using) sugar over each square of cake. (Uniced cake can be tightly wrapped and stored on the counter overnight, or frozen for up to 3 months.)

PER SERVING (WITH ICING OR GARNISHES): 159 CALORIES, 3.8 G TOTAL FAT, 0.8 G SATURATED FAT, 0 G TRANS FAT,
83 MG SODIUM, 29.8 G CARBOHYDRATE, 1 G FIBRE, 22 G SUGARS, 2 G PROTEIN

DIABETES FOOD CHOICE VALUES PER SERVING (WITH ICING): 2 CARBOHYDRATE, 1 FAT

PER SERVING (WITHOUT ICING OR GARNISHES): 95 CALORIES, 2.5 G TOTAL FAT, 0.3 G SATURATED FAT, 0 G TRANS FAT, 71 MG SODIUM, 18 G CARBOHYDRATE, 0.6 G FIBRE, 11 G SUGARS, 1.8 G PROTEIN

DIABETES FOOD CHOICE VALUES PER SERVING (WITHOUT ICING): 1 CARBOHYDRATE, ½ FAT

MENU

Winter

A CANDLELIT DINNER FOR FOUR

Sweet and Spicy Walnuts (page 254)

Moroccan Chicken (page 334)

My All-Time Favourite Whole-Grain Side Dish (page 145)

Steamed Broccoli (page 92)

Baked Blueberries with Oat Topping (page 335)

•

WINE LIST

To drink with the main course:

Jackson-Triggs Merlot 2009 (Ontario)

or

Cedar Creek Cabernet Merlot 2007 (British Columbia)

WINTER MENU GAME PLAN

THE DAY BEFORE:

- Prepare the walnuts (page 254)

THE DAY OF:

- Put the walnuts in a serving bowl and set aside at room temperature

AT LEAST 2 HOURS BEFORE:

- Preheat the oven for the dessert
- Assemble and bake the dessert (page 335)
- While the dessert is baking, assemble the chicken dish (page 334), then cover and refrigerate it until you're ready to cook it
- When the dessert is ready, remove it from the oven and set aside at room temperature
- If your company is always on time, put the chicken in the oven, adding 10 to 15 minutes to the baking time because it's been refrigerated (if your guests are usually late, start baking the chicken 1 hour before you plan to eat it)
- Once you put the chicken in the oven, set the timer for 55 or 60 minutes
- When the timer goes off, check the internal temperature of the chicken, and cook it for a little longer if necessary
- Make the whole-grain side dish (page 145). Set the timer for 45 minutes
- When the timer goes off, check the whole-grain side dish (if it's done, fluff with a fork, cover, and set aside; even if the chicken takes another 20 minutes, the side dish will be fine)

WHEN EVERYONE'S ARRIVED:

- Serve the walnuts
- When the chicken is ready, remove it from oven, cover, and set aside (both the chicken and the whole-grain side dish will be fine while the broccoli cooks)
- Steam the broccoli (page 92)
- Plate and serve the main course
- Enjoy the wine and fabulous conversation

AFTER YOU'VE EATEN THE MAIN COURSE:

- Plate the dessert and serve with vanilla frozen yogurt sprinkled with cinnamon if desired

Moroccan Chicken

My dear friend Zahava moved to Spain in 2009 and I miss her tons. So to honour her, I decided to make a recipe with some Spanish flair. I think I must have headed a bit too far south, because after many incarnations the dish ended up with Moroccan flavours. But I still think of Zahava every time I make it.

If you have never before cooked protein with dried fruit, adding the prunes will sound really weird, but their sweetness rounds out the flavours. Even my 83-year-old mother, who always picks out the "different stuff" and puts it on the side of her plate, loves this dish.

MAKES 4 SERVINGS | ONE SERVING = 1½ TO 2 THIGHS

INGREDIENTS

- 4 cloves garlic
- 1 lb (500 g) skinless, boneless chicken thighs (6 to 8 thighs)
- 8 pimento-stuffed green olives, coarsely chopped (don't go crazy; you want to be able to recognize that they were once olives)
- 1 tbsp (15 mL) dried oregano leaves
- 1 tbsp (15 mL) capers, drained and rinsed (see page 12)
- 1 tsp (5 mL) dried basil leaves
- ½ tsp (2.5 mL) Spanish smoked sweet paprika or regular paprika
- ½ tsp (2.5 mL) cracked black pepper
- One 14 oz (398 mL) can diced tomatoes
- ¼ cup (60 mL) dry red wine (optional)
- 12 pitted prunes, cut in half

1 Mince the garlic and set aside.

2 Preheat the oven to 400°F (200°C). Line a non-metallic 11- × 7-inch (2 L) baking dish with wet parchment paper (see page 11).

3 Place the chicken thighs in the prepared dish and sprinkle evenly with the garlic, olives, oregano, capers, basil, paprika, and black pepper.

4 Spread the tomatoes evenly over the chicken. Pour over the wine (if using). Scatter the prunes evenly over the chicken, pushing them down into the liquid with a spoon so they'll plump up during cooking.

5 Bake, uncovered, until the chicken is no longer pink inside and a meat thermometer inserted into each piece of chicken registers 165°F (74°C), 45 to 50 minutes.

PER SERVING: 339 CALORIES, 10 G TOTAL FAT, 2.9 G SATURATED FAT, 0 G TRANS FAT, 436 MG SODIUM, 36.1 G CARBOHYDRATE, 4 G FIBRE, 12.5 G SUGARS, 27 G PROTEIN

DIABETES FOOD CHOICE VALUES PER SERVING: 2 CARBOHYDRATE, 3 MEAT AND ALTERNATIVES

FAMILY FAVOURITE

My reality tester Larry and his wife, Jill, have now made this their house specialty. Not only does your whole house smell amazing while it's cooking, any leftovers taste even better the next day.

Baked Blueberries with Oat Topping

I love to use frozen fruits and berries in the middle of winter. It really makes me feel like a bit of summer has crept into the house.

To glam this up, serve it warm in wide, rimmed soup bowls. Sprinkle each portion with a little cinnamon and add a small scoop of vanilla frozen yogurt to each bowl.

MAKES 8 SERVINGS | ONE SERVING = APPROX ¾ CUP (185 ML)

BAKED BLUEBERRIES

- 6 cups (1.5 L) frozen cultivated blueberries (see below)
- 1 tbsp (15 mL) quick-cooking tapioca
- 1 tbsp (15 mL) fresh lemon juice
- 1 tsp (5 mL) cinnamon

OAT TOPPING

- ¾ cup (185 mL) large-flake rolled oats
- ½ cup (125 mL) whole wheat flour
- ½ cup (125 mL) packed dark brown sugar
- ¼ cup (60 mL) oat bran
- 1 tbsp (15 mL) cinnamon
- 6 tbsp (90 mL) canola oil

1 Preheat the oven to 350°F (180°C). Line an 8-inch (20 cm) square baking dish with wet parchment paper (see page 11). Set aside.

2 For the baked blueberries, place the berries in the prepared dish. Sprinkle the tapioca, lemon juice, and cinnamon evenly over the berries. Set aside.

3 For the oat topping, stir together the oats, flour, brown sugar, oat bran, and cinnamon in a medium bowl. Using a large spoon, stir in the oil until well combined. The mixture should look wet.

4 Pour the topping evenly over the berries and press down lightly.

5 Bake until the blueberries are bubbling and the topping is a deep golden brown, 60 to 70 minutes. Serve warm or cold. (The dessert can be covered and refrigerated for up to 2 days.)

PER SERVING: 285 CALORIES, 12.5 G TOTAL FAT, 1 G SATURATED FAT, 0.3 G TRANS FAT, 2 MG SODIUM, 43.3 G CARBOHYDRATE, 6 G FIBRE, 22.5 G SUGARS, 3 G PROTEIN

DIABETES FOOD CHOICE VALUES PER SERVING: 2½ CARBOHYDRATE, 2½ FAT

DON'T GO WILD

Don't be tempted to use wild blueberries in this recipe. They are a lot smaller and tend to dry out in this baked dish. Trust me; I tried it once with wild berries, and "disaster" is the only word to describe the result (see page 309 for the gory details).

Bibliography

ABOUT THIS BOOK

Gu, Yian et al. "Food Combination and Alzheimer Disease Risk: A Protective Diet," *Archives of Neurology* 67(6) (June 2010): 699–706.

A CONSTELLATION ON YOUR PLATE

American Institute for Cancer Research, "Foods That Fight Cancer," www.aicr.org.

Canadian Diabetes Association, www.diabetes.ca.

DIABETES FOOD CHOICE VALUES

"Beyond the Basics: Meal Planning for Healthy Eating, Diabetes Prevention and Management," © Canadian Diabetes Association (2005).

THE RECIPES

Gu, Yian et al. "Food Combination and Alzheimer Disease Risk: A Protective Diet," *Archives of Neurology* 67(6) (June 2010): 699–706.

APPLES: THE PERFECT FRUIT

Boyer, Jeanelle, and Rui Hai Liu. "Apple Phytochemicals and Their Health Benefits," *Nutrition Journal* 3:5 (2004).

Reagan-Shaw, Shannon et al. "Antiproliferative Effects of Apple Peel Extract Against Cancer Cells," *Nutrition and Cancer* 62, no. 4 (May 2010): 517–24.

BERRIES: ANTIOXIDANTS TO THE RESCUE!

Basu, Arpita et al. "Berries: Emerging Impact on Cardiovascular Health," *Nutrition Reviews* 68, no. 3 (2010): 168–77.

BROCCOLI, BRUSSELS SPROUTS, CABBAGE, AND CAULIFLOWER: THE CRUCIFEROUS FAMILY OF SUPERHEROES

American Institute for Cancer Research, "Foods That Fight Cancer," www.aicr.org.

Gu, Yian et al. "Food Combination and Alzheimer Disease Risk: A Protective Diet," *Archives of Neurology* 67(6) (June 2010): 699–706.

Lee, Sang-Ah et al. "Cruciferous Vegetables, the GSTP1 Ile(105)Val Genetic Polymorphism, and Breast Cancer Risk," *American Journal of Clinical Nutrition* 87, no. 3 (March 2008): 753–60.

National Cancer Institute, www.cancer.gov.

Servan-Schreiber, David. *Anticancer: A New Way of Life.* HarperCollins, 2008.

FISH: GET YOUR OMEGA-3S!

Yurko-Mauro, Karin et al. "Beneficial Effects of Docosahexaenoic Acid on Cognition in Age-Related Cognitive Decline," *Alzheimer's & Dementia: The Journal of the Alzheimer's Association.* Published online May 3, 2010.

THE GLYCEMIC INDEX

Willett, Walter et al. "Glycemic Index, Glycemic Load, and Risk of Type 2 Diabetes 1, 2, 3," *American Journal of Clinical Nutrition* 76(1) (July 2002): 274S–280S.

GRAINS: THREE PLUSES IN ONE TINY PACKAGE

Hu, Frank B. "Are refined carbohydrates worse than saturated fat?" *American Journal of Clinical Nutrition* 91 (2010): 1541–42.

Katcher, Heather I. et al. "The Effects of a Whole Grain–Enriched Hypocaloric Diet on Cardiovascular Disease Risk Factors in Men and Women with Metabolic Syndrome," *American Journal of Clinical Nutrition* 87 (2008): 79–90.

McKeown, Nicola M. et al. "Whole-Grain Intake and Cereal Fiber Are Associated with Lower Abdominal Adiposity in Older Adults," *Journal of Nutrition* 139 (2009): 1950–55.

GREENS: NATURE'S PERFECT COLOUR

American Heart Association, www.heart.org.

Center for Young Women's Health, Children's Hospital Boston, youngwomenshealth.org/leafy.

Reiter, Maximilian et al. "Antioxidant Effects of Quercetin and Coenzyme Q10 in Mini Organ Cultures of Human Nasal Mucosa Cells," *Anticancer Research* 29(1) (1 January 2009): 33–39.

Olthof, Margreet R. et al. "Effect of Homocysteine-Lowering Nutrients on Blood Lipids: Results from Four Randomised, Placebo-Controlled Studies in Healthy Humans," *Public Library of Science Medicine* (published online May 2005).

Tokuyama, J. et al. "Tyrosine Kinase Inhibitor SU6668 Inhibits Peritoneal Dissemination of Gastric Cancer *via* Suppression of Tumor Angiogenesis," *Anticancer Research* 25 (January 2005): 17–22.

HERBS AND SPICES: A LITTLE BIT GOES A LONG WAY

Dearlove, Rebecca P. et al. "Inhibition of Protein Glycation by Extracts of Culinary Herbs and Spices," *Journal of Medicinal Food* 11(2) (June 2008): 275–81.

Fung, Daniel Y. C. Department of Animal Sciences and Industry and Food Science Institute, Kansas State University.

MUSHROOMS: NOT YOUR AVERAGE LITTLE BALLS OF FUNGI

Adams, L .S., S. Phung, X. Wu, L. Ki, and S. Chen. "White Button Mushroom (Agaricus Bisporus) Exhibits Anti-Proliferative and Pro-Apoptotic Properties and Inhibits Prostate Tumor Growth in Athymic Mice," *Nutrition and Cancer* 60(6) (2008): 744–56.

Min Zhang, Jian Huang, Xing Xie, C. D'Arcy, and J. Holman. "Dietary Intakes of Mushrooms and Green Tea Combine to Reduce the Risk of Breast Cancer in Chinese Women," *International Journal of Cancer* 124(6) (March 15, 2009): 1404–08.

Savoie, J. M., N. Minvielle, and M. L. Largeteau. "Radical-Scavenging Properties of Extracts from the White Button Mushroom, Agaricus Bisporus," *Journal of the Science of Food and Agriculture* 88 (2008): 970–75.

OATS: MAKING BETA GLUCAN YOUR FRIEND

American Heart Association, "Whole Grains and Fiber," www.heart.org.

Canadian Diabetes Association, www.diabetes.ca.

Saltzman, E., S. K. Das, A. H. Lichtenstein, et al. "An Oat-Containing Hypo-Caloric Diet Reduces Systolic Blood Pressure and Improves Lipid Profile beyond Effects of Weight Loss in Men and Women," *Journal of Nutrition* 131(5) (May 2001): 1465–70.

Van Horn, L., K. Liu, J. Gerber, et al. "Oats and Soy in Lipid-Lowering Diets for Women with Hypercholesterolemia: Is There Synergy?" *Journal of American Dietetic Association* 101(11) (November 2001): 1319–25.

ORANGES, GRAPEFRUIT, LEMONS, AND LIMES: MAKE DINNER MORE A-PEELING

Hakim, I. A. et al. "Citrus Peel Use Is Associated with Reduced Risk of Squamous Cell Carcinoma of the Skin," *Nutrition and Cancer* 37(2) (2000): 161–68.

Acknowledgements

If it takes a village to raise a child, then it takes a flotilla of friends to write a cookbook.

First of all, thanks to my publisher, Robert McCullough, who asked me to write another cookbook. I wasn't sure if I wanted to put my life on hold again while I created 100-plus recipes, but my inner cookbook author said "yes"—a resounding "yes." Thank goodness for gut feelings, and for Robert.

I would be *so up a creek* without the wonderfully fun, enthusiastic, and talented Whitecap staff. To Taryn Boyd for being my champion and running the show, and to Grace Yaginuma, Viola Funk, Michelle Furbacher, Jeffrey Bryan, and Grace Partridge—thank you for all the work and support you have given me and my baby! Hats off to a fabulous crew.

A very special thank-you to Joanne Sigal, who braved rush hour traffic from Oakville to Toronto to test recipes for me. The best perk of all was, after cooking in my Lilliputian kitchen, she reorganized the whole place.

Thanks to six pairs of eyes: my friends—professional home economist Barb Holland, registered dietitian Cary Greenberg, Jill Harland, Michale Brode, and Jann Stefoff—and my partner, Scott, for reading the book and offering their advice and expertise before I sent it off to the publisher.

Thanks to Yvonne MacRae, RD, CDE, for her work on the Diabetes Food Choice Values. I wanted this book to be diabetes friendly, so Yvonne deserves a huge thank-you for the work she did.

Big thanks to Nancy Au for the wonderful work she did deciphering my recipes and coming up with all the nutrient breakdowns.

A huge thank-you to Erin Spencer, my neighbour and Diva #4, for her work on styling all the still-life shots.

Big thanks to chef Jen Mattka, Diva #2, for doing the wine pairings in the Throwing a Dinner Party without Losing Your Mind chapter.

Thanks to professional home economists Joan Ttooulias and Barb Holland, Joan's assistants Sara and Andrew, and my friend Michale Brode for schlepping all their food props and toys to my house on four sweltering days in August to shoot the photographs for the book. Who knew I was so clueless at food styling? The pictures are a total credit to their expertise. I now bow at their collective feet.

Thanks to my neighbour and friend Evelyne Carter for making that fabulous green apron for the inserts.

Thanks to Heather, Diva #1, for her support, laughter, and general help during the photo shoot.

Thanks to photographer Mike McColl and his assistant, Sasha Kuzmicz, who not only worked with seven women every day of the photo shoot but remained calm, kept their sense of humour, and produced the amazing photographs of the recipes, the still-life shots, and the picture of us partying.

And thanks to my friend Pierre Gautreau who shot the cover on the fifth hottest day of August, and kept me smiling the entire time, even when I was melting!

Hairdressers are a girl's best friend. Thanks to Evangelia Calafato, my hairdresser for the past 12 years, who made my hair look great for the cover shot.

Loving thanks and a full-on hug to my partner in life, Scott, for his words of wisdom, the foot rubs, and all his support, and especially for listening when I was having another mini breakdown.

Thanks to my son, Andrew, for being a great taster and tester, and for all the work he did around the house while I was cooking up a storm in the kitchen.

Thanks to Liz Pearson, my friend and the co-author of the two *Ultimate* books, for her support during the whole cookbook-writing process.

All the recipes were "reality tested" by a legion of friends and friends of friends. Special thanks to these amazing people: Liz Arkwright, Michale Brode, Maggie Butterfield, Simone Demers-Collins, Orla Gaughan, Cary Greenberg, Barb Holland, Kim Jones, Larry Mannell (who also gets a gold star for testing the most recipes), Jen Mattka, Robert McCullough, Joanne Sigal, Donna Trimble, Elise Yanover, Vivien Yellowlees, Heather (Diva #1), my partner, Scott, and my son, Andrew.

This book became a better book after one of my foodie heroes edited it. I am forever in her debt. Thank you, Julia Aitken.

from left to right: Evelyn, Michale, Joan (standing), me, Barb, (standing behind) Sasha, Andrew, Erin, and Heather

Index

Cc

Dd

Ee

Ff

Gg

Hh

Ii

Jj

Kk

Ll

Mm

Nn

Oo

Pp

Qq

Rr

Ss

Tt

Uu

Vv

Ww

Yy

Zz